The Mighty Works of God

DIVINE PROVIDENCE

A Child's History of the United States of America

Ruth J. Smith • Lynn Meier • Jeanette Whittaker

First Edition
Copyright © 2005, by Ruth J. Smith

Published by
Bradford Press
South Bend, Indiana

All Scripture quotations are taken from the King James Version of the Bible.
All definitions are from the *American Dictionary of the English Language,* 1828.

ISBN 978-0-9705618-6-2

Library of Congress Catalog Number 2005901625

Cover Art and Illustrations by Lisa M. Mikler. Selected maps by
Mountain High Maps ® Copyright © 1993 Digital Wisdom, Inc.

ACKNOWLEDGMENTS

Many years of study and teaching are represented in this work designed to restore to the children of America the record of God's mighty work in bringing forth this nation. The accomplishment of the project could not have been reached without the help and encouragement of family and friends.

The work is dedicated to my grandchildren, Cari, Courtney, John, Jonathan, Chad, Christina, Kaylynn, and Beth. Their eagerness to learn was the inspiration to produce the work that had been in my heart and mind for many years. My prayer is that this work will be not only for my grandchildren, but for the children and children's children in many families and the students in many classrooms, who will enjoy learning of God's work in the lives of men and nations.

What a blessing it has been to labor with my three daughters in producing this work. Mrs. Lynn Meier and Mrs. Jeanette Whittaker have sacrificially given untold hours to editing, writing, and sharing ideas which they have used in their teaching. Mrs. Charlene Trowbridge has spent hours in formatting and designing the volume and the student materials.

I want to express my heartfelt thanks to Mrs. Lisa Mikler, who was able to share the vision of the volume and illustrate the content of the volume in a manner consistent with the ideas presented. The detailed, delightful pictures work together with the text to bring the historic events to life. Her work has helped to produce a book which will be treasured by children both in their homes and in the classroom.

Let me express my appreciation to a few individuals who, each, in their own way, gave of their time, effort, and expertise to the publication of this volume :

Mrs. Lyona Hannahs
Mrs. Dixie Thompson
Mr. Craig Trowbridge
Mr. Jay Young

The children's history volume is enhanced by the research and writing of Mrs. Penelope Paquette, Mrs. Jeanette Whittaker, and Mrs. Lynn Meier in the chapters on the Battle of Saratoga, James Madison, and the Wright brothers.

This series for children could not be produced without the prayers and generous contributions of many friends who share the vision for a Providential history for the children of the 21st Century in America. My appreciation is extended to these friends, including the following:

Mrs. Edna English
Mr. and Mrs. Brian Gregory
Mr. and Mrs. Lanny Husebo
Lighthouse Foundation
Mr. and Mrs. Don McNeill
Mr. and Mrs. Robert Thompson
Rhema Foundation

Special gifts for this project were given in memory of Allen Smith, who shared the vision for preserving America's Christian history and the development of materials for children. A special thank you to the following:

Mr. and Mrs. Scott Meier

Mr. and Mrs. Craig Trowbridge

A special thank you goes to Miss Katherine Dang, President of Philomath Foundation. Her knowledge, expertise and counsel during the production of this work has been a blessing. Her charts for the research and teaching of American History, as published in *A Guide to American Christian Education for the Home and School,* were the basis of several of the charts produced for children in this work. We appreciate the direction she has given which helps to make complex ideas simple enough for children to comprehend.

I want to thank Mr. James Rose, President of American Christian History Institute, associate for many years, for his advancement of the ideas for teaching America's Christian History in the elementary classroom through *A Guide to American Christian Education for the Home and School,* the classic work on American Christian education, published in 1987. This first published expression is the foundation on which this work has been built. For these many years, Mr. Rose has encouraged the teaching and expansion of that work. His continued interest and support helped to bring the project to completion.

My heart's desire in publishing this work is that American Christians will be prepared to teach the children of the next generation the Mighty Works of God, that the next generation will have the character to remember His works, and that there might be a *healing* in our land. "That the generations to come might know *them, even* the children which should be born; *who* should arise and declare *them* to their children: That they might set their hope in God, and not forget the works of God, but keep his commandments." Psalm 78:7-8.

— Ruth J. Smith

TABLE OF CONTENTS

PREFACE

This volume, the third in a series for elementary children, began about 1972. My husband and I attended a class at our church in which we were introduced to the idea that America had a Christian history. My education had included many history courses, whose facts had been promptly forgotten, but none which brought me to recognize the Biblical truth of God's Providential direction in the lives of men and *nations*.

This class began a journey of learning which revolutionized our lives and home. As we studied the Biblical principles of government which formed the United States of America, we recognized that these principles had both individual and national application. The primary historical works which guided this journey were *The Christian History of the Constitution of the United States of America,* by Verna M. Hall, and its companion volume, *Teaching and Learning America's Christian History,* by Rosalie J. Slater.

As my heart and life changed, the Lord opened doors in the field of education, first in the classroom with students, and later teaching adults.

In the Christian school classroom, it soon became apparent that most teaching materials were simply a study of dates, facts, names, and events, with no consideration to their cause and effect. It became my desire to pass on to students the *joy* of learning America's Providential history. Rather than history being re-

garded as *dull* and *boring*, students could understand the *cause* of history and the individual's importance in His Story. Studying history with an effort to determine the cause and effect of events gives *life* to the subject.

Nearly 30 years ago, I accepted the challenge of developing a plan for teaching America's Christian history to children. Ideas were identified, expanded, confirmed, and taught to students and in countless workshops.

Through the American Christian philosophy and curriculum, children have grown to love and appreciate the unique individual liberty which has prospered in America as Christian self government was exercised, Christian character cultivated and practiced, property valued, and discernment exercised in establishing and maintaining a form of government built upon Scriptural principles. In 1987, the plan was published in *A Guide to American Christian Education for the Home and School.*

In 1992, two Teacher's Guides were produced and published by Pilgrim Institute. The first was co-authored with Jeanette Smith, *An American Christian Approach for Teaching Christopher Columbus in the Primary Grades,* and the second was co-authored with Lynn Meier, *An American Christian Approach for Teaching Christopher Columbus and the Discovery of the New World.*

For more than a decade, educators in

homes and classrooms expressed repeatedly the need for more detailed history materials. Thus, the arduous task of writing Student Texts and Teacher's Guides began.

In 2002, the first in the series, *The Mighty Works of God: Self Government* was published, a primary level history for the home and school. The challenge of Self Government, first in the life of the individual, and then its historic development in the city, state, and nation is presented in vocabulary for the young student. Readers consider Christ as the cause of Self Government, the Bible in English and its effect in history, God's Hand in the discovery of the New World, the individuals and events which God used to produce a new nation built upon the idea of Self Government, and the expansion of the nation.

In 2003, the second in the series, *The Mighty Works of God: Liberty and Justice for All,* was published, an elementary level history for the home and school. Focusing on Christ as the source of liberty, both individual and national, emphasis is made upon the individuals and events God used to bring forth American liberty, and the fruit of liberty, America's growth and expansion. Children delight in American patriots and their love for liberty, as well as the adventures of the explorers and mountain men used by God to open the West.

The Mighty Works of God: Divine Providence provides a clear and engaging presentation of God's marvelous Hand working since the beginning of time. The reader sees God's Divine plan in the placement of men in nations; the fundamental laws of self and civil government; Christ's fulfillment of the law and His gift of internal liberty; Christianity's answer to the pagan ideas of ancient nations; the westward movement of Christianity and liberty, and the adventures and accomplishments of the explorers and colonists. The Revolutionary Period records abundant evidence of Divine Providence as Americans struggled to preserve the precious gift of American liberty. Individuals and a nation at liberty move forward into a fascinating era of invention and progress, leading into the 20th century and the worldwide struggle to protect liberty against the threat of tyranny.

This present work is designed to further assist families and educators who recognize the responsibility for perpetuating a nation's ideals and principles, and who desire to place before their children the story of how God uses individuals and nations to forward His Story.

—Ruth J. Smith

Part I

TEACHING AMERICA'S CHRISTIAN HISTORY IN THE ELEMENTARY SCHOOL

God commands His people to remember all He has done for them as individuals and nations (Deut. 7:18; 8:2; Joshua 4:1-9). Noah Webster stated that "to remember is to have in the mind an idea which had been in the mind before, and which recurs to the mind without effort." Indeed, as Emma Willard observed, ". . . if we expect that memory will treasure up the objects of attention," it would help to acknowledge that "Each individual is to himself the centre of his own world and the more intimately he connects his knowledge with himself, the better will it be remembered . . ."[1] Hence, if the individual rejoices upon every remembrance of the grace of God in his *personal* history and world, he errs in forgetting God's Providence—His immediate, sovereign care and supervision—in his *nation's* unique history.

Today, the study of history has become a study of dates, facts, names, and events, with no consideration for their cause and effect. This approach to history has produced students who regard history as *dull* and *boring* and who have some knowledge of *facts* (or effects) of history, but no understanding of the *cause* of history and the individual's importance in His Story. Studying history with an effort to determine the cause and effect of events gives *life* to the subject.

The individual Christian must determine what is the cause of all events in his own personal history and his nation's history. Rev. S. W. Foljambe declared a causal relationship in his Annual Election Sermon, January 5, 1876, "It has been said that history is the biography of communities; in another, and profounder, sense, it is the autobiography of him 'who worketh all things after the counsel of his own will' (Eph. 1:11), and who is graciously timing all events in the interests of his Christ, and of the kingdom of God on earth."[2]

Recognizing God as the cause of events of history will make the study of history truly Christian. How the Holy Spirit must be grieved when history is attributed to other than the true source!

A study of history from the premise that God is in control will cause the individual to recognize that God has a plan for each individual and nation. After Christ brought Christianity, Christianity through God's Divine direction moved westward with its effect in civil liberty. This westward march of Christianity produced America, the world's first Christian Republic established with a Christian form of government.

In many classrooms, history loses its identity when it is blended into a social studies course. The teaching of social studies produces an individual who has no mastery of history and who has a philosophy based upon man as causative, with a great emphasis upon societies rather than the individual. As early as 1876, the Centennial of American Independence, Rev. Foljambe cautioned Americans against a failure to study Providential history: "The more thoroughly a nation deals with its history, the more decidedly will it recognize and own an overruling Providence therein, and the more religious a nation will it become; while the more superficially it deals with its history, seeing only secondary causes and human agencies, the more irreligious will it be."[3]

The failure to teach history produces an irreligious people who attribute all advancement to man's efforts. History studied from original source documents enables individuals to see God's Hand moving to fulfill His plan and purpose and to therefore give God, not man, the glory.

American Christians must *again*, as the forefathers did, recognize that America is the direct result of Christianity and its relationship to all areas of life, including the sphere of civil government. American Christians must recognize the link between internal Christian liberty and external religious and civil liberty. If the foundations of America are to be restored, these premises must become an integral part of the teacher's philosophy of history and government and thus direct how and what he teaches in the classroom.

Developing the Elementary Christian History Program

History records the evidence of God's use of individual men and nations to move Christianity westward. This westward movement produced America and her Christian form of government.

The Mighty Works of God: Divine Providence identifies nine major links used by God to move Christianity westward.

In *The Christian History of the Constitution of the United States of America*, historian Verna Hall identified individuals, events, and nations, used of God, to bring forth America and her form of government. These nine links were derived from that work.[4]

Christianity Moved Westward

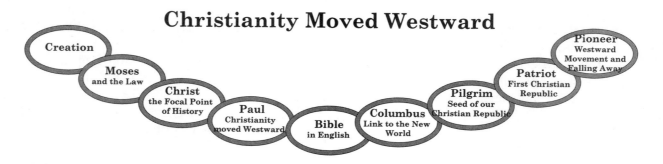

Each link is studied each year with the seed of the link being presented in kindergarten and expanded through the elementary grades. This allows the teacher to review the materials learned in the previous year(s) and build upon that foundation. By building the elementary history program upon expanding links the student will complete his elementary education with a great mastery of Christianity's effect upon the domestic, ecclesiastical, and civil sphere, i.e., the relationship between Christian liberty and external religious and civil liberty.

Christianity Moved Westward
Expanding the Links Through the Elementary School

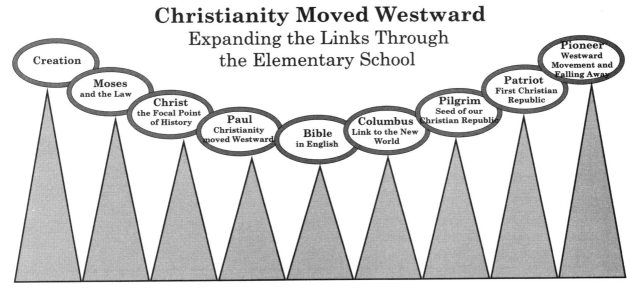

The question is often asked: how can the same link be taught each year without being repetitious? The goal is to expand each link through the elementary years with a diversity of ideas thereby teaching without repetition.

The following chart provides the overview of ideas which may be included each year in the elementary school. The ideas for *The Mighty Works of God: Divine Providence* were derived and expanded from the Fourth year of the chart.

Kindergarten—Sixth Grade
Christianity Moved Westward

	CREATION	MOSES and the Law	CHRIST Focal Point of History	PAUL Westward Movement	BIBLE in English	CHRISTOPHER COLUMBUS Link to the New World	PILGRIM Seed of our Christian Republic	PATRIOT First Christian Republic	PIONEER Westward Movement & Falling Away
FIRST YEAR (Kindergarten)	God's Principle of Individuality — God as Creator — Christian Individuality	Moses Preserved By God — Infancy	Jesus: Birth and Reason for Coming	Story of Paul	John Wycliffe	Christopher Columbus	Thanksgiving Story	George Washington Father of our Country	Abraham Lincoln
SECOND YEAR (First Grade)	Man is God's Property •••••••••••••••• Geographic Individuals	Moses Preserved by God for His purpose as First Historian and First Lawgiver — First 40 Years	Jesus Christ — The basis for Christian self government	Christianity moved Westward to Europe — Macedonian Call	John Wycliffe •••••••••••••••• William Tyndale	Christopher Columbus	America's Heritage of Christian Character — Brotherly love & Christian care	George Washington Father of our Country	Abraham Lincoln
THIRD YEAR (Second Grade)	God's Character Revealed in Creation — Infinity, Diversity, Individuality	Moses Prepared to Lead Children of Israel from Captivity — Last 80 years — Principle of Representation. Deut. 1	Jesus coming changed history B.C.—A.D.	Paul's internal change — from persecutor to missionary	Geneva Bible	Providential Preparation of Columbus — Marco Polo's voyages	America's Heritage of Christian Character — Faith and Steadfastness — Diligence and Industry	Declaration of Independence — America declares herself an individual nation	Lewis and Clark

	CREATION	MOSES and the Law	CHRIST Focal Point of History	PAUL Westward Movement	BIBLE in English	CHRISTOPHER COLUMBUS Link to the New World	PILGRIM Seed of our Christian Republic	PATRIOT First Christian Republic	PIONEER Westward Movement & Falling Away
FOURTH YEAR (Third Grade)	Origin & dispersion of the Races — Noah's 3 sons	Ten Commandments — Dual Form of Government	Christ came to fulfill the law Matt. 5:17-20	Paul on Mars Hill	King James Bible	Providence of God — Prince Henry and Navigational Instruments — America Preserved until He had a people ready	Providence of God — Bible — Holland — John Smith	God's Providence in American Revolution	Land of the Free
FIFTH YEAR (Fourth Grade)	Establishment of Civil Gov't. Gen. 9:6	Ten Commandments — God's law the basis of civil law	Law and the Gospel—the basis of our Government	Purpose of God's law as identified by Paul	Magna Charta — Individual rights protected by written law	Origin of the name America •••••••••••••••••• Cabot's claim to North America	Voluntary Consent: Key to Self Government — Mayflower Compact	Samuel Adams — Christian Patriot	State History
SIXTH YEAR (Fifth Grade)	Christian Idea of Man and Gov't/ Pagan Idea of Man and Gov't	Hebrew Republic vs. Monarchy I Sam. 8	"In the fullness of time Christ came" — Greece & Rome prepared the soil for Christianity	Purpose of civil government as declared in Paul's writings	Bible — Basis of Reformation	Mexico and Canada claimed by Spain/France	Contrast Jamestown/ Plymouth	Patriotic Letters — Committees of Correspondence •••••••••••••••••• Boston Patriots and Boston Tea Party	Herbert Hoover
SEVENTH YEAR (Sixth Grade)	Creation vs. Evolution	Distinctives of Moral law, Ritual law, Civil law	Two Systems of Law — Roman Civil Law — English Common Law — External/ Internal	New Testament Church —"a little Republic"	Bible and the Constitution	Contribution of Columbus to Westward Movement	Communism vs. Free Enterprise	Our Constitution: Law of the Land •••••••••••••••••• Republic vs. Democracy — Prin. of Rep.; 3 branches of gov't; Dual Form of gov't	Ronald Reagan American Federalism

This overview has been developed with the intent of building line upon line, precept upon precept. The chart was originally published in *A Guide to American Christian Education for the Home and School.*

Part II

USING THE TEACHER'S GUIDE

Teacher Preparation

As the American Christian educator considers the teaching of any event or individual, the key is to determine the *Leading Ideas* to be presented to the students. The classroom content should be centered around the Idea to be taught, and supported by the facts and material selected for classroom use. The Ideas chosen must support the general Course Objectives. The following suggested general Course Objectives are reasoned from a Providential interpretation of history:

Course Objectives

1. To recognize the Providential Hand of God in all events, past, present, and future.

2. To recognize the importance of each individual in God's plan of history.

3. To teach the key links God used to move Christianity westward.

4. To teach the Biblical principles of government which formed the American Christian Constitutional Republic.

5. To learn to reason from cause to effect in historic events.

6. To recognize the stewardship responsibility of the American Christian for this nation.

Developing a General Course Overview

To direct the planning of the elementary history course, the teacher should prepare an overview for the year to determine the number of days or weeks to be spent on each of the nine links and its expansion. The length of time spent on each link will vary within the year, and from year to year. For example, one might spend one or two weeks on most links but six to eight weeks on just one.

Following is a suggested Course Overview based upon the ideas identified in the Teacher's Guide. Each teacher must individualize his Overview to reflect the peculiar needs and background of the students being taught.

Suggested Course Overview

I. Introduction   2-3 weeks

    A. Divine Providence
        1. Definition
        2. Biblical and historic examples
    B. Definitions—history, government, self-government
    C. Civil Government
    D. Christianity moved westward

II. Creation   1½-2 weeks

    A. The Lord God made all things
    B. Origin & dispersion of the races

III. Moses and the Law   1½-2 weeks

    A. The ten commandments
    B. Dual form of government

IV. Christ—the Focal Point of History   1-1½ weeks

    A. Christ came to fulfill the law
    B. The two great commandments

V. Paul and the Westward Movement of Christianity   1-1½ weeks

    A. The link for the Gospel from Asia to Europe
    B. Paul on Mars Hill

VI. Bible in English   1½-2 weeks

    A. King James Bible
    B. Peak of the English language

VII. Christopher Columbus—Link to the New World   1½-2 weeks

    A. God's Providence in opening the New World for exploration
    B. Prince Henry and navigational instruments
    C. America preserved until He had a people ready

VIII. Pilgrim—Seed of our Christian Republic   5-5½ weeks

    A. God's Providence in preparing the way for the Pilgrims
    B. John Smith
    C. William Bradford
    D. Peter Stuyvesant

IX. Patriot - First Christian Republic   8-11 weeks

    A. God's Providence in the American Revolution
    B. The battle of Bunker Hill
    C. George Washington: *Commander-in-Chief*
    D. The Declaration of Independence
    E. The battle of Long Island
    F. The battle of Saratoga
    G. A winter at Valley Forge
    H. Battle of the kegs
    I. George Rogers Clark
    J. A traitor in the camp
    K. The Swamp Fox
    L. The surrender of Cornwallis
    M. Uniting the States
    N. James Madison

X. Pioneer - Westward Movement   6-8 weeks

    A. God's protection in the War of 1812
    B. The Star Spangled Banner
    C. Land of the free
        1. Robert Fulton and the steamboat
        2. A path to the west
        3. The railroad
        4. The automobile
        5. A dream to fly
    D. The World at War
    E. "In God We trust"

XI. Conclusion   ½ week

Expanding the Course Overview

After the teacher has determined the general topics to be covered during the year, i.e., the General Course Overview, he should expand the Overview to include the specific ideas to be covered with the students.

The Expanded Course Overview will identify the Leading Ideas for each general topic and the number of days for teaching each idea. Beginning on page 15 of the Teacher's Guide, suggested Leading Ideas have been included for each chapter of the Student Text. The teacher may select from the suggested Leading Ideas or include additional Ideas of his own choosing.

The following Expanded Course Overview is for the Introduction to the course.

Expanded Course Overview

Introduction   2-3 Weeks

   A. **Divine Providence — *Chapter 1***   3-4 Days
      1. Divine Providence
      2. God controls the battle
      3. God is timing all events

   B. **History — *Chapter 2***   1-2 Days
      1. History reveals the Hand of God
      2. History is the record of God working in the lives
         of men and nations.

   C. **Government — *Chapter 3***   3-4 Days

      1. Government is direction, control, and restraint
      2. "For as he thinketh in his heart, so is he."
      3. Self government is direction, control and restraint
         of one's self
      4. Man looks at the outward appearance but God looks
         at the heart

   D. **Civil Government — *Chapter 4***   3-4 Days

      1. God planned for civil government to protect
         each person's life, liberty and property
      2. "Civil government is the flow of power and
         force in society"
      3. Each person has a responsibility for the kind
         of civil government

   E. **Christianity Moved Westward**   1-2 Days

Developing Lesson Plans

Part III of the Teacher's Guide is designed to assist the teacher in developing lesson plans for daily instruction. The Idea to be comprehended by the student must be clearly identified by the teacher and must govern the content of the classtime and any student work. Suggested Leading Ideas have been given for each chapter of the Student Text. The teacher may select from these Ideas, or add additional Ideas.

Several essentials should be included in the lesson plan: summary statement of the leading idea to be covered, reading, discussion, notes, and student written work.

Teachers might find it beneficial to prepare lesson plans for a complete section of their expanded overview at one time. When beginning the lesson plans for each section of the overview, the teacher could write the Leading Idea for each day into the lesson plan before including the specific information necessary for the class. Planning for one or two weeks at a time helps insure that the teacher will cover the amount of material necessary during that time and also allows for a continuous train of thought rather than individual, isolated lessons.

To provide a classroom which will produce a love of learning in the student, a variety of approaches to the daily classtime should be included in the plans—consideration must always be given to the age and capacity of the students. Elementary students may read the book aloud together during the classtime, reason concerning the main ideas, record simple notes, answer written questions, outline maps, and color pictures. Students of all ages enjoy special projects and events which enhance the material and bring it to life. Part III of the Teacher's Guide identifies many suggestions to aid in developing the student's ability to reflect and reason concerning historic events.

Selected materials have been included on the CD as *Teacher Resource Pages*. These pages provide additional resources for the teacher's preparation. Each *Teacher Resource Page* is noted within the related lesson in Part III of the Teacher's Guide

As stated previously, a key ingredient in preparing lessons is variety; the teacher should attempt to incorporate into the lesson plans different teaching methodologies, including various types of discussion, notes, and student work.

Suggestions for *Supplemental Activities* have been included. These activities provide opportunities for additional study, special celebrations, or field trips, which will enhance the course of study.

Student Recording

The main Ideas to be remembered by the student should become a part of their permanent record in the notebook, with adequate facts to support the Idea. This recording may be accomplished in a variety of ways:

Sentences which reflect the Leading Idea may be recorded. Charts showing contrasts, comparisons, cause to effect, or effect to cause are effective in developing reasoning skills. Timelines demonstrate the Providence of God in events of history. The student may simply record a list which reflects the fruit of reasoning from the Leading Idea.

Outlines may be utilized by the teacher, but should be limited to one day or unit of teaching, keeping the teacher and student from becoming encumbered by the tedium of the outline.

For the elementary student, the charts, timelines, or outlines are kept simple in their form and content.

A variety of *Suggested Student Notes* have been included in Part III of the Teacher's Guide.

Student Written Work

The confirmation of the Idea being taught will occur as the student has the opportunity to reflect and reason concerning the Idea taught. Suggestions for student written work are included in Part III of the Teacher's Guide, in the section *Cultivating Student Mastery*.

Student Activity Pages are included on the CD with the Teacher's Guide. These pages provide many opportunities for the student to reason with the Ideas presented in the Student Text.

The student work should be devised

to demand reasoning from the Leading Idea being considered, not just the recording of facts. These exercises must be evaluated as to their appropriateness for the capacity of the students and the preparation given during the classtime.

Drawing or coloring pictures illustrating the events studied will be enjoyed by students of all ages. Original art may be checked as to its accuracy in representation of the event.

Maps provide an excellent opportunity for the student to produce a geographical essay which confirms his comprehension of the Idea covered.

Questions which involve short answers may be given. Consider that questions asking who, what, when, and where are fact-centered and identify the student's comprehension, but do not require reasoning. Questions addressing why, considering cause to effect or effect to cause, or expecting the student to draw conclusions demand that the student exercise reasoning. The teacher should keep in mind that questions which demand reasoning will require more time in answering than simply reproducing facts which have been presented.

Short essays may be written by the elementary student. Essays should be specifically related to the Idea which the teacher has presented in the classroom.

Simple guided research may be performed by the elementary student. The teacher would probably find it best to have available in the classroom the resources which are appropriate for the grade level, and provide questions which would guide the student in his research.

Map Instructions

Preparation of maps will confirm the geographic setting of historic events in the student's mind. Historian Katherine

Dang identified instructions for map work in *A Guide to American Christian Education for the Home and School.* The following simplified instructions have been derived from that work.

1. Map work is mainly outlining and lettering. There is no filling-in of areas with solid coloring.
2. Rivers, shorelines of lakes, coastlines of seas and oceans are outlined with blue. Rivers are outlined along *one side* of the drawn line.
3. Outlining will follow along the exact course of the printed lines.
4. Labeling is to be straight and even on the map. Drawing two lines with a ruler will provide control of the size of letter.
5. All labeling is in manuscript. The size of letters may vary, i.e. names of countries will be larger than names of cities.[5]

Sample Lesson Plans

Following are sample lesson plans for teaching the Leading Ideas for the first two chapters of the Student Text. They are intended for an elementary classroom, with a classtime of approximately thirty to forty minutes.

Sample Lesson Plan

Divine Providence

Leading Idea: Divine Providence

Read: Page 1 of Student Text

Reflection and Reasoning:
- What is Divine Providence?
- Reason and discuss from the Student Text to identify key ideas of God's Providence. Following are suggestions:
    God cares for all of His creatures — the birds, fish, and animals.
    God cares even more for each person. He has a plan for each person.
    God has a plan for each nation.

Student Activity:
- Use *Student Activity Page 1-1* and *1-2*. Record key ideas above and *Suggested Student Notes*. Cut and glue appropriate picture next to statement.

Student Notes:
    Providence is God's care and control of His creation, including men and nations.
    - His plan
    - His provision
    - His protection

Sample Lesson Plan

Divine Providence

Leading Idea: God controls the battle.

Introducing the lesson:
- Review the definition of Providence.

Read: Pages 2-3 of Student Text.

Reflection and Reasoning:
- Who has a plan for each person? Who has a plan for nations? God guides and controls nations when they must go to war. He is the one who gives the victory or defeat.
- The story of the fall of Jericho is probably familiar to the students. What challenges were faced by the Israelites as they marched around Jericho? Can you imagine what the people in Jericho were thinking? Was this "attack" what they expected? Did the people of Jericho think the walls would fall down?

Student Activity:
- Color the picture of the battle of Jericho. Record *Suggested Student Notes* on the coloring page.
- Dramatize God's defeat of the city of Jericho

Suggested Student Notes
> God controls the battle. "Shout; for the Lord hath given you the city." Joshua 6:16b

Cultivating Student Mastery
1. Read Joshua 6:2. What did God promise Joshua before the Israelites went to battle against Jericho?
2. Read Joshua 6:16. When the time came for Jericho to be overcome, what did Joshua tell the Israelites?
3. From God's promise and Joshua's command, how do we know who was in control of the battle?

Divine Providence

Leading Idea: God controls the battle.

Introducing the lesson:
- Locate Pennsylvania, New York, New Jersey, Delaware River, and Trenton on a map.

Read: Pages 4-6 of Student Text.

Reflection and Reasoning:
- Who are the Hessians? The use of hired soldiers was a common practice during the 1700's. Would the Hessians have been as interested in victory as the British? Why or why not?
- Reason with the students to compile a list of the events which allowed the Americans, under the direction of General George Washington, to defeat the British at Trenton:
  - The Hessian soldiers not on guard.
  - The fishermen knew how to row through the storm.
  - Only two of Washington's men died in the cold.
  - In only one hour, Washington was master of the place.
- Consider the picture of George Washington crossing the Delaware. Note the details included in the picture.

Student Activity:
- Listen to the music, *The Battle of Trenton*. How can the various events be "heard" in the music?

Divine Providence

Leading Idea: God is timing all events.

Introducing the lesson:
- Locate Princeton on a map.

Read: Pages 6-8 of Student Text.

Reflection and Reasoning:
- What Providential events allowed the Americans under the direction of General George Washington to defeat the British at both Trenton and Princeton? List the events on the board.

Student Activity
- *Student Activity Page 1-4.* Students record the Providential events.

Cultivating Student Mastery
1. In what way did the cold weather help Washington and the Americans?
2. How did God's control of the weather hinder the British?
3. In the Battle of Trenton, how did God prove to be the God of the battle?

Divine Providence

British Army	American Army
1. More troops	
2. Sure that Washington was trapped	2. Slipped away in the night
	3. Roads froze and they could travel
4. Streams thawed and blocked their troops	
	5. Safe for the winter

History

Leading Idea: History reveals the Hand of God.

Read: Pages 9-10 of Student Text.

Reflection and Reasoning:
- Who is the subject or focus of history, men or God? What should our study of history teach us about God?

Student Activity:
- Students read selected Scriptures to find God's commands to remember His mighty works:
    - Deuteronomy 10:20-21
    - I Chronicles 16:12
    - I Samuel 12:24
    - Psalm 77:11, 14
    - Psalm 105:5
    - Psalm 111:4
    - Psalm 143:5
    - Psalm 145:4-7

Cultivating Student Mastery
1. Why do we study history?
2. What does history show us about God?

History

Leading Idea: History is the record of God working in the lives of men and nations.

Introducing the lesson:
- Review: What is History?

Read: Page 10 of Student Text.

Reflection and Reasoning:
- How does God work in the lives of individual boys, girls, men and women? Is God interested in each of your activities?
- What is a nation? In what nation do we live? Who are our closest neighbors as a nation?
- Look at a globe or map — How are nations distinguished?
- How does studying the record of God working in the lives of men and nations encourage us to love Him more?

Introduce Ideas (To be studied later in year):
- How does God work in a nation? Could He work in the lives of the rulers? How would He work in the lives of the people of the nation?
- Reason with the students that liberty begins with Christ, internally. It took centuries for people to identify Biblical ideas of liberty and develop laws which protected liberty. Why did people need the Bible to have liberty?
- Does America have more liberty than other nations? Do nations which do not believe in the Bible have as much liberty as Americans? This year we will be studying the relationship between Christ, Christianity and liberty.

Suggested Student Notes:
History is the record of God working in the lives of men and nations.

Part III

INTRODUCTION
Chapters 1-4
2-3 Weeks

Each year the history course should begin with the basic concepts which are the premise for reasoning throughout the entire study. These basic truths reflect the philosophy of history on which the course is built.

The rudiments of the history course must be introduced, even to the youngest student. These elements are simplified or deepened according to the age of the child.

Chapters 1-4 of the Student Text contain the introductory philosophy of history and the major premises to guide the student's reasoning.

Caution: Do not oversimplify. The young child can understand such words as history, government, and Providence.

Leading Ideas

When presenting each day's lesson, the teacher should have specific goals. The main goal should be to teach a Leading Idea through the reading, facts, discussion, and other class activities. *This leading idea is a conclusion to which the teacher should reason with the students.*

Suggested Leading Ideas are highlighted in boxes. Pages from the Student Text are identified below the Leading Idea. Some Ideas may be taught with no reading in the Student Text.

Explanatory material, for the teacher, may follow the Leading Idea.

Chapter 1
Divine Providence
3-4 Days

Leading Idea	*Divine Providence*
	Student Text, page 1

• Webster defined *divine* as "Pertaining to the true God; (4) Proceeding from God."

• *Providence* is defined as "the care and superintendence which God exercises over his creatures."

• "Essentially, there are only two interpretations of History, two views of God—that which is Biblical and that which is unbiblical—the Providential interpretation and the pagan interpretation.

"The pagan mind refuses to receive Christianity and is disposed to reject and oppose the authority of the Bible, God's Word. Everything pertaining to life and living is approached from the standpoint of what the human intellect can gather, systematize, and formulate through the experiences of the physical senses . . .

"In contrast to the pagan interpretation of History is the Providential interpretation of History . . .

"The Providential approach to History presupposes order and purpose, deliberateness on the part of God the Creator, whose manner it is to overrule the purposes and cross purposes of men, to bring about the actual events of history. From this approach to history, men and nations become, in effect, the peculiar agents of Divine Providence which governs and directs the course of this world, moving it forward to its destined conclusion."[7]
Katherine Dang, *Universal History, Volume I*

• There are various elements of God's Providence which may be discerned throughout Scripture, as well as in the study of history.
  • God cares for His creation
  • God "superintends" or governs His creation
  • God controls events according to His plan. Genesis 50:20.

• God controls His creation. He is the one who gives life and takes life. He has a design for each individual's life. He also has a plan for each nation.

• See Rev. S. W. Foljambe's statements regarding history, Teacher's Guide, pages 1 and 2.

For Reflection and Reasoning

• What is Divine Providence? Use *Student Activity Page 1-1* to record *Suggested Student Notes* at the top of the page.

Reason and discuss from the Student Text to identify key ideas of God's Providence. Following are suggestions:
  • **God cares for all of His creatures—** the birds, fish, and animals.

• **God cares even more for each person.** He has a plan for each person.

• **God has a plan for each nation.**

The students may record these statements. Cut and glue the appropriate picture next to each statement, *Student Activity Page 1-2.*

Suggested Student Notes

Providence is God's care and control of His creation, including men and nations.
- His plan
- His provision
- His protection

Leading Idea

God controls the battle.

Student Text, pages 2-3

• As God is "timing all events in the interest of his Christ", He guides the outcome of each battle with the enemy. This battle may be in the daily walks of life or on the battlefield.

• As David faced Goliath, he went forth in confidence, knowing "the battle is the Lord's."

"David speaks with as much assurance as Goliath had done, but upon better ground; it is his faith that says, '*This day will the Lord deliver thee into my hand,* and not only thy carcase, but the carcases of the host of the Philistines, shall be given to the birds and beasts of prey.' (3.) He devotes the praise and glory of all to God. He did not, like Goliath, seek his own honour, but the honour of God, not doubting but by the success of this action, [1.] All the world should be made to know that there is a God, and that the God of Israel is the one only living and true God, and all other pretended deities are vanity and a lie. [2.] All Israel . . . shall *know that the Lord saveth not with sword and spear (v.* 47), but can, when he pleases, save without either and against both, Ps. xlvi. 9. . . ."

Matthew Henry, *Commentary*

• II Chronicles 20:15. "'*Be not afraid;* you

have admitted fear enough to bring you to God, do not now admit that which will drive you from him again. *The battle is not yours;* it is not in your own strength, not for your own cause, that you engage; the *battle is God's:* he does and will, as you have desired, interest himself in the cause.'"

Matthew Henry, *Commentary*

• When the Israelites faced Jericho, the Lord gave them unique instructions for carrying out the conquest. Note Matthew Henry's comments regarding this plan: "(4.) it was to try the faith, obedience, and patience, of the people, to try when they would observe a precept which to human policy seemed foolish to obey and believe a promise which in human probability seemed impossible to be performed. They were also proved whether they could patiently bear the reproaches of their enemies and patiently wait for the salvation of the Lord. Thus by faith, not by force, the walls of Jericho fell down. . . . The strongest and highest walls cannot hold out against Omnipotence; they needed not to fight, and therefore needed not to fear, because God fought for them."

Matthew Henry, *Commentary*

For Reflection and Reasoning

● Review: What is Divine Providence?

● Who has a plan for each person? Who has a plan for nations? God guides and controls nations when they must go to war. He is the one who gives the victory or defeat.

● The story of the fall of Jericho is probably familiar to the students. What challenges were faced by the Israelites as they marched around Jericho? Can you imagine what the people in Jericho were thinking? Was this "attack" what they expected? Did the people of Jericho think the walls would fall down?

● Students would enjoy dramatizing God's defeat of the city of Jericho.

● *Student Activity Page 1-3.* Students may color the picture of the battle of Jericho. Record *Suggested Student Notes* on the coloring page.

Suggested Student Notes

**God controls the battle.
"Shout; for the Lord hath given you the city." Joshua 6:16b**

Cultivating Student Mastery

1. Read Joshua 6:2. What did God promise Joshua before the Israelites went to battle against Jericho?

2. Read Joshua 6:16. When the time came for Jericho to be overcome, what did Joshua tell the Israelites?

3. From God's promise and Joshua's command, how do we know who was in control of the battle?

Leading Idea

God controls the battle.

Student Text, pages 4-6

● Sometimes God's control of the battle is effected through the weather. Sometimes it is effected through the individual leading the battle. The American War for Independence provides many examples of God's "care and superintendence" being exercised over battles. The events of Christmas 1776, certainly provide a dramatic example of God's perfect timing.

● "It has been said that Christmas night was fixed upon for the enterprise, because the Germans are prone to revel and carouse on that festival, and it was supposed a great part of the troops would be intoxicated, and in a state of disorder and confusion; but in truth Washington would have chosen an earlier day, had it been in his power. 'We could not ripen matters for the attack before the time mentioned,' said he in his letter to Reed . . .

"Early on the eventful evening (Dec. 25th), the troops destined for Washington's part of the attack, about two thousand four hundred strong, with a train of twenty small pieces, were paraded near McKonkey's Ferry, ready to pass as soon as it grew dark, in the hope of being all on the other side by twelve o'clock. Washington repaired to the ground accompanied by Generals Greene, Sullivan, Mercer, Stephen, and Lord Stirling. . . .

"Boats being in readiness, the troops began to cross about sunset. The weather was intensely cold; the wind was high, the current strong, and the river full of floating ice. . . . They were men accustomed to battle with the elements, yet with all their skill and experience, the crossing was difficult and perilous. Washington, who had crossed with the troops, stood anxiously, yet patiently on the eastern bank, while one precious hour after another elapsed, until the transportation of the artillery should be effected. The night was dark and tempestuous, the drifting ice drove the boats out of their course, and threatened them with destruction. Colonel Knox, who attended to the crossing of the artillery, assisted with his labors, but still more with his 'stentorian lungs,' giving orders and directions.

"It was three o'clock before the artillery was landed, and nearly four before the troops took up their line of march. Trenton was nine miles distant; and not to be reached before daylight. To surprise it, therefore, was out of the question. There was no making a retreat without being discovered, and harassed in repassing the river. Beside, the troops from the other points might have crossed, and co-operation was essential to their safety. Washington resolved to push forward, and trust to Providence. . . .

"The Hessian journals before us enable us to give the reader a glance into the opposite camp on this eventful night. The situation of Washington was more critical than he was aware. Notwithstanding the secrecy with which his plans had been conducted, Colonel Rahl had received a warning from General Grant, at Princeton, of the intended attack, and of the very time it was to be made, but stating that it was to be by a detachment under Lord Stirling. Rahl was accordingly on the alert.

"It so happened that about dusk of this very evening, when Washington must have been preparing to cross the Delaware, there were alarm guns and firing at the Trenton outpost. The whole garrison was instantly drawn out under arms, and Colonel Rahl hastened to the outpost. It was found in confusion, and six men wounded. A body of men had emerged from the woods, fired upon the picket, and immediately retired. Colonel Rahl, with two companies and a field-piece marched through the woods, and made the rounds of the outposts, but seeing and hearing nothing, and finding all quiet, returned. Supposing this to be the attack against which he had been warned, and that it was 'a mere flash in the pan,' he relapsed into his feeling of security; and, as the night was cold and stormy, permitted the troops to return to their quarters and lay aside their arms. Thus the garrison and its unwary commander slept in fancied security, at the very time that Washington and his troops were making their toilsome way across the Delaware. How perilous would have been their situation had their enemy been more vigilant!

"It began to hail and snow as the troops commenced their march, and increased in violence as they advanced, the storm driving the sleet in their faces. So bitter was the cold that two of the men were frozen to death that night. . . .

"It was about eight o'clock when Washington's column arrived in the vicinity of the village. The storm, which had rendered the march intolerable, had kept every one within doors, and the snow had deadened the tread of the troops and the rumbling of the artillery . . .

"The advance guard was led by a brave young officer, Captain William A. Washington, seconded by Lieutenant James Monroe (in after years President of the United States). . . .

"Washington had been exposed to the most imminent hazard. The force with which he had crossed, twenty-four hundred men, raw troops, was not enough to cope with the veteran garrison, had it been properly on its guard; and then there were the troops under Donop at hand to co-operate with it. Nothing saved him but the utter panic of the enemy; their want of proper alarm places, and their exaggerated idea of his forces. . .

"'For our whole ill luck,' writes he [Lieutenant Piel], 'we have to thank Colonel Rahl. It never occurred to him that the rebels might attack us; and, therefore, he had taken scarce any precautions against such an event. In truth I must confess we have universally thought too little of the rebels, who, until now, have never on any occasion been able to withstand us. Our brigadier (Rahl) was too proud to retire a step before such an enemy; although nothing remained for us but to retreat. . ." [8]

Washington Irving,
Life of George Washington

For Reflection and Reasoning

● Locate Pennsylvania, New York, New Jersey, Delaware River, and Trenton on a map.

● Who are the Hessians? The use of hired soldiers was a common practice during the 1700's. Would the Hessians have been as interested in victory as the British? Why or why not?

● Reason with the students to compile a list of the events which allowed the Americans, under the direction of General George Washington, to defeat the British at Trenton:

　· Hessian soldiers were not on guard.
　· The fishermen knew how to row through the storm.
　· Only two of Washington's men died in the cold.
　· In only one hour, Washington was master of the place.
If desired, these may be recorded for Student Notes.

● Consider the picture of George Washington crossing the Delaware. Note the details included in the picture.

● Listen to the music, *The Battle of Trenton,* by James Hewitt. How can the various events be "heard" in the music?

Leading Idea

God is timing all events.

Students Text, pages 6-8

● "General Howe was taking his ease in winter quarters at New York, waiting for the freezing of the Delaware to pursue his triumphant march to Philadelphia, when tidings were brought him of the surprise and capture of the Hessians at Trenton. . . . He instantly stopped Lord Cornwallis, who was on the point of embarking for England, and sent him back in all haste to resume the command in the Jerseys. . . .

　"Early on the morning of the 2d, came certain word that Cornwallis was approaching with all his force. . . .

　"What must have been the feelings of the commander-in-chief, as he anxiously patrolled his camp, and considered his desperate position? A small stream, fordable in several places, was all that separated his raw, inexperienced army, from an enemy vastly superior in numbers and discipline, and stung to action by the mortification of a late defeat. . . .

　"In this darkest of moments a gleam of hope flashed upon his mind; a bold expedient suggested itself. Almost the whole of the enemy's force must by this time be drawn out of Princeton, and advancing by detachments toward Trenton, while their baggage and principal stores must remain weakly guarded at Brunswick. Was it not possible by a rapid night-march along the Quaker road, a different road from that on which General Leslie with the rear-guard was resting, to get past that force undiscovered, come by surprise on those left at Princeton, capture or destroy what stores were left there, and then push on to Brunswick? This would save the army from being cut off; would avoid the appearance of a defeat; and might draw the enemy away from Trenton, while some fortunate stroke might give additional reputation to the American arms. . . .

"Such was the plan which Washington revolved in his mind... and which he laid before his officers in a council of war . . . One formidable difficulty presented itself. The weather was unusually mild; there was a thaw, by which the roads might be rendered deep and miry, and almost impassable. Fortunately, or rather providentially, as Washington was prone to consider it, the wind veered to the north in the course of the evening; the weather became intensely cold, and in two hours the roads were once more hard and frostbound. In the mean time, the baggage of the army was silently removed to Burlington, and every other preparation was made for a rapid march. To deceive the enemy, men were employed to dig trenches near the bridge within hearing of the British sentries, with orders to continue noisily at work until daybreak; others were to go the rounds; relieve guards at the bridge and fords; keep up the camp fires, and maintain all the appearance of a regular encampment. At daybreak they were to hasten after the army."[9]

Washington Irving,
Life of George Washington

For Reflection and Reasoning

• Locate Princeton on a map.

• *Student Activity Page 1-4.* Reason with the students to produce a timeline of Providential events which allowed the Americans under the direction of General George Washington to defeat the British at both Trenton and Princeton. Discuss and answer question regarding Cornwallis and Washington.

Cultivating Student Mastery

1. In what way did the cold weather help Washington and the Americans?

2. How did God's control of the weather hinder the British?

3. In the Battle of Trenton, how did God prove to be the God of the battle?

Divine Providence	
British Army	**American Army**
1. More troops	
2. Sure that Washington was trapped	2. Slipped away in the night
	3. Roads froze and they could travel
4. Streams thawed and blocked their troops	
	5. Safe for the winter

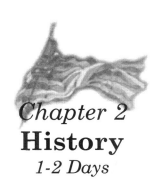

Chapter 2
History
1-2 Days

Leading Idea

History reveals the Hand of God.

Student Text, pages 9-10

● This Providential History series for children was entitled *The Mighty Works of God* in order to focus the attention of the next generation on the true meaning of history. A study of history as His Story prepares each individual to see himself as part of God's continuing plan for His creation.

The Biblical command to remember the mighty works of God influences every academic discipline. The intricacies of the natural world, the order of mathematical relationships, the vastness of the universe, and the beauty with which God has graciously endowed His creation all reveal dimensions of the character of God. In the study of history, the due consideration of His mighty works draws attention away from man and focuses on God, ". . . showing to the generation to come the praises of the Lord, and his strength, and his wonderful works that he hath done. . . That the generation to come might know them. . . That they might set their hope in God, and not forget the works of God, but keep his commandments." Psalm 78:4-7.

Does your teaching of history cause the student to increase his respect and reverence for God as the author of history? As Moses considered the mighty works of God on Israel, how did the people respond? "he hath triumphed gloriously. . . The Lord is my strength and song. . . Thy right hand, O Lord, is become glorious in power. . . Who is like unto thee, O Lord, among the gods? Who is like unto thee, glorious in holiness, fearful in praises, doing wonders?" Exodus 15:1-11.

For Reflection and Reasoning

● Who is the subject or focus of history, men or God? What should our study of history teach us about God?

● Selecting from the following list, have students read Scriptures related to remembering the mighty works of God:
    I Chronicles 16:12
    I Samuel 12:24
    Deuteronomy 10:20-21

Psalm 77:11, 14
Psalm 105:5
Psalm 111:4
Psalm 143:5
Psalm 145:4-7

Cultivating Student Mastery

1. Why do we study history?

2. What does history show us about God?

Leading Idea

History is the record of God working in the lives of men and nations.

Student Text, page 10

• Webster defined *history*: "An account of facts, particularly of facts respecting nations or states; a narration of events in the order in which they happened, with their cause and effect." The last phrase of this definition, "with their cause and effect" distinguishes a Providential view of history.

• Review Rev. Foljambe's statements regarding history, Teacher's Guide, pages 1 and 2.

• As a teacher, what view of history does your teaching advance, the view that history is the "biography of communities" or that history is "the autobiography of God"?

• The Scriptures reveal the fact that God has been working in the lives of men and nations since the beginning of time. Therefore, History is His Story or God's Story. It is the record of God working in the lives of men and nations.

• Webster identified *nation* as "A body of people inhabiting the same country, or united under the same sovereign or government. . . The word *nation* usually denotes a body of people speaking the same language."

For Reflection and Reasoning

• Review: What is History?

• How does God work in the lives of individual boys, girls, men and women? Is God interested in each of your activities?

• What is a nation? In what nation do we live? Who are our closest neighbors as a nation? Using a globe or map, identify how nations are distinguished.

• How does God work in a nation? Could He work in the lives of the rulers? How would He work in the lives of the people of the nation?

• A study of history shows us that liberty for the individual begins with Christ. Throughout the centuries, the Biblical ideas of liberty have gradually been identified and protected by law.

Why did people need the Bible to have liberty?

• Does America have more liberty than other nations? Do nations which do not believe in the Bible have as much liberty as Americans? Our study this year will help to identify the relationship between Christ, Christianity and liberty.

Note: The above ideas should simply be introduced, as they will be expanded throughout the year.

• How does studying the record of God working in the lives of men and nations encourage us to love God more?

Suggested Student Notes

History is the record of God working in the lives of men and nations.

Chapter 3

Government

3-4 Days

Leading Idea

Government is direction, control, and restraint

Student Text, page 11

● Webster's definition of *government* is "Direction, regulation, control, restraint."

● *Direction*—"Aim at a certain point; a pointing towards . . . The act of governing; administration; management; guidance; superintendence. . . ."

● *Regulate*—"To adjust by rule. . . To put in good order . . . To subject to rules or restrictions . . . "

● *Control*—"To check; to restrain; to govern."

● *Restraint*—"The act or operation of holding back or hindering from motion, in any manner, hinderance of the will, or of any action, physical, moral or mental . . . Limitation; restriction."

For Reflection and Reasoning

Note: For students who have studied the earlier volumes of *The Mighty Works of God*, this should be a review.

● Review: What is history? Why should we study history?

● To understand history, each person must consider several important questions. What are they? The next few chapters teach ideas about men and nations. This will help you to understand history. A study of history prepares you to think about men and nations today.

● Define government: "Government is direction, control, and restraint."

● Does direction (aiming at a certain point) help you to accomplish something? Could you bake cookies without directions? Could you find a new place without directions? Can you accomplish the right things in your life without direction? Direction keeps us on the right path, and protects us.

How does a policeman direct traffic? Is he governing the drivers? How?

How does a choir director govern a choir?

● How could a driver lose control of a car or bicycle? What happens when a vehicle gets out of control?

How do people control their anger?

Rules help control our actions. Do you enjoy playing games with someone who does not follow the rules? Why? Is that person controlling himself?

• To restrain is to hold back or keep something within the right boundaries. A driver uses the brakes to restrain the vehicle. A seatbelt is a type of restraint. It protects from injuries.

How is a horse restrained? How are cattle or sheep restrained?

A young child has to be restrained from touching a hot stove, so that he doesn't get hurt. How are toddlers restrained from dangers? How are you restrained from dangers? Do you look for cars before crossing a street?

We must learn to restrain our actions. When you want to do something that you know is wrong, how do you restrain yourself?

Suggested Student Notes

Government is direction, control, and restraint.

"For as he thinketh in his heart, so is he."

Student Text, pages 11-12

• As we consider the topic of government, the American Christian often thinks first of civil government. However, government begins first in the internal sphere of the individual — in the heart. "For as a man thinketh in his heart, so is he." The individual makes choices which control his actions.

• "(1) 'Judge of the man as his mind is.

Thou thinkest to pay thy respect to him as a friend, so thou takest him to be, because he compliments thee, but *as he thinks in his heart so is he,* not as he speaks with his tongue.' We are that really, both to God and man, which we are inwardly; and neither religion nor friendship is worth any thing further than it is sincere."

Matthew Henry, *Commentary*

For Reflection and Reasoning

• Review: What is history? What is government?

• Read Proverbs 23:7.

• What activities have you done today? Have you brushed your teeth? Made your bed? Eaten breakfast? Dressed for school? Had other classes? Finished some arithmetic problems or grammar?

• How did you decide to do today's activities? Do you have chores that you do each morning? Did you do your chores without being told? Or, did someone have to remind you? Were you *told* to make your bed? Or, did you know that your bed must be made, so you made it?

• What were your thoughts? Did you know that you had certain responsibilities? Did you decide on your own to complete them? When you were instructed to do something, did you do it immediately? Or, did you think that it would be more fun to play, and did someone have to remind you of your responsibilities?

• When you play with your friends, how do you decide what to play? Do you have *ideas* in your mind of what you want to play? Are there certain rules about what you can and cannot do when you play with your friends? Do these rules help you to decide what you play?

• Do you ever disobey your parents or your teacher? What thoughts are in your mind? Is what you want to do more important than obedience?

• *Student Activity Page 3-1.* Record Proverbs 23:7 at the top of the chart. Divide the verse: Left—"For as he thinketh in his heart" and Right—"So is he." Read the action listed on the right side of the chart. Record the idea or thought that would be in the heart to produce that action. The student may use a red pencil or red pen to draw a heart on the chart.

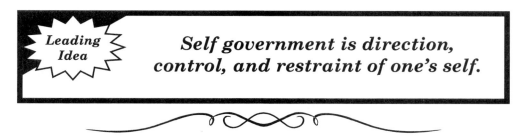

Leading Idea

Self government is direction, control, and restraint of one's self.

For Reflection and Reasoning

• Review: What is government? How does the heart control our actions?

• Each man, woman, boy and girl must govern his own actions. What does it mean to govern your actions? To govern is to direct, control, or restrain them. This is self government.

• The Word of God will help me to control my thoughts and my actions.

• *Student Activity Page 3-2.* Label the two spheres of government: internal and external. What is in the internal? What is in the external? Complete the chart in the course of the discussion. Use examples appropriate for the students. Which controls — the internal or the external? Have the students draw an arrow from the internal to the external. How does the internal govern the external?

Review Proverbs 23:7. What is the heart that is referred to in this verse — the internal or the external? The students may draw a heart on the internal side of the chart.

The balance of the *Student Activity Page* will be completed in a later lesson.

• The Word of God can control our ideas, thoughts, desires, etc. (the internal). As the internal is governed by God, the external will be governed by God. This is

self government.

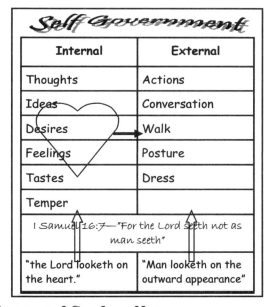

Self Government	
Internal	**External**
Thoughts	Actions
Ideas	Conversation
Desires	Walk
Feelings	Posture
Tastes	Dress
Temper	
I Samuel 16:7—"For the Lord seeth not as man seeth"	
"the Lord looketh on the heart."	"Man looketh on the outward appearance"

Suggested Student Notes

Self government is direction, control, and restraint of one's self.

Cultivating Student Mastery

1. Who or what must control and direct (govern) the internal? How?

2. If a person's external actions or words are wrong, what must change?

Leading Idea

> ## Man looks at the outward appearance but God looks at the heart.
>
> Student Text, pages 12-14

● "If the sons of Jesse were told that God would provide himself a king among them (as he said, *v.* 1), we may well suppose they all made the best appearance they could, and each hoped he should be the man; but here we are told,

"I. How all the elder sons, who stood fairest for the preferment, were passed by.

"1. Eliab, the eldest, was privately presented first to Samuel, probably none being present but Jesse only, and Samuel thought he must needs be the man: *Surely this is the Lord's anointed, v.* 6 . . . *Look not on his countenance, v.* 7. It was strange that Samuel, who had been so wretchedly disappointed in Saul, whose countenance and stature recommended him as much as any man's could, should be so forward to judge of a man by that rule. When God would please the people with a king he chose a comely man; but, when he would have one after his own heart, he should not be chosen by the outside. Men judge by the sight of the eyes, but God does not, Isa. xi. 3. *The Lord looks on the heart,* that is, (1.) He knows it. We can tell how men look, but he can tell what they are. Man looks on the eyes . . . and is pleased with the liveliness, and sprightliness that appear in them; but God looks on the heart, and sees the thoughts and intents of that.

Matthew Henry, *Commentary*

For Reflection and Reasoning

● Review: What is government? What does it mean to have self government?

● Review: What controls our actions? Our conversation? Who we choose as friends?

● Why did Samuel think Eliab, or one of the older brothers would be the man God would choose to be the King of Israel? Is that internal or external? When God looks at a man, what does He think is the most important part, the internal or the external?

● What do you see when you look at another person? You see the external. Using the chart, *Student Activity Page 3-2,* consider what is external: actions, conversation, walk, posture, dress.

● What is it that God sees when He looks at the individual man, woman, boy, or girl? He sees the heart. Using the chart, *Student Activity Page 3-2,* consider what is internal: thoughts, ideas, desires, feelings, tastes, temper.

● Read I Chronicles 28:9. What does the Lord see?

● Reasoning from I Samuel 16:7, complete the chart, *Student Activity Page 3-2.* What is your countenance? What is your stature?

● God knows who we really are. He knows what no person knows. He sees our heart. We must, therefore, direct our thoughts and ideas according to the Word of God.

Chapter 4
Civil Government
3-4 Days

 **Leading Idea** — *God planned for civil government to protect each person's life, liberty and property.*

Student Text, page 15

• I Peter 2:13-14—"Submit yourselves to every ordinance of man for the Lord's sake: whether it be to the king, as supreme; Or unto governors, as unto them that are sent by him for the punishment of evildoers, and for the praise of them that do well."

• Romans 13:1-4—"Let every soul be subject unto the higher powers. For there is no power but of God: the powers that be are ordained of God. Whosoever therefore resisteth the power, resisteth the ordinance of God: and they that resist shall receive to themselves damnation. For rulers are not a terror to good works, but to the evil. Wilt thou then not be afraid of the power? Do that which is good, and thou shalt have praise of the same: For he is the minister of God to thee for good. But if thou do that which is evil, be afraid; for he beareth not the sword in vain: for he is the minister of God, a revenger to execute wrath upon him that doeth evil."

• Galatians 6:10—"As we have therefore opportunity, let us do good unto all men, especially unto them who are of the household of faith."

• "Where an excess of power prevails, property of no sort is duly respected. No man is safe in his opinions, his person, his faculties, or his possessions. Where there is an excess of liberty, the effect is the same. . . Government is instituted to protect property of every sort. . . This being the end of government."[10]

James Madison, *Property*

For Reflection and Reasoning

• Review: What is government? How does God want boys and girls or men and women to govern (direct and control) themselves?

• Review the relationship between internal and external.

• Discuss: What is a city? A state? A nation? How do these different spheres compare in size? Discuss both population and geographic size. Review with the students the name of their city, state, and nation.

• Since we are sinners, do boys and girls or men and women always govern themselves properly? If your neighbor does not govern himself would your property be safe? What might happen to it? If you do not govern yourself, what might you do with your neighbor's property?

● As men live together in a city, state, or nation, there must be government to protect each person's life, liberty and property. This is called civil government.

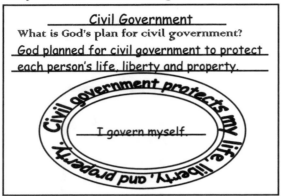

Civil Government
What is God's plan for civil government?
God planned for civil government to protect each person's life, liberty and property.

Civil government protects my life, liberty, and property.

I govern myself.

● *Student Activity Page 4-1.* Students title and label the chart. Consider the question: What is God's plan for civil government? Record the response on the chart.

Note: For the students who have been studying the series, *The Mighty Works of God,* the chart should be a review and expansion from previous years' studies.

Cultivating Student Mastery

1. Why is civil government necessary?

Leading Idea

"Civil government is the flow of power and force in society."

Student Text, page 15-16

● *"Where* he has this power; in *heaven and in earth,* comprehending the universe. Christ is the sole universal Monarch, he is *Lord of all,* Acts x: 36. He has all *power in heaven.* He has power of dominion over the angels, they are all his humble servants, Eph. i. 20, 21. He has power of intercession with his Father, in the virtue of his satisfaction and atonement; he intercedes, not as a suppliant, but as a demandant; *Father, I will.* He has *all power on earth* too; having prevailed with God, by the sacrifice of atonement, he prevails with men, and deals with them as one having authority, by the ministry of reconciliation. He is indeed, in all causes and over all persons, supreme Moderator and Governor. *By him kings reign."*

Matthew Henry *Commentary*

● Noah Webster has extensive definitions for the word, *power.* Selected terms include "force," "strength," "command," "the right of governing" and "authority." We could, therefore, say that God has force, strength, command, and authority.

● Historian Verna Hall defined civil government as "the flow of power and force in society."[11]

● The Christian idea of civil government deduced from the Scriptures is that all power comes from God to the individual. That power can then be delegated by the individual to the sphere of civil government. Civil government is given the power by the people to govern the city, state, or nation.

For Reflection and Reasoning

● Review: What is government?

● When we discuss *civil government,* what do we mean? Review the idea of civil government directing and controlling the city, state, and nation.

● Review: What is the purpose of civil government?

● Read Matthew 28:18. What is power? Identify a simple definition for the students to record, see *Suggested Student Notes*. Record additional ideas concerning God's direction and control. How much of the creation does God govern? Does He control the universe?

A songwriter has described God's power in these words, "He's big enough to rule the mighty universe, yet small enough to live within my heart." These words describe how God rules the physical world externally by His awesome power, but His relationship with man is internal, and He rules us as we allow Him to control our heart.

● Read selected verses which identify God's power or control over civil government, i.e. Proverbs 8:15; Daniel 2:20-21; Daniel 2:37. How does God control civil government? Who places the rulers on the throne? Ultimately, it is God.

● Reason with the students concerning the chart, Student Text, page 16. What is God's plan for civil government?
  · Review Matthew 28:18—What is the source of all power?
  · We know of God's power through the Word of God. Read Hebrews 4:12a.
  · To whom does God give His power? God gives His power to each person who believes.

· How does civil government receive power? The individual delegates authority to civil government. What does it mean to delegate authority? Illustrate how the student receives delegated authority to carry out a task for another person — his parent or teacher.
· Conclude the discussion by reviewing the steps of the flow of power.

● *Student Activity Pages 4-2* and *4-3*. Record a definition of civil government and complete the chart.

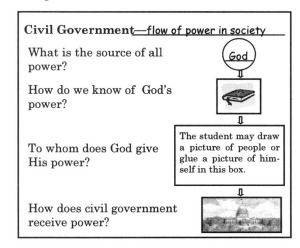

Civil Government—flow of power in society

What is the source of all power?

How do we know of God's power?

To whom does God give His power?

The student may draw a picture of people or glue a picture of himself in this box.

How does civil government receive power?

Suggested Student Notes

Power is force, authority, or the right of governing. All power comes from God. He has the right to govern all things.

Leading Idea

Each person has a responsibility for the kind of civil government.

Student Text, page 16

● "*Rulers are not a terror to good works, but to the evil, &c.* Magistracy was designed to be, [1.] A terror to evil works and evil workers. They bear the sword; not only the sword of war, but the sword of justice. They are *heirs of restraint*, to put offenders to shame; Laish wanted

such, Judg. xviii. 7. Such is the power of sin and corruption that many will not be restrained from the greatest enormities, and such as are most pernicious to human society, by any regard to the law of God and nature or the wrath to come; but only by the fear of temporal punishments, which the wilfulness and perverseness of degenerate mankind have made necessary. Hence it appears that laws with penalties for the lawless and disobedient (1 Tim. i. 9) must be constituted in Christian nations, and are agreeable with, and not contradictory to, the gospel. When men are become such beasts, such ravenous beasts, one to another they must be dealt with accordingly, taken and destroyed *in terrorem—to deter others*. The horse and the mule must thus be held in with bit and bridle. In this work the magistrate is the *minister of God, v. 4.* He acts as God's agent, to whom vengeance belongs . . ."

Matthew Henry, *Commentary*

For Reflection and Reasoning

● Review the relationship between internal and external government.

● Review: What is self government? What is civil government? What is the purpose of civil government? How does civil government receive power?

● If you do not govern your own actions in your home, what will your parents do? If you do govern your own actions at home, what happens?

● If you do not govern your own actions at school, what must the teacher do? If you do govern your own actions at school, what happens?

● In the neighborhood, if you do not govern your own actions, what will the police do? If you do govern your own actions, what happens?

● Read Romans 13:1-4 and I Timothy 1:9a.

● What will decide how much civil government we need? Will it relate to the amount of self government we practice in our lives? Draw charts on the board to illustrate how the amount of government can be divided between the internal and external. If there is a large amount of self government, there will be a smaller amount of civil government. If there is a small amount of self government, there will be a large amount of civil government. If time permits, the charts could first relate to the idea of the balance

between self and home or family government. This idea could then be extended and illustrated for family and civil government.

Who needs civil government the most? Who needs civil government the least? The charts will be a review to the students who have studied previous volumes of *The Mighty Works of God.*

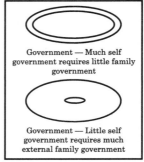

Government — Much self government requires little family government

Government — Little self government requires much external family government

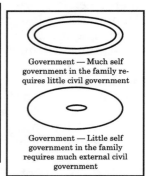

Government — Much self government in the family requires little civil government

Government — Little self government in the family requires much external civil government

● As Americans, how do we protect the quality of civil government, so that it stays true to its Biblical responsibility?

● How do we choose representatives in civil government? What is an election? What is a ballot? How many people must be on the ballot for one job to make it truly an election? Some nations which do not have Christian ideas hold elections, but there is only one person on the ballot. Is this truly an election?

Cultivating Student Mastery

1. How can you control how much external government you have in your life?

2. What opportunity do Americans have to protect the quality of civil government?

Christianity Moved Westward

1-2 Days

> **Leading Idea**
>
> **God used individual men and nations to move the Gospel westward.**

● History records the evidence of God's use of individual men and nations to move Christianity westward with its effect in the civil sphere. This westward movement produced America and her Christian form of government.

Historian Verna Hall identified individuals, events, and nations used of God to bring forth America and her form of government. See *The Christian History of the Constitution,* page 6A.

● *The Mighty Works of God: Divine Providence* identifies key links used by God to move Christianity westward. See *Teacher's Guide,* pages 2 and 3, for the links to be included in this year's study.

For Reflection and Reasoning

● Review: What is History? What is Providence?

● Our study of history this year — *The Mighty Works of God: Divine Providence* — will be looking at individuals God used to give us our nation, the United States of America. Each individual is important, like the links on a chain.

● Review the names of the continents. When Christ came to the earth, on which continent did he live? Christianity was first on the continent of Asia. The Gospel was taken from Asia to Europe. Whom did God use to take the Gospel from Asia to Europe? After many centu-

ries, the Gospel was taken to North America. The Gospel was the basis of the ideas found in our nation's constitution.

● Look at a chain and discuss the importance of each link. Relate that God has used individuals to move the Gospel westward to produce our nation. Each one is important in His Story.

● *Student Activity Pages 4-4* and *4-5.* Briefly introduce the students to the key links to be studied this year in history class. Students may cut and glue the pictures representing Christ, Paul, the Pilgrim and the Patriot links. As desired, review individuals and events which have been studied in previous years.

Christianity Moved Westward

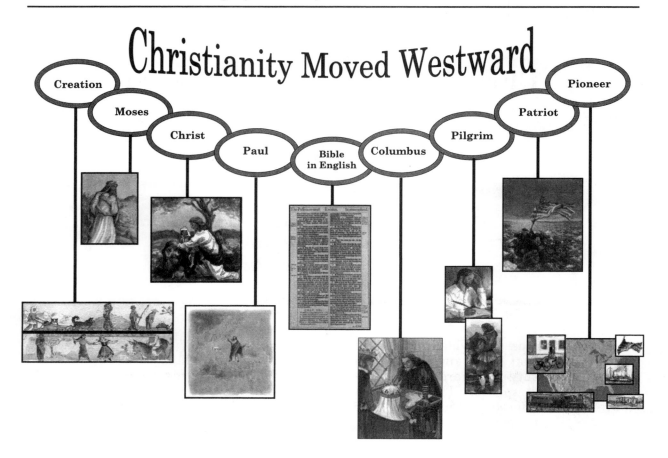

CREATION

1½-2 Weeks

Chapter 5
Beginnings

9-10 Days

>
> **Leading Idea**
>
> ## *"All things bright and beautiful, the Lord God made them all."*
>
> Student Text, page 17

- Webster defined *lord* as "A master; a person possessing supreme power and authority; a ruler; a governor. (7) In *Scripture*, the Supreme Being; Jehovah."

- *Almighty* is defined by Webster as "The Omnipotent God."

For Reflection and Reasoning

- Read Colossians 1:16.

- As needed, review the story of creation from Genesis 1.

- *Student Activity Page 5-1.* Students may circle the words which identify the variety of things which God created, i.e. creatures, flowers, birds, rich men, poor men, etc. Discuss how each is described by the poet.

- Discuss the governmental meaning of "Lord". What is a lord? How is God the

Lord of His creation?

- What does it mean to be almighty? How is God almighty?

Cultivating Student Mastery

Reason from the poem to answer these questions:

1. What does creation teach us about God?

2. What does creation teach us about all the things He made?

History began with creation.

Student Text, page 18

• The individual's view of God and man is foundational to his view of history. This lesson serves as a review of who God is and who man is. Depending on the student's background, this lesson may be expanded.

• Webster defined *infinite* as "Without limits; unbounded; boundless. . . Applied to *time, space,* or *quantity.*"

• Often we think of infinite or infinity as relating only to the sphere of time. This is only one aspect of God's infinity. God is not bound by any of man's limits. He is not limited by time, space, or quantity. The concept of no beginning or ending may be difficult for adults or students to comprehend.

For Reflection and Reasoning

• When is your birthday? Your birthday celebrates the day you were born. Why does God have no birthday? Read Revelation 22:13 again. Alpha and Omega are words representing the first and last letter of the Greek alphabet. What do they mean? The verse gives us the definition. *Student Activity Page 5-2,* record the definition of Alpha and Omega.

• Review: What is history? Why can history only begin at creation?

• Before God could work in the lives of men and nations, He had to create the place for men and nations. He is the author of history and has always been in control of history.

• How large is the universe? How many kinds of plants and animals did God create? In how many days did God create this great universe? Where do we look to find the record of creation? What does the Bible teach us is special about the creation of man?

• Sing songs which identify who God is in relation to creation and God's infinite character — no beginning or ending: *And God Said; Yesterday, Today, Forever; I Sing the Mighty Power of God; My God is So Big; He is Able; For the Beauty of the Earth.*

Cultivating Student Mastery

1. *Student Activity Page 5-2.*

"Wherefore, as by one man sin entered into the world."

Student Text, page 18

• "(1.) How Adam, as a public person, communicated sin and death to all his

posterity (*v.* 12): *By one man sin entered.* We see the world under a deluge of sin and death, full of iniquities and full of calamities. Now, it is worth while to enquire what is the spring that feeds it, and you will find it to be the general corruption of nature; and at what gap it entered, and you will find it to have been Adam's first sin. It was *by one man,* and he the first man . . . That one man from whom, as from the root, we all spring. [1.] By him *sin entered.* When God pronounced all very good (Gen. i. 31) there was no sin in the world; it was when Adam ate forbidden fruit that sin made its entry. Sin had before entered into the world of angels, when many of them revolted from their allegiance and left their first estate; but it never entered into the world of mankind till Adam sinned. Then it entered as an enemy, to kill and destroy, as a thief, to rob and despoil; and a dismal entry it was. Then entered the guilt of Adam's sin imputed to posterity, and a general corruption and depravedness of nature. . . Sin entered into the world by Adam for in him we all sinned. As, 1 Cor. xv. 22, *in Adam all die;* so here, *in him all have sinned;* for it is agreeable to the law of all nations that the acts of a public person be accounted theirs whom they represent; and what a whole body does every member of the same body may be said to do. Now Adam acted thus as a public person, by the sovereign ordination and appointment of God, and yet that founded upon a natural necessity; for God, as the author of nature, had made this the law of nature, that man should beget in his own likeness, and so the other creatures. In Adam therefore, as in a common receptacle, the whole nature of man was reposited, from him to flow down in a channel to his posterity; for all mankind are made *of one blood* (Acts xvii. 26) so that according as this nature proves through his standing or accordingly it is propagated from him, nature became guilty and corrupt, and is so derived. Thus in him all have sinned. [2.] *Death by sin,* for death is the wages of sin. Sin, when it is finished, brings forth death. When sin came, of course death came with it. Death is here put for all that misery which is the due desert of sin, temporal, spiritual, eternal death. If Adam had not sinned, he had not died; the threatening was *In the day thou eatest thou shall surely die,* Gen. ii. 17. [3] *So death passed,* that is, a sentence of death was passed, as upon a criminal . . . It is the universal fate, without exception: death passes upon all. There are common calamities incident to human life which do abundantly prove this."

Matthew Henry, *Commentary*

For Reflection and Reasoning

• Review: What was special about the creation of man?

• Read Genesis 2:8-9. Would the Garden of Eden have been beautiful? Can we even begin to imagine what the Garden of Eden was like? Would there have been weeds in the Garden?

• Review: What is government?

• What is sin? Consider the chart, *Student Activity Page 3-2.* How does sin affect the internal thoughts, ideas, etc.? How is life today different than Adam and Eve's lives before they sinned?

• *Student Activity Page 5-3.* Record a simple definition of sin from the Student Text, see *Suggested Student Notes.* What does it mean to disobey? Reason from the Student Text to draw conclusions for the state of Adam and Eve in the Garden of Eden before sin and what was their state after sin. Some ideas will have to be reasoned from knowing the opposite.

Before Sin	After Sin
• Walked and talked with God	• Could not walk and talk with God
• Enjoyed the Garden of Eden	• Adam had to till the ground
	(continued on next page)

Before Sin	After Sin
• God provided everything Adam and Eve needed	• Sent from the Garden of Eden
• No weeds	• Thorns and thistles
• No death	• Death came into the world
• No grief and sorrow	• Grief and sorrow

Suggested Student Notes

Sin is disobeying God.

Leading Idea

God rules in the affairs of men.

Student Text, page 19

• Ussher's chronology places creation at 4004 B.C. and the flood at 2348 B.C. This indicates there was 1,656 years between creation and the flood.

• "Here is, I. God's resentment of man's wickedness. He did not see it as an unconcerned spectator, but as one injured and affronted by it; he saw it as a tender father sees the folly and stubbornness of a rebellious and disobedient child, which not only angers him, but grieves him, and makes him wish he had been written childless. *It repented the Lord that he had made man upon the earth,* that he had made a creature of such noble powers and faculties, and had put him on the earth, which he built and furnished on purpose to be a convenient, comfortable, habitation for him; *and it grieved him at his heart.* These are expressions after the manner of men, and must be understood so as not to reflect upon the honour of God's immutability or felicity. 1. This language does not imply any passion or uneasiness in God (nothing can create disturbance to the Eternal Mind), but it expresses his just and holy displeasure against sin and sinners, against sin as odious to his holiness and against sinners as obnoxious to his justice. He is pressed by the sins of his creatures (Amos ii. 13), wearied (Isa. xliii. 24), broken (Ezek. vi. 9), grieved (Ps. xcv. 10), and here *grieved to the heart,* as men are when they are wronged and abused by those they have

been very kind to, and therefore repent of their kindness, and wish they had never fostered that snake in their bosom which now hisses in their face and stings them to the heart. Does God thus hate sin? And shall we not hate it? Has our sin grieved him to the heart? And shall not we be grieved and pricked to the heart for it? O that this consideration may humble us and shame us, and that we may look on him whom we have thus grieved, and mourn! Zech. xii. 10. 2. It does not imply any change of God's mind; for *he is in one mind, and who can turn him?* With him *there is no variableness.* But it expresses a change of his way. When God had made man upright, *he rested and was refreshed (Exod. xxxi. 17),* and his way towards him such as showed he was pleased with the work of his own hands; but, now that man had apostatized, he could not do otherwise than show himself displeased; so that the change was in man, not in God. God repented that he had made man; but we never find him repenting that he redeemed man (though that was a work of much greater expense), because special and effectual grace is given to secure the great ends of redemption; so that those *gifts and callings are without repentance,* Rom. xi. 29.

"II. God's resolution to destroy man for his wickedness, *v.* 7. Observe, 1. When God repented that he had made man, he resolved to destroy man. . . . 3. He speaks of man as his own creature even when he resolved upon his ruin: *Man whom I have created. . . . 4.* Even the brute-creatures were to be involved in this destruction—*Beasts, and creeping things, and the fowls of the air.* These were made for man, and therefore must be destroyed with man; for it follows: *It repenteth me that I have made them;* for the end of their creation also was frustrated. They were made that man might serve and honour God with them; and therefore were destroyed because he had served his lusts with them, and made them subject to vanity. 5. God took up this resolution concerning man after his Spirit had been long striving with him in vain. None are ruined by the justice of God but those that hate to be reformed by the grace of God."

Matthew Henry, *Commentary*

● Webster defined *repent* as "To feel pain, sorrow or regret for something done or spoken" or "*Applied to the Supreme Being,* to change the course of providential dealings."

For Reflection and Reasoning

● Review: How did history begin? How did sin affect man? the earth?

● If the students are familiar with the terms of B.C. and A.D., identify that creation was approximately 4004 B.C. How much time passed between creation and Christ's birth?

● Ussher dated the flood at 2348 B.C. How many years passed between creation and the flood?

● How many people were on the earth? We don't really know, but after over 1500 years there would have been many, many people.

● What did God see when He looked at man? What does "it repented the Lord" mean? Why was He grieved? What does it mean to be grieved?

● Why could God destroy man? Had He created man? Who controls the lives of men?

Cultivating Student Mastery

1. Why did God choose to destroy man from the face of the earth?

2. If God can destroy man, what does this teach us about God?

Leading Idea

"Noah found grace in the eyes of the Lord."

Student Text, pages 20-21

● "We have here Noah distinguished from the rest of the world, and a peculiar mark of honour put upon him. 1. When God was displeased with the rest of the world, he favoured Noah: *But Noah found grace in the eyes of the Lord, v.* 8. This vindicates God's justice in his displeasure against the world, and shows that he had strictly examined the character of every person in it before he pronounced it universally corrupt; for, there being one good man, he found him out, and smiled upon him. It also magnifies his grace towards Noah that he was made a vessel of God's mercy when all mankind besides had become the generation of his wrath: distinguishing favours bring under peculiarly strong obligations. Probably Noah did not find favour in the eyes of men . . .

"Now observe his character. [1] He *was a just man* . . . [2] He was *perfect,* not with a sinless perfection, but a perfection of sincerity . . . [3] He *walked with God,* as Enoch had done before him. He was not only honest, but devout. . . . But, [4] That which crowns his character is that thus he was, and thus he did, *in his generation,* in that corrupt degenerate age in which his lot was cast. It is easy to be religious when religion is in fashion; but it is an evidence of strong faith and resolution to swim against a stream to heaven, and to appear for God when no one else appears for him: so Noah did, and it is upon record, to his immortal honour. . . .

"1. God directs Noah to *make an ark, v.* 14-16. This ark was like the bulk of a ship, fitted not to sail upon the waters (there was no occasion for that, when there should be no shore to sail to), but to float upon the waters, waiting for their fall. God could have secured Noah by the ministration of angels, without putting him to any care, or pains, or trouble, himself; but he chose to employ him in making that which was to be the means of his preservation. . . . Both the providence of God, and the grace of God, own and crown the endeavours of the obedient and diligent. God gave him very particular instructions concerning this building, which could not but be admirably well fitted for the purpose when Infinite Wisdom itself was the architect. . . ."

Matthew Henry, *Commentary*

For Reflection and Reasoning

● The story of Noah and the flood should be a review for the students. As needed, read selected passages from Genesis 6-8.

● Of all the people on the face of the earth, God found only one man who walked with Him. God judged the character of every person individually. He punished all who were wicked, and preserved Noah because of his righteousness. God did not punish Noah for other men's sins.

● As Noah followed God's instructions in building the ark, how did those who watched him probably act? What character does it take to stand alone against all other people?

● How did God control the building and filling of the ark? Could God have saved Noah and his family in another way?

● Read Genesis 7:17-24.

● *Student Activity Page 5-4.*

Leading Idea

God blessed Noah.

Student Text, page 20

● Genesis 9:8-11. "Here is, I. The general establishment of God's covenant with this new world, and the extent of that covenant, *v.* 9, 10. Here observe, 1. That God is graciously pleased to deal with man in the way of a covenant, wherein God

greatly magnifies his condescending favour, and greatly encourages man's duty and obedience, as a reasonable and gainful service. 2. That all God's covenants with man are of his own making: *I, behold, I.* It is thus expressed both to raise our admiration—'Behold, and wonder, that though God be high yet he has this respect to man,' and to confirm our assurances of the validity of the covenant—'Behold and see, I make it; I that am faithful and able to make it good.' 3. That God's covenants are established more firmly than the pillars of heaven or the foundations of the earth, and cannot be disannulled. 4. That God's covenants are made with the covenanters and with their seed; the promise is to them and their children. 5. That those may be taken into covenant with God, and receive the benefits of it, who yet are not capable of restipulating, or giving their own consent. For this covenant is made with *every living creature, every beast of the earth.*"

Matthew Henry, *Commentary*

● Webster defined *covenant* as "A mutual consent or agreement of two or more persons, to do or to forbear some act or thing; a contract; stipulation."

For Reflection and Reasoning

● Because Noah was obedient and trusted God, God made a covenant with Noah. A covenant means that two people agree together either to do something, or not to do something. A covenant is a strict promise.

● What kinds of covenants do people make with one another? How does a covenant govern your actions?

● God's covenants always included a promise and a command.

● What was the covenant between God and Noah? What was God's promise? What was His command? What sign did God give to remind men of His covenant?

● Review: Who caused the waters to flood the earth? Why? Why did Noah find grace in God's eyes?

● When God sent the flood, the pressure of the water was so strong, that some animals were pressed into the mud, which later hardened into rock. These rocks are very special. Do you know what they are called? The creation of fossils shows how powerful God is.

Look at pictures of fossils, or use modeling clay to make a fossil. Flatten the clay and press a green leaf, small toy animal, or seashell into the clay. When the leaf or toy is removed, the shape will remain. This resembles a fossil.

● *Student Activity Page 5-5.*

Leading Idea

"And hath made of one blood all nations of men."

Student Text, page 21

● "The Mosaic history informs us, that Shem and his descendants dwelt in Eastern and Southern Asia; Ham and his posterity, Canaan and others, in Western Asia and Africa and that the 'Isles of the Gentiles,' meaning probably the Mediterranean, European and Caucasian regions, were divided among the children of Japheth. Modern physiologists have classed the human species under three corresponding races, namely, the *Mongol,* the *Negro,* and the *Caucasian.* . . .

"We cannot indeed tell exactly, what places on the earth's surface were designated by the names of the countries mentioned at very remote periods; for it was not until ages after that geography was cultivated as a science, or that accurate maps existed. The sacred historian, after speaking of the location of the descendants of Noah, informs us, that they all collected on the plain of Shinar with the impious design to build a tower whose top should reach to heaven. God confounded their language, and they then separated; wandering to distant countries.

"We soon begin to find traces of such connections among particular families or tribes, as gave them the name of nations. The earliest mentioned are the *Assyrians,* the *Babylonians* or *Chaldeans,* the *Egyptians,* and the *Jews.* Some obscure accounts of Phoeœnicia also extend back to this period, and in Greece, Sicyon is supposed by some to have been founded. . . ."[12]

Emma Willard, *Universal History*

• Webster defined *ancestor* as "One from whom a person descends, either by the father or mother. . ."

• *Race* is defined as "The lineage of a family, or continued series of descendants from a parent who is called the stock."

For Reflection and Reasoning

• The families of men all came from one ancestor, Noah. What is an ancestor? Shem, Ham and Japheth were the sons of Noah. Shem, Ham, and Japheth were the ancestors from which God made the races of men.

• Read Acts 17:26. What does "one blood" mean? If men are all made of "one blood", then is any race of people better than any other?

• Draw a simple family tree showing Noah and his three sons.

• Sing: *Jesus Loves the Little Children.*

Suggested Student Notes

All races of men came from one ancestor.

Leading Idea

God planned a home for each of Noah's sons.

Student Text, pages 21-22

For Reflection and Reasoning

• Review: What command did God give Noah and his sons after the flood?

• How is Noah the ancestor of all men and races?

• Read selected verses from Genesis 10.

● *Student Activity Page 5-6.* Label the continents. On each continent, record the name of the son of Noah whose family settled that land. Record Genesis 10:32.

Leading Idea	**God is able to defeat the designs of men.**

Student Text, page 22

● "(1.) It seems designed for an affront to God himself; for they would build a tower *whose top might reach to heaven,* which bespeaks a defiance of God, or at least a rivalship with him. . . (2.) They hoped hereby to make themselves a name; they would do something to be talked of now, and to give posterity to know that there had been such men as they in the world. Rather than die and leave no memorandum behind them, they would leave this monument of their pride, and ambition, and folly. (3) They did it to prevent their dispersion: *Lest we be scattered abroad upon the face of the earth.* 'It was done' (says Josephus) 'in disobedience to that command (*ch. ix.* 1), *Replenish the earth.*' God orders them to disperse. 'No,' say they, 'we will not, we will live and die together.' In order hereunto, they engage themselves and one another in this vast undertaking. That they might unite in one glorious empire, they resolve to build this city and tower, to be the metropolis of their kingdom and the centre of their unity....."

"III. The execution of these counsels of God, to the blasting and defeating of the counsels of men, *v.* 8, 9. God made them know *whose word should stand, his or theirs,* as the expression is, Jer. xliv. 28. Notwithstanding their oneness and obstinacy, God was too hard for them, and wherein they dealt proudly he was above them; for *who ever hardened his heart against him and prospered?* Three things were done:—

"1. Their language was confounded. God, who, when he made man, taught him to speak, and put words into his mouth fit to express the conceptions of his mind by, now caused these builders to forget their former language, and to speak and understand a new one, which yet was common to those of the same tribe or family, but not to others: those of one colony could converse together, but not with those of another. Now, (1.) This was a great miracle, and a proof of the power which God has upon the minds and tongues of men, which he turns as the rivers of water. . . .

"2. Their building was stopped: *They left off to build the city.* This was the effect of the confusion of their tongues; for it not only incapacitated them for helping one another, but probably struck such a damp upon their spirits that they could not proceed, since they saw, in this, the hand of the Lord gone out against them. Note, (1.) It is wisdom to leave off that which we see God fights against. (2.) God is able to blast and bring to nought all the devices and designs of Babel-builders. He sits in heaven, and laughs at the counsels of the kings of the earth against him and his anointed; and will force them to confess that there is no wisdom nor counsel against the Lord. Prov. xxi. 30; Isa. viii. 9, 10.

"3. The builders were scattered abroad upon the face of the whole earth, *v.* 8, 9. They departed in companies, with their families, and after their tongues (*ch.* x. 5, 20, 31), to the several countries and places allotted to them in the division that had been made, which they knew before, but would not go to take possession of till now that they were forced to it. . . . (2.) It was God's work: *The Lord scattered them.* God's hand is to be acknowledged in all scattering providences. . ."

Matthew Henry, *Commentary*

● "The ancient fathers were of opinion that the distribution of mankind was not left to be settled at random, but that a formal division of the world, as known to him, was made by Noah, the sole proprietor, among his three sons, a considerable time before any migrations were made.

They suppose Noah to have acted in this case by divine direction. This hypothesis is strongly favoured by mere probability; and though many writers have discountenanced it, it is adopted by Dr. Hales, who quotes the striking passages, Deut. xxxii, 7-9, and Acts xvii, 26, as tending strongly to support it."[13]

John Frost, *Pictorial History of the World*

For Reflection and Reasoning

● Review: What were the promise and the command that were part of God's covenant with Noah? Did men obey His command?

● Reasoning from the Scriptures included in the Student Text, identify why the people wanted to build a high tower (2 reasons). How did this show disobedience to God?

● Speak to the students in a foreign language. Perhaps give an instruction, or say something with great feeling. Ask the students why they did not understand what was said? Could you work well with someone who does not speak the same language as you?

● Why did God cause some groups of people to speak different languages? Since God is an orderly God, do you think He caused members of one family to speak different languages? Why not?

● Why did speaking different languages cause people to separate and live in different places? Was that God's original plan?

● God is always in control of the plans of men. Men think they can have their own plans and do what they wish to do, no matter what God says. When men disobey God, He can overturn their plans and punish them for their disobedience.

Suggested Student Notes

God governs the affairs of men.

God's Plan	Man's Plan
God's command to men after the Flood was to "multiply and replenish the earth."	Men chose not to obey God, but to build a huge tower, and "make us a name, lest we be scattered abroad."

God's Plan

God confounded their language and "scattered them abroad."

Cultivating Student Mastery

1. How did God take action at the Tower of Babel to cause men to obey His plan?

MOSES AND THE LAW

1½-2 Weeks

Chapter 6
Moses and the Law

8-10 Days

> **Leading Idea**
>
> ***God gave Moses the Ten Commandments to control and direct man's actions.***
>
> Student Text, pages 23-26

● Noah Webster defined *commandment* as "A command; a mandate; an order or injunction given by authority; charge; precept." He also defined *moral law* as "a law which prescribes to men their religious and social duties, in other words, their duties to God and to each other. The moral law is summarily contained in the Decalogue or ten commandments, written by the finger of God on two tables of stone, and delivered to Moses on mount Sinai."

● "The law of the ten commandments is, 1. A law of God's making. They are enjoined by the infinite eternal Majesty of heaven and earth. . . 2. It is a law of his own speaking. God has many ways of speaking to the children of men. . . by his Spirit, by conscience, by providences, by his voice, all which we ought carefully to attend to; but he never spoke, at any time, upon any occasion, as he spoke the ten commandments, which therefore we ought to hear with *more earnest heed*. . . This law God had given to man before (it was written in his heart by nature); but sin had so defaced that writing that it was necessary, in this manner, to revive the knowledge of it.

". . . God asserts his own authority to enact this law in general. . . He that gives being may give law."

Matthew Henry, *Commentary*

● "II. The delivering of the two tables of testimony to Moses. God had promised him these tables when he called him up into the mount (*ch.* xxiv. 12), and now, when he was sending him down, he delivered them to him, to be carefully and honourably deposited in the ark, *v.* 18. 1. The ten commandments which God had spoken upon mount Sinai in the hearing of all the people were now written, *in perpetuam rei memoriam—for a perpetual memorial,* because that which is written remains. 2. They were written in *tables of stone,* prepared, not by Moses, as it should seem (for it is intimated, *ch. xxiv.* 12, that he found them ready written when he went up to the mount), but, as some think, by the ministry of angels. The law was written in *tables of stone,* to denote the perpetual duration of it (what can be supposed to last longer than that which is written in stone, and laid up?), to denote likewise the hardness of our hearts; one might more easily write in stone than write any thing that is good in our corrupt and sinful hearts. 3. They were written *with the finger of God,* that is, by his will and power immediately, without the use of any instrument. It is God only that can write his law in the heart; he *gives a heart of flesh, and then, by his Spirit,* which is the *finger of God,* he writes his will in the *fleshly tables of the heart,* 2 Cor. iii. 3. 4. They were written in two tables, being designed to direct us in our duty both towards God and towards man. 5. They are called *tables of testimony,* because this written law testified both the will of God concerning them and his good-will towards them, and would be a testimony against them if they were disobedient. . . ."

Matthew Henry, *Commentary*

For Reflection and Reasoning

• Can you imagine how it must have been for Moses to see the Ten Commandments being written onto stone by the finger of God? Can you write words onto stone? Why not? Why could God do it? What does it picture that God wrote them on stone? God's laws last forever.

• What is a commandment? A person who has authority or power over you can give you a command or order. They can instruct you to do something. They can give you rules or precepts that control, direct, or restrain your actions. What people have the right and responsibility to govern you? Why? Must you obey?

• Because God created man, He has the authority and power to govern and control each one of us. The Ten Commandments are commands or precepts (rules) He has given us to obey. We sometimes call them God's law. They are very important, because they come from God. All people should obey the Ten Commandments.

• In what two ways do God's laws or commandments govern us? They control our thoughts (internal) our actions (external).

• Our thoughts, on the inside, are very important. Before you do an action, do you usually think about it? That means that the thought comes first, then the action. The kinds of thoughts you have determine what your actions will be. If your thoughts please God, will they cause your actions to please God? Will obeying God's commandments please Him?

• Read selected verses regarding obeying God's commandments or precepts. Suggestions: Psalm 119:4; Psalm 119:11; Proverbs 6:23.

• *Student Activity Page 6-1.* Record the definition of commandment: "A commandment is a command or order given by an authority." Complete the statement: God's law "governs our thoughts and actions." The remainder of the chart will be completed in following lessons.

Cultivating Student Mastery

1. Why did God give the Ten Commandments to the Israelites?

2. What is a commandment?

3. In what two ways do God's laws govern us?

4. What must please God before our actions will please God?

The Ten Commandments teach us our duty to God and duty to other men.

Student Text, pages 24-25

● "The first four of the ten commandments. . . we have in these verses. It was fit that those should be put first, because man had a Maker to love before he had a neighbor to love; and justice and charity are acceptable acts of obedience to God only when they flow from the principles of piety. It cannot be expected that he should be true to his brother who is false to his God. . ."

Matthew Henry, *Commentary*

For Reflection and Reasoning

● The Ten Commandments are often called the Moral Law. They do not give instructions about what to wear or eat. They are not rules about how fast to drive or how to build our houses. They are commands or precepts that govern our actions and manners toward God and toward people around us in our homes, churches, and our community.

● Do you know what a duty is? A *duty* is "that which a person owes to another . . . To pay, do, or perform."

● The diagram in the Student Text, pages 24-25, shows that the Ten Commandments are placed in a special order.

First, we find the commandments which govern our duty to God. What are the four commandments that teach us what thoughts and actions we should have toward God? The students may read the abbreviated statements of the first four commandments in the Student Text, or read Exodus 20:1-11.

● As we look at the rest of the commandments, we will see that they all govern our thoughts and actions toward our neighbors — those around us in our home and community.

● Why do you suppose God placed the commandments governing our relationship and actions toward Himself first? If we do not have the right thoughts and ideas in our hearts, we will not have right actions toward Him. If we do not have right thoughts and actions toward God, we will not be able to have right actions toward those around us.

● *Student Activity Page 6-1.* Draw arrow from Me to God. To the left of the arrow, record: "Duty to God" and a statement of the first four commandments.

Cultivating Student Mastery

1. Why does our duty to God come before our duty to man?

The Ten Commandments teach us our duty regarding our respect and worship of God.

Student Text, pages 24-25

● "I. The first commandment concerns the object of our worship, Jehovah, and him only. . . The sin against this commandment which *we* are most in danger of is giving the glory and honour to any creature which are due to God only. . . whatever is esteemed or loved, feared or served, delighted in or depended on, more than God, that (whatever it is) we do in effect make a god of. This prohibition includes a precept which is the foundation of the whole law, that we take the Lord for our God, acknowledge that he is God, accept him for ours, adore him with admiration and humble reverence, and set our affections entirely upon him."

Matthew Henry, *Commentary*

● "The second commandment concerns the ordinances of worship, or the way in which God will be worshipped, which it is fit that he himself should have the appointing of. Here is, (1.) The prohibition: we are here forbidden to worship even the true God by images . . . Our religious worship must be governed by the power of faith, not by the power of imagination. They must not make such images or pictures as the heathen worshipped, lest they also should be tempted to worship them. Those who would be kept from sin must keep themselves from the occasions of it. . ."

Matthew Henry, *Commentary*

● "The third commandment concerns the manner of our worship, that it be done with all possible reverence and seriousness . . . We take God's name in vain, [1.] By hypocrisy, making a profession of God's name, but not living up to that profession. . . [3.] By rash swearing,

mentioning the name of God, or any of his attributes, in the form of an oath, without any just occasion for it, or due application of mind to it, but as a by-word, to no purpose at all, or to no good purpose."

Matthew Henry, *Commentary*

● Noah Webster defined the *Sabbath* as "The day which God appointed to be observed by the Jews as a day of rest from all secular labor or employments, and to be kept holy and consecrated to his service and worship. This was originally the seventh day of the week, the day on which God rested from the work of creation; and this day is still observed by the Jews and some christians. . ."

● *Holy* is defined by Webster as "Hallowed; consecrated or set apart to a sacred use, or to the service or worship of God; a sense frequent in Scripture; as the holy sabbath. . ."

● "How it must be observed. *First,* as a day of rest; they were to do no manner of work on this day in their callings or worldly business. *Secondly*, As a holy day, set apart to the honour of the holy God, and to be spent in holy exercises. God, by blessing it, had made it holy; they, by solemnly blessing him, must keep it holy, and not alienate it to any other purpose than that for which the difference between it and other days was instituted."

Matthew Henry, *Commentary*

For Reflection and Reasoning

● Review: What is a commandment? What is the purpose of the Ten Commandments? How do the Ten Commandments govern us in two ways? Why is our duty to God the most important?

● Read the first commandment, Exodus 20:3.

The people in Egypt, where the Israelites had been slaves, worshiped false gods. They worshiped animals, the sun, the wind, and other things. Can you

imagine praying to a cat or a dog? Why not?

● God is the only true God. He is the most important One in our lives. His first commandment tells us to worship Him. In everything we do, we should make sure to honor and obey Him. We must allow God to govern every part of our lives. We must not love, delight in, or depend on anything else more than God. What is most important in your life? Is it God? Is it friends? Is it having fun? Is it your toys? Is it sports? We break this commandment when we are selfish, and do what we want to do instead of what we know God wants us to do.

• Read the second commandment, Exodus 20:4-6.

What did God tell us not to make? *Graven* means engraved, or carved. This commandment tells us not to make an idol to represent God.

• God is infinite, awesome, and all-powerful. No idol could ever truly represent God, and an idol would tempt us to forget how truly amazing God is. God wants us to worship Him as our Creator, our Provider, our Protector, our Guide, our Savior, and much more. An idol would limit God to something very simple, instead of our truly great God.

• This commandment forbids worshipping idols of any kind. God says that He is jealous. He wants us to love and worship only Him, not anything else. He becomes angry when His people ignore Him, do not worship Him, or worship false gods. Can you remember any Bible story in which people worshipped idols rather than the true God? What did God do?

• Read the third commandment, Exodus 20:7.

The third commandment teaches us to always say the name of God carefully, never thoughtlessly, or as a swear word. This commandment emphasizes that we should always respect and honor God.

• The commandment also teaches us that if we say we love God, we should act like it as well. What would people think if you say that you are a Christian, but they see you being mean, stealing, lying, or doing other wrong things? They would think that being a Christian isn't any different from not being a Christian. That would be taking God's name in vain.

• Read the fourth commandment, Exodus 20:8-11. Discuss the meaning of the sabbath.

God created the Sabbath when He created the earth. Read Genesis 2:2-3. From the very beginning of time, He planned for a day of rest and worship.

• Sunday is the first day of the week, and we honor Sunday as the day to worship God. We worship on Sunday, following the example of the New Testament churches. The first day of the week is the day when Jesus was resurrected from the grave. Even though we do not observe the Sabbath as the Israelites did, we still should honor and obey the fourth commandment.

How can we make Sunday a holy day? In order to obey this commandment, what should not be done on Sunday?

Cultivating Student Mastery

1. Complete the chart, *Student Activity Page 6-2.*

Leading Idea

The Ten Commandments govern our actions toward other men.

Student Text, pages 24-25

• "We have here the laws of the second table, as they are commonly called, the last six of the ten commandments, comprehending our duty to ourselves and to one another..."
Matthew Henry, *Commentary*

For Reflection and Reasoning

● Review: What is a commandment? Who had the authority to give man the Ten Commandments? Why?

● Review: How did God give the commandments to Moses? As we read the Ten Commandments, we are reminded that the commandments were put into order by God. He placed the commandments which govern our walk with Him first. After that, He gave six commandments which govern our duty to ourselves and those around us.

● Review: What is a duty? What is our duty to God? We have a duty to respect God, worship Him and obey Him because He is our Creator.

● We also have a duty to ourselves and to other people. We have that duty because man is God's creation. The last six commandments govern our thoughts and actions toward ourselves and others.

● Students may read the abbreviated statements of the last six commandments in the Student Text, or read Exodus 20:12-17.

● *Student Activity Page 6-1.* Draw arrow from Me to Others. Below the arrow, record: "Duty to others" and a statement of the last six commandments.

Leading Idea

Honor thy father and thy mother.

● "The fifth commandment concerns the duties we owe to our relations; those of children to their parents are alone specified: *Honour thy father and thy mother,* which includes, 1. A decent respect to their persons, an inward esteem of them outwardly expressed upon all occasions in our conduct towards them. *Fear them* (Lev. 19:3), *give them reverence,* Heb. 12:9. The contrary to this is mocking at them and despising them, Proverbs 30:17. 2. Obedience to their lawful commands; so it is expounded (Eph. 6:1-3): *Children, obey your parents,* come when they call you, go where they send you, do what they bid you, refrain from what they forbid you; and this, as children, cheerfully, and from a principle of love.... 3. Submission to their rebukes, instructions, and corrections; not only to the good and gentle, but also to the froward, out of conscience towards God. 4. Disposing of themselves with the advice, direction, and consent, of parents, not alienating their property, but with their approbation. 5. Endeavoring, in every thing, to be the comfort of their parents, and to make their old age easy to them, maintaining them if they stand in need of support, which our Saviour makes to be particularly intended in this commandment, Matt. 15:4-6. The reason annexed to this commandment is a promise. . . a long life is. . . promised particularly to obedient children. . ."
Matthew Henry, *Commentary*

● Webster defined *honor* as "To revere; to respect; to treat with deference and submission, and perform relative duties to."

For Reflection and Reasoning

● Review: Who is supposed to obey the Ten Commandments? What relationship is governed by the first four commandments? By the last six?

● Read the fifth commandment, Exodus 20:12.

What does it mean to *honor* someone? A child who truly honors his parents honors them in his heart and externally at the same time. That means you must have a good heart attitude as you obey your parents.

● A story has been told about a little boy whose mother asked him to sit down. He sat down, but he said to his mother, "I'm standing up on the inside." He did not obey with his heart. God wants you to obey with your heart and your actions.

● Read selected verses regarding obedience to parents. Suggestions: Ephesians 6:1-3; Colossians 3:20; Matthew 15:4; Proverbs 1:8; 6:20.

● Read and discuss the statement by Matthew Henry on *Student Activity Page 6-3.*

● How are children tempted to break the fifth commandment? How do children obey the fifth commandment internally and externally?

● What promise did God make to children who obey the fifth commandment?

● *Student Activity Page 6-3.* Complete the Obedience Chart, showing the relationship of the internal and external in obedience to parents.

Cultivating Student Mastery

1. How are children tempted to break the fifth commandment?

2. How do children obey the fifth commandment internally and externally?

3. What promise did God make to children who obey the fifth commandment?

Leading Idea

We are commanded to respect the life and person of others.

● "The sixth commandment concerns our own and our neighbour's life (*v.* 13): *'Thou shalt not kill;* thou shalt not do any thing hurtful or injurious to the health, ease, and life, of thy own body, or any other person's unjustly.' This is one of the laws of nature and was strongly enforced by the precepts given to Noah and his sons, Gen. 9:5, 6. It does not forbid killing in lawful war, or in our own necessary defence, nor the magistrate's putting offenders to death, for those things tend to the preserving of life; but it forbids all malice and hatred to the person of any (for *he that hateth his brother is a murderer),* and all personal revenge arising therefrom; also all rash anger upon sudden provocations, and hurt said or done, or aimed to be done, in passion: Matt. 5:22. And, as that which is worst of all, it forbids persecu-

tion, laying wait for the blood of the innocent and excellent ones of the earth."
Matthew Henry, *Commentary*

● "The seventh commandment concerns our own and our neighbor's chastity: *Thou shalt not commit adultery, v.* 14. This is put before the sixth by our Saviour (Mark 10:19): *Do not commit adultery, do not kill;* for our chastity should be as dear to us as our lives, and we should be as much afraid of that which defiles the body as of that which destroys it. This commandment forbids all acts of uncleanness, with all those fleshly lusts which produce those acts and war against the soul, and all those practices which cherish and excite those fleshly lusts, as looking, in order to lust, which Christ tells us, is forbidden in this commandment, Matt. 5:28."
Matthew Henry, *Commentary*

For Reflection and Reasoning

● Read the sixth commandment, Exodus 20:13.

Who created life? In whose image is man created? God, as creator, chooses when we are born and when we should die. God has a plan and purpose for each individual, including the length of his life. No man, therefore, should murder another person.

● In the New Testament, Jesus taught that hating someone is just as wrong as killing them. In order to keep this commandment, we must ask Jesus to help us love one another, our brothers and sisters, our parents, other family members, friends, and other people.

● This commandment teaches that life is a gift from God. We should not do anything that would harm our own bodies or another person. You may be tempted to do something that sounds enjoyable, but would actually be harmful to you. Consciously harming your health and life breaks the sixth commandment.

● Read the seventh commandment, Exodus 20:14.

In the seventh commandment, God explained His plan for a man to love a woman, to marry her, and to always love her, and her only, as his wife. God created Adam and Eve. God gave Adam one wife to love for the rest of his life. Someday, if God plans for you to be married, you should have a very special kind of married love for the one person God planned to be your husband or wife.

Cultivating Student Mastery

1. Why is it wrong to kill another person?

2. What did Jesus say was just as wrong as killing someone?

3. When a man and woman get married, how can they keep the seventh commandment?

Leading Idea

We are commanded to respect the internal and external property of others.

● "The eighth commandment concerns our own and our neighbour's wealth, estate, and goods: *Thou shalt not steal, v.* 15. . . . This command forbids us to rob ourselves of what we have by sinful spending, or the use and comfort of it by sinful sparing, and to rob others by removing the ancient landmarks, invading our neighbour's rights, taking his goods from his person, or house, or field, forcibly or clandestinely, over-reaching in bargains, not restoring what is borrowed or found, withholding just debts, rents, or wages, and (which is worst of all) to rob the public in the coin or revenue, or that which is dedicated to the service of religion."

Matthew Henry, *Commentary*

● "The ninth commandment concerns our own and our neighbour's good name: *Thou shalt not bear false witness, v.* 16. This forbids, 1. Speaking falsely in any matter, lying, equivocating, and any way devising and designing to deceive our neighbour. 2. Speaking unjustly against our neighbour, to the prejudice of his reputation. . . 3. Bearing false witness against him, laying to his charge things that he knows not, either judicially, upon oath. . . or extrajudicially, in common converse, slandering, backbiting, talebearing, aggravating what is done amiss and making it worse than it is, and any way endeavouring to raise our own reputation on the ruin of our neighbour's."

Matthew Henry, *Commentary*

• Webster defined *witness* as "Testimony; attestation of a fact or event."

• "The tenth commandment strikes at the root: *Thou shalt not covet, v. 17.* The foregoing commands implicitly forbid all desire of doing that which will be an injury to our neighbour; this forbids all inordinate desire of having that which will be a gratification to ourselves. 'O that such a man's house were mine! Such a man's wife mine! Such a man's estate mine!' This is certainly the language of discontent at our own lot, and envy at our neighbour's; and these are the sins principally forbidden here. St. Paul. . . perceived that this law. . . forbade all those irregular appetites and desires which are the first-born of the corrupt nature, the first risings of the sin that dwelleth in us, and the beginnings of all the sin that is committed by us. . ."

Matthew Henry, *Commentary*

• To *covet* is defined by Webster as "To desire inordinately; to desire that which it is unlawful to obtain or possess."

For Reflection and Reasoning

• Review: What is the relationship between the Ten Commandments and our lives?

• Read the eighth commandment, Exodus 20:15.

Property is anything that a person owns. This commandment reminds us that God gave property to people. What kind of property do you have? How did God provide it for you? Usually property is earned, or received as a gift.

• What does it mean to steal? What does God say about stealing?

• If someone has something that we would really like, perhaps it could be apples growing on a tree in their back yard, what should we do? What should we not do?

• If Mom made delicious cookies, and they are cooling on the counter, what might we be tempted to do? What would be the right thing to do?

• This commandment also teaches that we should not be wasteful of money or property that God has given to us. Nor should we be selfish and stingy.

• Just as we would want other people to respect our property, we must respect the property of others. We must be careful of our own property, and careful not to hurt property that belongs to someone else. You should not think it is funny to draw pictures on someone else's paper, or walk on their books, etc. That does not respect their property and does not keep the eighth commandment.

If we promise to pay something, we must keep our promise. If you borrow a toy from a friend, and ask to keep it for one week, what should you do at the end of the week?

• Read the ninth commandment, Exodus 20:16.

Do you know what a witness is? A witness tells what happened.

• The ninth commandment instructs us to be truthful when we speak, especially when we speak about others. We should be honest about the character and actions of others.

• If something happens while Mom or

Dad is out of the room, what will he or she ask the children? How should the children answer the question? Sometimes, we are tempted to lie, because we think it will keep us out of trouble. What will actually happen when we lie?

● Read the tenth commandment, Exodus 20:17.

What does it mean to covet? To covet means to want another person's property. When we see things which belong to others, we may admire them, and we may think that it would be nice to have something similar. But, we must never want their property.

● How would coveting another person's property lead to breaking another commandment? If we want something that belongs to someone else, and we continually think about how much we want it, what will we be tempted to do? If we actually stole something, what else might we be tempted to do when people started asking questions about the missing property.

● Can someone see you covet? Why or why not?

● Can another person see you breaking the ninth or tenth commandments? Why or why not? Can God see you?

The Ten Commandments are the Moral Law, teaching us our duty to God and to men.

Student Text, page 26

● "God give us all to see our face in the glass of this law, and to lay our hearts under the government of it!"

Matthew Henry, *Commentary*

For Reflection and Reasoning

● Review: What is a commandment? How did we get the Ten Commandments?

● Man has two relationships — a relationship to God and a relationship to others. The Ten Commandments govern both relationships.

What do the first four commandments govern?

What do the last six commandments govern?

Why does our duty to God come before our duty to man?

● Why is it so important to govern our thoughts?

● How can breaking one commandment lead to breaking another commandment? Give an example.

● Using familiar Bible stories, guide the students to recognize the consequences of obeying or disobeying the Ten Commandments. Identify the individuals, what commandment did they keep or break? What were the consequences? Suggestions: Cain; Achan; David and Bathsheba; Daniel; Shadrach, Meshach, and Abednego; Ahab and Naboth.

● *Student Activity Page 6-4*. Read Isaac Watt's poem, "The Ten Commandments."

CHRIST
The Focal Point of History
1-1½ Week

Chapter 7
Christ Changed History
5-7 Days

Leading Idea

Sin requires a sacrifice for forgiveness.

Student Text, page 27

• "All men by sin had become guilty before God, had forfeited their inheritance, their liberties, and their very lives, into the hands of divine justice; but God, being willing to show the greatness of his mercy, proclaimed a covenant of grace, and ordered it to be typically administered under the Old Testament, but not without the blood and life of the creature; and God accepted the blood of bulls and goats, as typifying the blood of Christ; and by these means the covenant of grace was ratified under the former dispensation."

Matthew Henry, *Commentary*

For Reflection and Reasoning

• Review: What is sin? Why is there sin in the world?

• Sin created a break in man's relationship with God. Review *Student Activity Page 5-3*. What changes took place in Adam and Eve's lives because of sin?

• Read Romans 5:12. Because sin is passed down from parent to child, all people are born as sinners. Did anyone have to *teach* you to disobey? to be selfish? to be unkind?

• *Student Activity Page 7-1.* Each one of us was born with a sin nature. We began to sin at a very early age. Sin has broken our relationship with God — it separates us from Him because He is holy and right-

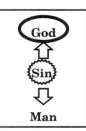

eous. Discuss the illustration of sin's effect on man's relationship with God.

● *Student Activity Page 7-3.* Reason with the students concerning how Christ affected the relationship of man to God.
    • Students may record "Old Testament" on the left side of the cross and "New Testament" on the right.
    • On the lines below "Old Testament", students may record Hebrews 9:22b.
    • Below the verse, students record "animal sacrifices required". Students may draw an arrow on the left pointing to the cross, showing that the sacrifices of the Old Testament looked forward or foretold His coming.

The remainder of the chart will be completed in the following lesson.

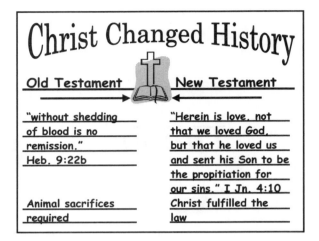

Christ came to fulfill the law.

Student Text, pages 27-28

● "Christ commands nothing now which was forbidden either by the law of nature or the moral law, nor forbids any thing which those laws had enjoined; it is a great mistake to think he does, and he here takes care to rectify the mistake; *I am not come to destroy.* The Saviour of souls is the *destroyer* of nothing but the *works of the devil,* of nothing that comes from God, much less of those excellent dictates which we have from Moses and the prophets. No, he came to *fulfil* them. That is, [1.] To obey the commands of the law, for he was *made under the law,* Gal. iv. 4. He in all respects yielded obedience to the law, honoured his parents, sanctified the sabbath, prayed, gave alms, and did that which never any one else did, obeyed perfectly, and never broke the law in any thing. [2.] To make good the promises of the law, and the predictions of the prophets, which did all bear witness to him. The covenant of grace is, for substance, the same now that it was then, and Christ the Mediator of it. [3.] To answer the types of the law; thus (as bishop Tillotson expresses it), he did not make *void,* but make *good,* the ceremonial law, and manifested himself to be the Substance of all those shadows. [4.] To fill up the defects of it, and so to complete and perfect it. . . [5.] To carry on the same design; the Christian institutes are so far from thwarting and contradicting that which was the main design of the Jewish religion, that they promote it to the highest degree. The gospel is the *time of reformation* (Heb. ix. 10), not the repeal of the law, but the amendment of it, and, consequently, its establishment."

Matthew Henry, *Commentary*

For Reflection and Reasoning

● Review: What is a law? What did the Old Testament law require for men's sins to be forgiven? The law was God's way of governing men.

● What does it mean to fulfill something?

Can men fulfill God's law? Why? Why could Christ fulfill God's law?

● Old Testament prophets foretold Christ's coming, His death and His resurrection to fulfill the law and pay the penalty for man's sin. The book of Isaiah, written approximately 700 years before Christ's birth, described Christ's death. Students may read selected passages in Isaiah. Which foretell Christ's suffering? Compare them with the New Testament accounts written after Christ became man's sacrifice.

Isaiah 53:4	He bore our sins	I Peter 2:24; Matthew 8:17
Isaiah 53:5	He was wounded for our sins, that we might be forgiven	II Cor. 5:21
Isaiah 53:6	He bore the sins of all men	Hebrews 9:28a
Isaiah 53:7	He is the Lamb of God	John 1:36

● Review the Chart, *Student Activity Page 7-1.* What separates each of us from God? Who can pay the penalty for that sin? Read I John 4:10.

To depict Christ's death on the cross paying for man's sin, have the students cut out the cross, *Student Activity Page 7-*

2. Students may tape the top of the cross on *Student Activity Page 7-1,* so that it covers the broken arrows and "sin" between God and man.

● *Student Activity Page 7-3.* Consider how Christ changed history.
 • On the right side, under "New Testament", have the students record a verse, such as I John 4:10, which identifies that Christ is the means of salvation. Animal sacrifices are no longer needed. Christ's death, burial and resurrection provide man with eternal salvation.
 • In the right lower section, below the verse, the student may record, "Christ fulfilled the law."
 • Students may draw an arrow on the right pointing to the cross, showing that Christ paid for the penalty for all sin.

Note: This lesson will require two classtimes.

Cultivating Student Mastery

1. Why did God give men His law?

2. Why couldn't man keep God's law?

3. What was God's way of fulfilling the law?

Leading Idea

"On these two commandments hang all the law and the prophets."

Student Text, pages 28-29

● "This is the sum and substance of all those precepts relating to practical religion which were written in men's hearts by nature, revived by Moses, and backed and enforced by the preaching and writing of the prophets. All hang upon the law of love; take away this, and all falls to the ground, and comes to nothing. Rituals and ceremonials must give way to these, as must all spiritual gifts, for love is the more excellent way. This is the spirit of the law, which animates it, the cement of the law, which joins it; it is the root and spring of all other duties, the compendium of the whole Bible, not only of the law and the prophets, but of the gospel too, only supposing this love to be the fruit of faith, and that we love God in Christ, and our neighbour for his sake. All hangs on these two commandments, as the effect doth both on its efficient and on its final cause; for *the fulfilling of the law is love* (Rom. xiii. 10), and *the end of the law is love,* 1 Tim. i. 5. The law of love is the nail, is the *nail in the sure place, fastened by the masters of assemblies* (Eccl. xii. 11), on which is hung all *the glory of the law and the prophets* (Isa. xxii. 24)... *Love never faileth.* Into these two great commandments therefore let our hearts be delivered as into a mould; in the defence and evidence of these let us spend our zeal, and not in notions, names, and strifes of words, as if those were the mighty things on which the law and the prophets hung, and to them the love of God and our neighbour must be sacrificed; but to the commanding power of these let every thing else be made to bow."

Matthew Henry, *Commentary*

For Reflection and Reasoning

● Review: What is the law? What do the Ten Commandments teach us? What relationships do the Ten Commandments govern? What are some of the commandments which deal with our relationship to God? What are some of the commandments which deal with our relationship to other people?

● Jesus was questioned by the Jewish leaders concerning the laws. What are the two "new" commandments which Jesus gave these men? To which of the Ten Commandments does the first commandment relate? To which of the Ten Commandments does the second commandment relate? How do these commandments show that God does not change?

● *Student Activity Page 7-4.* Record the first of the two commandments showing the relationship of man to God. Below this commandment, record "First four commandments". Below the arrow showing relationship of man to man, students record the second commandment of the New Testament. Following the commandment, students record "Last six commandments."

● Which of these relationships is most important: our relationship to God or our relationship to other people? How will it affect the other relationship?

● What does it mean to love God? to love our neighbors?

● If we truly love God, will we want to respect Him—
  • As the only true God to worship
  • Not worshipping idols
  • Respecting His name and using it rightly
  • Setting aside a day to worship Him

● If we truly love our neighbors, will we respect them—
  • Honoring and obeying our parents
  • Protecting the life and person of others, and not harming them
  • Respecting our bodies as belonging to God, and keeping them pure
  • Respecting the property of others, not taking or harming it in any way
  • Protecting the reputation of others, by telling the truth
  • Being content with our own possessions, not being greedy or covetous of what others have

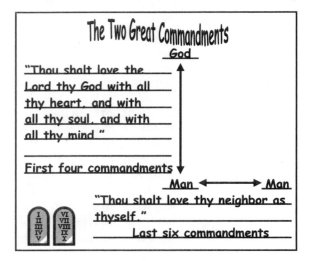

The Two Great Commandments

God

"Thou shalt love the Lord thy God with all thy heart, and with all thy soul, and with all thy mind."

First four commandments

Man ← → Man

"Thou shalt love thy neighbor as thyself."

Last six commandments

Leading Idea

The law is our Schoolmaster.

Student Text, page 29

● Webster defined *schoolmaster* as "He or that which disciplines, instructs and leads."

● "As it declared the mind and will of God concerning them, and at the same time denounced a curse against them for every failure in their duty, so it was proper to convince them of their lost and undone condition in themselves, and to let them see the weakness and insufficiency of their own righteousness to recommend them to God. . . And thus it was their schoolmaster, to instruct and govern them in their state of minority, or . . . To lead and conduct them to Christ . . . That they might be more fully instructed by him as their schoolmaster, in the true

way of justification and salvation, which is only by faith in him... Thus the apostle acquaints us for what uses and purposes the law served; and, from what he says concerning this matter, we may observe,

"1. The goodness of God to his people of old, in giving the law to them. . . It furnished them with sufficient means and helps both to direct them in their duty to God and to encourage their hopes in him.

"2. . . . Whereas it was never designed to be the rule of their justification, but only a means of convincing them of their guilt and of their need of a Saviour, and of directing them to Christ, and faith in him, as the only way of obtaining this privilege. See Rom. ix. 31, 32; x. 3, 4."

Matthew Henry, *Commentary*

For Reflection and Reasoning

● Review: What is the law? Note: Although the law contains more than the Ten Commandments, for our study with the students, refer specifically to this aspect of the law.

● Do you have a teacher? What does your teacher do? Does your teacher instruct you in your lessons? Does your teacher correct you if you are wrong? Does your teacher help you to develop good habits? Are you taught to know what is right or wrong? This is the job of a *schoolmaster*.

● Read Galatians 3:24. What does this verse teach is to be our "schoolmaster"?

● In the study of the Ten Commandments, did we learn that it would be hard for us to keep all of the commandments? Why is this true? Does this show that, as

sinners, we each need a Saviour?

● How can the law be a *schoolmaster* to us? How does the law instruct us? How does the law teach us whether our actions are right or wrong? Does the law teach us we are sinners? How? How does the law help us to develop good habits?

Suggested Student Notes

Schoolmaster — One who instructs and leads.

The law is our schoolmaster to bring us to Christ.

Cultivating Student Mastery

1. What does the law teach us?

2. How does the law bring us to Christ?

Leading Idea

Internal liberty produces external liberty.

Student text, pages 29-30

• "Reflect upon this: When Christ Jesus came, He gave individual, internal, *spiritual liberty* to every one who accepted Christ by grace through faith. The gift of individual salvation is the gift of spiritual liberty. (Eph. 2:8-9) When one is redeemed from bondage to internal sin and spiritual death, he is given spiritual liberty. The same principle of liberty is identified in the Scriptures '. . . the law of the Spirit of life in Christ Jesus hath made me free from the law of sin and death.' *Romans 8:2* 'And ye shall know the truth and the truth shall make you free. . . If the Son therefore shall make you free, ye shall be free indeed.' *John 8:32, 36.* Also consider *Romans 6:22, II Corinthians 3:17, Galatians 5:1, James 1:25*

"Christ's free man, throughout all ages, has desired, striven for, and often died for religious freedom. Christianity purposes to work positively to effect laws for the lawless and liberty for the righteous under the Law.

". . . After the English Bible was printed and promulgated, did the individual enjoy more or less liberty? Surely, thoughtful men discern there was *more*, not less liberty for the individual. And, when the Bible was brought to America by the Pilgrims in 1620, and, then, the Puritans in 1630, did individuals enjoy more or less liberty? Indeed, liberty abounded *even more* than before! And, when the constitution of the United States of America was finally ratified in 1789, the local church enjoyed *the greatest expression of individual liberty the world had ever witnessed!*"[14]
James Rose, *Spiritual Liberty is Causative to Religious and Civil Liberty*

For Reflection and Reasoning

• Review: What is liberty? Government? Self government? How is our liberty related to our self government?

• What happens to our hearts when we accept Jesus as our Saviour? How does Christ govern our heart? How does He govern our actions?

• If we govern our own actions, will we need as many civil laws? Why? Review the relationship between internal and external government. See Chapter 4.

• What gives liberty in our home? What laws must control the home to have liberty?

• In the first century after Christ, many small churches began. How does this show that they had internal liberty?

• Once people had liberty in their own lives, in their family, and in their church, they wanted liberty in their nation. This took many centuries. What is a century?

• *Student Activity Page 7-5.* Christ began working in the hearts of Christians when He came to earth. With Christ, the individual had internal liberty. This was *spiritual liberty.* History teaches that liberty to worship God freely came after many centuries. This was *religious liberty.* The greatest amount of *civil liberty* did not appear until the United States of America. Students may record *Suggested Student Notes* on *Student Activity Page 7-5.*

Suggested Student Notes

Christ and Christianity gave spiritual liberty. This produced religious liberty and civil liberty.

PAUL
Westward Movement
1-1½ Weeks

Chapter 8
Paul on Mars Hill
5-7 Days

> **Leading Idea** — *Paul was the link for the Gospel from Asia to Europe.*
>
> Student Text, pages 31-32

• Athens. "The capital and largest city of Greece. . . The city stands in a plain surrounded on three sides by mountains. . . . Athens is named after Athena, the ancient Greek goddess of wisdom. . . .

   "ANCIENT BUILDINGS. The ancient city centered about a flat-topped hill, called the Acropolis. This hill is surrounded by a wall and contains four beautiful structures: the Propylæa, a building of mixed Doric and Ionic style, which serves as a stately entrance to the enclosure; the Temple of Victory, a small Ionic edifice beside the Propylæa; the Parthenon, which is the classic example of a pure Doric temple and is justly famed as one of the world's most beautiful buildings; and, finally, the Erechtheum, known best for its Porch of the Maidens, in which the columns take the form of Greek maidens, often called Caryatids. These four buildings were all erected in the 5th century B. C., but they still preserve much of their original impressiveness."[15]

   The Lincoln Library of Essential Information

For Reflection and Reasoning

• Review: Locate each of the continents on a globe or world map. On which continent was Christ born? To which continent did the Gospel come first?

• Whom did God use to first take the Gospel to the people of Europe? What was special about Paul's conversion? Why did Paul go to Europe? As desired, read selected verses from Acts 9 and Acts 16 to summarize these events.

• Paul took several missionary journeys into Europe. On his second journey, he traveled to Athens, Greece. Locate Greece and Athens on a map. How did the location of Athens encourage travel to that city?

● *Student Activity Page 8-1.* Label Europe, Asia, Greece, Athens, Mediterranean Sea. Outline Greece. Title the map: "Paul was the link for the Gospel from Asia to Europe."

In preparation for the next day's study, the student may do simple research.

1. Find pictures of the Parthenon.

2. Define acropolis.

Leading Idea

The Parthenon — A wonder of Greek architecture

Student Text, page 32

● "The Parthenon, even in its ruined state, is one of the most beautiful buildings in the world. It was begun in the year 446 B.C. and finished 438 B.C. It is hard to realize that this glorious work of genius required only ten years to achieve.

"A study of the Parthenon ought to destroy some of our self-complacency with respect to modern achievement. To quarry the great blocks of marble out of the heart of Pentelicon, transport them to the city and lift them to the summit of the Acropolis, without our modern mechanical contrivances, that was a great accomplishment in itself. But those old craftsmen did more than pile the stones up in an enormous heap after the manner of the Egyptian pyramids. They took these blocks of marble, gleaming white, in which the sunshine seemed to be imprisoned, coming out in exquisite tones of

gold after weathering; they took this marble and fashioned it into this supremely beautiful building. By using a combination of straight lines they produced a building so marvelous in its proportions, in such perfect harmony that you lose the sense of rigidity, of severity, altogether.

"Somehow, the builders added beauty to strength; to severity grace and charm. A close examination reveals the fact that while the lines seem straight, they are not really so; they are curves, imperceptible except to very close scrutiny. The floor of the temple is built on a curve, said to come within one inch of being the same as the curve of the earth's surface. The lines of the columns taper to the top and are slightly convex in the middle."[16]

The Book of Life

For Reflection and Reasoning

● Review the student's definition of *acropolis.* What is the acropolis? Why was it important?

● Look at the picture of the Parthenon which the students found and the picture in the Student Text, page 33. What is unique about where the Parthenon was built? Since the building was a place of

worship, how did its location remind the people to worship?

● How was the building constructed? Today, if we build a large building, how do the workmen place the pieces of the building together? When it is very tall, what equipment do they use? How did the people of Greece construct the Parthenon?

Christianity confronted the pagan idea of God.

• A *pagan* is defined by Webster as "a person who worships false gods."

• Webster defines *God* as "The Supreme Being; Jehovah; the eternal and infinite spirit, the creator, and the sovereign of the universe. (2) A false god; a heathen deity; an idol."

For Reflection and Reasoning

• How do you worship the Lord? Do you worship more than one God? Why? Review the first four of the Ten Commandments and Christ's first great commandment. How do these govern our worship?

• When a person worships a god other than the God of the Bible, we identify them as a "pagan." What would decide if someone is a pagan or a Christian?

• What did Paul see when he arrived in Athens that told him the people did not believe in the God of the Bible? Where did the people worship? How many different places were there for worship?

• In Acts 14:12-14, Paul and Barnabas were saddened when the people of Lystra thought they were the gods Jupiter and Mercury.

• As desired, introduce the students to the names and position of some of the Greek gods. Note the limited power which the Greeks believed their gods possessed. When the Romans conquered much of the world, they claimed the Greek gods, but simply gave them a new name.

Greek god	Roman god	Power
Zeus	Jupiter	King of the gods
Hera	Juno	Queen of the gods
Ares	Mars	God of war
Hermes	Mercury	Messenger of the gods

• *Student Activity Page 8-2.* Using the definition of God, prepare a simple contrast between a Christian and pagan idea of God. The students may record Webster's definition of a pagan.

Paul confronted the pagan ideas in Athens with the Gospel.

Student Text, pages 32-33

• "I. Here is the impression which the abominable ignorance and superstition of the Athenians made upon Paul's spirit, *v.* 16. Observe, 1. The account here given of that city: it was *wholly given to idolatry.* This agrees with the account which the heathen writers give of it, that there were more idols in Athens than there were in all Greece besides put together, and that they had twice as many sacred feasts as others had. Whatever strange gods were recommended to them, they admitted them, and allowed them a temple and an altar, *so that they had almost as many gods as men . . .* It is observable that there, where human learning most flourished, idolatry most abounded, and the most absurd and ridiculous idolatry, which confirms that of the apostle, that when *they professed themselves to be wise they became fools* (Rom. i. 22), and, in the business of religion, were of all other the most *vain in their imaginations. . . .*

"He [Paul] did not. . . in the heat of his zeal break into the temples, pull down their images, demolish their altars, or fly in the face of their priests; nor did he run about the streets crying, 'You are all the bondslaves of the devil,' though it was too true; but he observed decorum, and kept himself within due bounds, doing that only which became a prudent man. 1. He *went to the synagogue of the Jews.* . . He discoursed *with the Jews,* reasoned fairly with them, and put it to them what reason they could give why, since they expected the Messiah, they would not receive Jesus. . . . 2. He entered into conversation with all that came in his way about matters of religion."

Matthew Henry, *Commentary*

For Reflection and Reasoning

● Review: What is a Christian? Whom do Christians worship? What is a pagan? How many gods did the people of Athens worship?

● Reason with the students concerning Paul's activities in Athens. Why was he troubled when he arrived there? What did he see? Historians tells us that Athens had more idols than any other part of Greece.

● What do we call the building in our county or state where we would go for any public business? Where was the public business completed in Greece?

● From the site of Mars Hill (the Areopagus), one could look across to the Parthenon and all of the temples to the idols. Why did the Greeks take Paul to the Areopagus?

● *Student Activity Page 8-3.* Students may answer the questions as class discussion, or as independent review.

Leading Idea

There is only one God.

Student Text, pages 33-34

● "Divers sermons we have had, which the apostles preached to the Jews, or such Gentiles as had an acquaintance with and veneration for the Old Testament, and were worshippers of the true and living God; and all they had to do with them was to open and allege *that Jesus is the Christ;* but here we have a sermon to heathens, that worshipped false gods, and were without the true God in the world, and to them the scope of their discourse was quite different from what it was to the other. In the former case their business was to lead their hearers by prophecies and miracles to the knowledge of the Redeemer, and faith in him; in the latter it was to lead them by the common works of providence to the knowledge of the Creator, and the worship of him. . . .

"I. He lays down this, as the scope of his discourse, that he aimed to bring them to *the knowledge of the only living and true God,* as the sole and proper object of their adoration. He is here obliged to lay the foundation, and to instruct them in the first principle of all religion, that there is a God, and that God is but one. When he preached against the gods they worshipped, he had no design to draw them to atheism, but to the service of the true Deity. . . Now he. . . does not introduce any new gods, but reduce them *to the knowledge of one God, the Ancient of days.*"

Matthew Henry, *Commentary*

For Reflection and Reasoning

• Review: What activities were held on Mars Hill?

• From the top of Mars Hill, what did Paul see? Remember, the people of Athens had many gods. When the Greeks were introduced to a new god, they simply added another temple and another altar.

• Paul did not want the people to just add another god to the many they already worshiped. He wanted them to know about the one, true God.

• *Student Activity Page 8-4.* Reason from the Student Text concerning Paul's sermon on Mars Hill. To bring the people of Athens to a belief in God, he taught them about God. List the characteristics of God which Paul identified. Discuss each idea more fully as it is recorded:

· **The Unknown God was the one, true God.** The Athenians had an altar to THE UNKNOWN GOD. Paul wanted to tell them of that God.

· **God created the world.** Review: God created the world and all that is in the heaven and the earth. God not only created the world, but He controls it. "He is Lord of heaven and earth." What verses can the students recall which teach that God created everything?

· **God gives each person life.** It is God who gives us life and breath.

· **God controls each person's life.** Review the definition of Providence, His plan, provision, and protection. He governs the lives of men and nations.

· **God will judge all men.** There will someday be a judgment and each person will be judged by God.

Cultivating Student Mastery

1. Paul told the Athenians that the Lord of heaven "giveth to all life, and breath, and all things." How does this show God's Providence?

2. What did Paul mean, He "hath made of one blood all nations of men"?

3. How do the following phrases reveal God's Providence?
· "hath determined the times before appointed"
· "and the bounds of their habitation"

4. What words in Paul's sermon describe God's government of men?

Leading Idea

Only Christianity could lay aside pagan ideas and give liberty.

Student Text, page 34

• "Where the Spirit of the Lord is, there is liberty." II Corinthians 3:17b. Paul was the instrument used by God to take the Gospel from Asia to Europe. Only as individuals received Jesus Christ could they have liberty within, internal spiritual liberty. The seed of the Gospel was planted by Paul. After centuries, that seed would flourish to bring forth not just internal, spiritual liberty, but liberty in all spheres of life—religious, economic, and civil.

For Reflection and Reasoning

• Review: What is liberty? Where will we first have liberty, internally or externally? How do we receive internal liberty?

• What is a pagan? If the pagan does not believe in Jesus Christ, can he have liberty?

• How do we know about Jesus Christ? If we did not have the Bible, would we, too, be ignorant of what Christ has done for us?

• How long had the people in Greece worshipped false gods? We know that God is creator, He has all power over heaven and earth, He is controlling the events of history. Whom did the Greeks credit for all of these things?

• The study of history will show how Paul's planting the seed of the Gospel in Europe was the beginning of Christian ideas in Europe. These ideas would later be carried to North America where a nation would be established based upon Christian ideas.

Cultivating Student Mastery

1. Before Paul came, what did the Greeks believe about the gods?

2. Name three things Paul taught the Greeks about God.

BIBLE IN ENGLISH

1½-2 Weeks

Chapter 9

A Bible for the People

7-10 Days

Leading Idea

The Scripture is profitable for instruction in righteousness

Student Text, pages 35-36

• Absence of the Word of God caused the period of history called the Dark Ages. The Scriptures warn of the darkness produced when a people are without the Word of God, Amos 8:11-12.

Without the light of the Scriptures people fell into error. Self-governing churches were replaced by centralized churches. Emphasis upon the individual's direct access to God through Jesus Christ was replaced by a church hierarchy.

A revival of truth was needed, through the light and the power of God's written word. The man God used to first penetrate the darkness was John Wycliffe, the Morning Star of the Reformation.

For Reflection and Reasoning

• Read II Timothy 3:16-17. Why is it important for each individual to have a Bible for himself?

• How were churches governed in the first century of Christianity?

• *Student Activity Page 9-1.* Record all material through Wycliffe. The chart will be completed in later lessons.

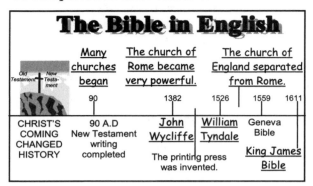

The Bible in English

	Many churches began	The church of Rome became very powerful.		The church of England separated from Rome.	
	90	1382	1526	1559	1611
CHRIST'S COMING CHANGED HISTORY	90 A.D New Testament writing completed	John Wycliffe _The printing press was invented._	William Tyndale	Geneva Bible King James Bible	

• Over the centuries of time, how did church government change?

• At the time of Wycliffe, what was being taught by the church in England instead of the Scripture?

• How did Wycliffe's translation affect learning?

Cultivating Student Mastery

1. What did John Wycliffe believe should be taught?

2. How did he put his belief into action?

3. What was the result?

> **Leading Idea**
>
> ### In God's timing, His Word was made available for the individual despite human opposition.
>
> Student Text, pages 36-37

• The Old Testament King, Jehoiakim, understood the power of God's Word and attempted to suppress it. In the same way, English religious and political leaders feared having their power limited by the teachings of Scripture. In spite of their efforts to the contrary, God, in His own marvelous way, brought His Word to His people.

In the process, men paid dearly for their efforts to translate, publish, and disseminate the Bible. But, their sufferings, their sacrifices, and even their deaths watered the seeds of spiritual and religious liberty in England.

For Reflection and Reasoning

• How did Tyndale's translation differ from Wycliffe's?

• What made *publication* of the Tyndale Bible easier than the publication of the Wycliffe Bible?

• Why did the church leaders oppose the Scriptures?

• How did William Tyndale show true brotherly love for King Henry VIII?

• What surprising decision did King Henry VIII make after William Tyndale's death?

• *Student Activity Page 9-1.* Add material on Tyndale to the timeline.

Leading Idea

The Bible in English brought many changes.

Student Text, page 37

● William Bradford, in his *History of Plymouth Plantation,* recorded the change which occurred in the hearts of the people when they had the Bible in their hands: "But that I may come more near my intendmente; when as by the travell & diligence of some godly & zealous preachers, & Gods blessing on their labours, as in other places of ye land, so in ye North parts, many became inlightened by ye word of God, and had their ignorance & sins discovered unto them, and begane by his grace to reforme their lives, the worke of God was no sooner manifest in them, but presently they were both scoffed and scorned by ye prophane multitude, and ye ministers urged with ye yoak of subscription, or els must be silenced; and ye poore people were so vexed with apparators, & pursuants, & ye comissarie courts, as truly their afflic-tion was not smale; which, notwithstanding, they bore sundrie years with much patience, till they were occasioned (by ye continuance & encrease of these troubls, and other means which ye Lord raised up in those days) to see further into things by the light of ye word of God. . . So many therfore of these proffessors as saw ye evill of these things, in thes parts, and whose harts ye Lord had touched with heavenly Zeale for his trueth, they shooke of this yoake of antichristian bondage, and as ye Lords free people, joyned them selves (by a covenant of the Lord) into a church estate, in ye felowship of ye gospell, to walke in all his wayes, make known or to be made known unto them, according to their best endeavours, whatsoever it should cost them, the Lord assisting them."[17]

For Reflection and Reasoning

● At the time of Wycliffe and Tyndale, what church was controlling most of Europe? King Henry VIII did not want to be a part of the Roman Church, so he separated from that church and began the Church of England, of which he was the head. At the time of the King James Bible, the state church was the Church of England.

● When the people of England had a Bible, what did they learn about salvation? Why did they need salvation? Identify other verses which the people of England might have read that would have told them of salvation?

● As the English people understood Scripture, they learned that each individual could govern his own actions. What does it mean to govern your own actions? What is government? How does the Bible teach the people they can govern their own actions?

● What does it mean to be a Puritan? The name of "Puritan" began to be used for the people who wanted to see things changed in the Church of England. It came from the idea that they wanted to worship according to the "pure" word of God.

Suggested Student Notes

Puritans — Christians who wanted to change the Church of England. They wanted to purify the church.

Cultivating Student Mastery

1. When the people of England read and studied the Bible, where did change first begin?

2. As they studied the Bible more, what other changes did they want to make?

Leading Idea

"No bishop, no king"

Student Text, pages 38-39

● "While the king was in his progress to London (April, 1603) the puritans presented their millenary petition, so called, because it was said to be subscribed by a thousand hands . . . It is entitled, 'the humble Petition of the Ministers of the Church of England, desiring Reformation of certain Ceremonies and Abuses of the church' . . .

". . . he agreed to have a conference with the two parties . . .

"The second day's conference was on Monday, January 16th . . . The king being seated in his chair, with his nobles and privy counsellors around him, let them know, he was now ready to hear their objections against the establishment. Whereupon Dr. Raynolds, in the name of his brethren, humbly requested, (1) That the doctrine of the church might be preserved pure, according to God's Word. (2) That good pastors might be planted in all churches, to preach the same. (3) That the Book of Common Prayer might be fitted to more increase of piety. (4) That church government might be sincerely ministered according to God's Word . . . Here the king broke out into a flame, and instead of hearing the doctor's reasons, or commanding his bishops to answer them, told the ministers, that he found they were aiming at a Scots presbytery, 'which', says he, 'agrees with monarchy as well as God and the devil; then Jack and Tom, Will and Dick, shall meet, and at their pleasure censure both me and my council' . . .

"Then turning to the bishops, he put his hand to his hat and said, 'My lords, I may thank you that these Puritans plead for my supremacy, for if once you are out and they in place, I know what would become of my supremacy, for, No bishop, no king' . . ."[18]
Daniel Neal, *History of the Puritans*

● The translators of the King James Bible wrote concerning that work: "The very historical truth is, that upon the importunate petitions of the Puritans, the Conference at Hampton Court having been appointed for hearing their complaints, when by force of reason they were put from all other grounds, *they had recourse at the last to this shift*, that they could not with good conscience subscribe to the Communion book (*i.e.*, the Prayer Book), since it maintained the Bible as it was there translated, which was, as they said, a most corrupted translation. And although this was judged to be but a very poor and empty shift, yet even hereupon did his Majesty begin to bethink himself of the good that might ensue by a new translation, and presently after gave orders for this translation which is now presented unto thee."[19]
H. W. Hoare, *The Evolution of the English Bible*

● Webster defined *piety* as "A compound of veneration or reverence of the Supreme Being and love of his character, or veneration accompanied with love."

For Reflection and Reasoning

● Review: What is a Puritan?

● What is a petition? Why was the Puritan's petition called the Millenary Petition?

● *Student Activity Page 9-2.* As each point of the petition is discussed, the students may record a simple understanding, see *Suggested Student Notes.*

● What is doctrine? What did the Puritans think had happened to the doctrine in the Church of England? How could that happen? Why is it important for us to read the Bible?

● What does the Puritans' second request suggest about their pastors? What did they want the pastors to preach?

● What was the book of common prayer? If the Puritans wanted the prayers to increase piety, what was it they wanted to have increased? What is reverence?

● What is church government? When the Puritans asked for church government to be according to God's Word, why did the King become angry? What did he fear?

Who are the bishops? What did the King think would happen to him if the church government changed?

● On the bottom line of *Student Activity Page 9-2,* the students may record King James' statement: "No bishop, no king."

● *Student Activity Page 9-3.* To review the events of the Hampton Court Conference, the students may read the play. The students would enjoy dramatizing the play, with simple costumes.

Suggested Student Notes

1. Teach the truth of the Word of God.

2. Pastors who preached the Word of God.

3. Prayers in prayer book showing love and reverence for God.

4. Churches governed by the Word of God.

Leading Idea

A new Bible for the people

Student Text, page 39

● "The first practical step had naturally been to select a competent committee of revisers. . . . It is evident, from what is known of the names on the list which was to come down to us, that all possible pains were taken to secure the services of the best available men. The only qualification which was held to be indispensable was that the revisers should be Biblical students of proved capacity. Puritan Churchmen and Anglican Churchmen, linguists and theologians, laymen and divines, worked harmoniously side by side. . ."[20]
H. W. Hoare, *The Evolution of the English Bible*

• The greatest care was to be given to the translation of the Scriptures. Specific instructions were given to the companies of men:

". . . Every particular man of each company to take the same chapter or chapters: and having translated or amended them severally by himself where he thinketh good, all to meet together, confer what they have done, and agree for their parts what shall stand.

"As any one company hath dispatched any one book in this manner, they shall send it to the rest to be considered of seriously and judiciously, for his Majesty is very careful in this point.

"If any company, upon the review of the book so sent, doubt or differ upon any place, to send them word thereof, note the place, and withal send the reasons: to which if they consent not, the difference to be compounded at the general meeting, which is to be of the chief persons of each company at the end of the work.

"When any place of special obscurity is doubted of, letters to be directed by authority to be sent to any learned man in the land for his judgment.

"Letters to be sent from every bishop to the rest of his clergy, admonishing them of this translation in hand, and to move and charge as many as being skilful in the tongues, and having taken pains in that kind, to send his particular observations to the company either at Westminster, Cambridge, or Oxford . . .

"These translations to be used when they agree better with the text than the Bishops' Bible: Tindale's, Matthew's, Coverdale's, Whitchurch's, Geneva . . ."[21]

H. W. Hoare, *The Evolution of the English Bible*

For Reflection and Reasoning

• Review: Why was the Hampton Court Conference called? Who were the Puritans? What did they want? Why did King James make the statement, "No bishop, no king"?

• Why did the Puritans want a change in the Prayer Book? What is a translation? What would make a translation good or bad?

• *Student Activity   Page 9-4*. When King James made the decision to have a new translation of the Bible, God led that great care was taken in making the translation. Reasoning from the Student Text, list steps which were taken to ensure the accuracy of the translation. Assist the students in writing summary statements regarding these steps. This should be completed in two class times. Following are suggestions:

1. Fifty-four leading Bible scholars were chosen.

2. The men were divided into six companies.

3. The translation of each chapter was reviewed and approved by all.

4. The translation took seven years.

5. The translators were humble men who trusted God to guide them.

• What is a Bible scholar? Why was it important that there were men from different walks of life?

• What does it mean when they said, he "had Hebrew at his finger ends"? How was this of benefit to their work?

• Consider the great care that was given to accuracy of the translation. How do we know they did not limit their work to the men who were part of the committees? Who else provided assistance?

Leading Idea

God used humble men to perform a great work.

Student Text, page 40

● Webster defined *humble* as "Lowly; modest; meek; submissive; opposed to *proud, haughty, arrogant,* or *assuming. . .*

God resisteth the proud, but giveth grace to the *humble*. James iv."

For Reflection and Reasoning

● *Student Activity Page 9-1.* Complete the timeline.

● What does it mean to be humble? When the men were willing to check with other translators or Biblical scholars, how did it show their humility? If there were changes to be made, did they make them?

● What other characteristics did the translators need?

● In what did translators trust? How do we know? Why was that so important?

● What did they mean when they prayed, " let me not be deceived in them"? When they prayed, "neither let me deceive by

them"?

● How was the character of these translators similar to that of John Wycliffe and William Tyndale?

● What is an anvil? What does it mean to bring "back to the anvil that which we had hammered"? What does it show of their character?

● Reason with the students to record a definition of humble.

Suggested Student Notes

God used humble men to perform the great work of translating the Scriptures.

Leading Idea

The King James Bible—the peak of the English Language

Student Text, page 40

● The King James Bible crystallized the English language, bringing it a great beauty, richness, and purity. With the Bible as the standard of the language, great

literature came forth from the pens of such men as Shakespeare, Spenser, and Bacon.

• Called the Authorized Version or the King James Bible, it became the standard for all translations which followed.

"It has held the first place throughout the English-speaking world for over three centuries."[22]

For Reflection and Reasoning

• Review: Who were the Puritans? What was the Puritans' desire?

• Review: Why did King James decide to order a translation of the Bible? Explain the method used to prepare the translation. What helped to preserve its accuracy?

• The King James Bible became the standard for the English language. What is a "standard"? How did literature reflect the language of the King James Bible?

Cultivating Student Mastery

1. How did God protect the accuracy of the King James Bible?

2. How could the Bible be the "standard" for literature?

CHRISTOPHER COLUMBUS
Link to the New World
1½-2 Weeks

Chapter 10
Opening a Path to the New World
8-10 Days

> **Leading Idea**
>
> **God prepares men and then He causes events.**
>
> Student Text, page 41

● "Consider and ponder the human events which take place when *one individual* recognizes the importance of the Bible in the hands of the individual! For down to the middle of the fourteenth century the individual was separated from the Word of God, but when Wycliffe not only saw the importance of the individual having his own Bible but began to do something about it in spite of the danger to his life, God honored him...

"Almost immediately following Wycliffe's translation of the whole Bible, God began to call forth men to develop the many scientific and economic fields which would be necessary to enable man to sail the seas, explore, and finally settle the lands across the vast Atlantic ocean.

With the correlation so plain and easily documented between the Bible being made available to the individual in England, and the almost sudden development of basic inventions necessary for sailing the seas, and colonizing America, it is strange this is not better known by American Christians who have so dramatically benefitted thereby. . . . God has been reserving the land we know as the original thirteen colonies to begin establishing the Christian form of civil government until there could be a handful of 'peculiar people' properly rooted and grounded in His Word."23

Verna M. Hall, *The Christian History of the American Revolution*

For Reflection and Reasoning

● Review: What is history? What is Providence? How did God Providentially give

His Word to the people of England?

● What is the Old World? What is the New World? Use a world map or globe to identify the two worlds.

• What geographic obstacle had kept the knowledge of the lands of the New World from the people of Europe in the 1300's and 1400's?

• As God works, He uses individuals from many parts of the world to bring forth an event. What individuals in England were preparing the way for a New World? How were people in England being prepared? Why would they need to know how to govern themselves? Why did they need the Bible?

• *Student Activity Page 10-1.* Label: Old World, New World. Optional: Label continents.

Leading Idea

In God's time, He raised up a leader to open the field of navigation.

Student Text, pages 41-42

•"Henry the Navigator, son of John I, king of Portugal, was born in 1394. He distinguished himself at the capture of Ceuta in 1415; took up his residence at Sagres, in Algarve; and devoted himself to extending geographical discovery. He erected an observatory and a school for navigation and dispatched some of his pupils on voyages that resulted in the discovery of the Madeira islands in 1420. . . . This maritime enterprise continued for a half century after Henry's death and resulted in the rounding of the Cape of Good Hope and the founding of Portuguese empires in India and Brazil. Died, 1460."[24]

Lincoln Library of Essential Information

• "The guiding spirit in this new habit of exploration was that scion of the royal family of Portugal who became famous eventually as Prince Henry, the Navigator. . . The Prince had assisted King João in the attack on the Moors at Ceuta, in 1415, and this success had opened to the Prince the prospect of possessing the Guinea coast, and of ultimately finding and passing the anticipated cape at the southern end of Africa.

"This was the mission to which the Prince early in the fifteenth century gave himself. His ships began to crawl down the western Barbary coast, and each season added to the extent of their explorations . . . 'We may wonder,' says Helps, 'that he never took personal command of any of his expeditions, but he may have thought that he served the cause better by remaining at home, and forming a centre whence the electric energy of enterprise was communicated to many discoverers and then again collected from them.'. . .

"He [Prince Henry] was a man, as his motto tells us, wished, and was able, to do well. He was shadowed with few infirmities of spirit. He joined with the pluck of his half-English blood — for he was the grandson of John of Gaunt — a training for endurance derived in his country's prolonged contests with the Moor. He was the staple and lofty examplar of this great age of discovery. He was more so than Columbus, and rendered the adventitious career of the Genoese possible. He knew how to manage men, and stuck devotedly to his work. He respected his helpers too much to drug them with deceit, and there is a straightforward honesty of purpose in his endeavors. He was a trainer of men, and they grew courageous under his instruction. To sail into the supposed burning zone beyond Cape Bojador, and to face the destruction of life which was believed to be inevitable, required a courage quite as conspicuous as to cleave the floating verdure of the Sargasso Sea, on a western passage. . . ."[25]

Justin Winsor, *Christopher Columbus*

76

● In 711 A.D. the Moors, followers of the Muslim religion from northern Africa, invaded Europe, holding control over both Spain and Portugal until 1249 A.D., when they were finally driven out of Portugal. For many years, the Moors continued to attack the Portuguese ships.

For Reflection and Reasoning

● *Student Activity Page 10-2.* Students record "1394" and "Prince Henry was born." *Student Activity Page* will be completed in later lessons.

In what year was Prince Henry of Portugal born? How did that relate to Wycliffe's translation of the Bible? Prince Henry would not have used the English Bible, because he lived in Portugal and did not speak English. Yet, at the same time that God was using Prince Henry to open the field of navigation and exploration, He was also using the Bible to change the hearts and lives of the Englishmen. Their descendants would later come to North America.

● Locate Portugal, Africa, and the Mediterranean Sea on a globe or world map. Why was it important that the ships from Portugal could sail freely on the Mediterranean Sea? How was Portugal's geographic position important to her becoming a leader in navigation and exploration?

● God created Prince Henry for a special purpose. How did Henry's position in the royal family enable him to pursue his dreams of sending ships to far-distant places?

● Could Prince Henry have gained great fame if he had chosen to lead great armies? Prince Henry probably gained greater fame with his contributions to the field of sailing than he would have as a leader of armies. Would he have known that when he made his decision?

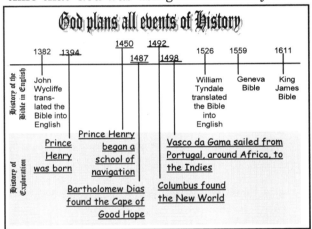

Leading Idea — ***Great accomplishments require great thinking and planning.***

Student Text, page 42

● "The prince, however, had set his mind on other and larger plans, involving no less than the hope of reaching India by the south point of Africa. . . . Accordingly in 1418-19 he took up his abode on the extreme south-western point of Europe, the promontory of Sagres, in Algarve, of which kingdom he was made governor in perpetuity, with the purpose of devoting himself to the study of astronomy and mathematics, and to the direction and encouragement of the expeditions which he proposed to send forth. There he erected an observatory, the first set up in

Portugal, and at great expense procured the services of one Mestre Jacome from Majorea, a man very skilful in the art of navigation and in the making of maps and instruments, to instruct the Portuguese officers in these sciences."[26]

Encyclopedia Brittanica

• Webster defined *geography* as "A description of the earth or terrestrial globe, particularly of the divisions of its surface, natural and artificial, and of the position of the several countries, kingdoms, states, cities, &c. As a science, geography includes the doctrine or knowledge of the astronomical circles or divisions of the sphere, by which the relative position of places on the globe may be ascertained. . ."

Navigation is "The art of conducting ships or vessels from one place to another. This art comprehends not only the management of the sails, but the directing and measuring of the course of ships by the laws of geometry, or by astronomical principles and observations."

• *Cartography* is "The science or art of making maps."[27]

For Reflection and Reasoning

• Why were the sailors of Prince Henry's day limited to sailing near land?

• What were Prince Henry's goals? What difficulties did he encounter? Some were real difficulties and some were imagined.

• Identify on a globe or world map the route which Prince Henry proposed around Africa to the Indies. At this time in history, the people of Europe knew only of the northern part of Africa, next to the Mediterranean Sea. The size or geography of the rest of Africa was unknown.

• How would the voyages be limited if the ships could only sail where they could see the shore? What if they could only sail during the daylight?

• Locate Sagres on a map. Why was this location ideal for Prince Henry to accomplish his goals?

• What steps did Prince Henry take to meet his goals? Why would he want to collect information on geography, navigation, and cartography? What is the study of geography? Geography is much more than just learning the names of countries, continents, and waterways. What are navigation and cartography? How would information in each of these areas have helped Prince Henry to accomplish his goals?

• *Student Activity Page 10-2.* Students record "1450" and "Prince Henry began a school of navigation."

• How would a school that taught navigation, astronomy, and cartography help Prince Henry to accomplish his goals?

• *Student Activity Page 10-3.* Students may complete the page as part of the classtime, or it may be used as independent work for the student to confirm the class discussion.

Prince Henry's Goals:

   1. Sail further from land.

   2. Sail around Africa to reach India.

Prince Henry's preparation to reach his goals:

   1. Studied geography, navigation, and cartography.

   2. Invited men to join him.

   3. Set up a school for navigators.

Leading Idea

Early navigation required mathematics and great faith.

Student Text, pages 42-44

• "Navigators use a special unit of measure called the *nautical mile.* The nautical mile is longer than the mile used in land measure. The mile used in land measure, . . . is 5280 feet long, while the nautical mile is now known to be about 6076. . . . Navigators like to use this unit, because it makes figuring distance sailed across the surface of the *round* earth easier.

"The cross-section of the earth, as in any other spherical object, is thought of as being divided into 360 degrees. [The choice of the number 360 for the number of degrees goes back to Old Testament times when the Hebrew people and the nations around them used a lunar calendar of 360 days. They added an extra month of 30 days every six years to keep up with the seasons.] Like any other unit of measure, degrees are subdivided into smaller units for the sake of accuracy. These units are called *minutes* and minutes are also divided into smaller units called *seconds.* Just as in the measurement of time, 60 seconds of circular measure equals one minute, and 60 minutes of circular measure equals one degree. Measuring the surface of the earth in this way, *on the equator or on any north-south line, one circular minute equals one nautical mile.* By using this unit of measurement, a navigator is able to simplify his arithmetic, when he converts his present position and some past position (both measured in degrees and minutes of latitude and longitude) into distance and direction. . . .

"Dead reckoning is based on two things: Keeping records of *direction* and *distance* sailed. The direction is found by using the magnetic compass. The distance sailed is found by using this formula: *distance = rate x time.*

"'Rate' is speed—miles per hour, on land, or at sea, nautical miles per hour (knots)—and 'time' is the length of time sailed at the given speed. According to this formula, if the ship were sailing at 30 knots for half an hour, the distance traveled would be 30 knots x 1/2 hour = 15 nautical miles. To use this formula, the rate must be known, so the navigator uses a device called the *log-line.* . . ."[28]

Darold Booton, Jr.

• Webster defines *log-line* as "A line or cord about a hundred and fifty fathoms in length, fastened to the log by means of two legs. This is wound on a reel, called the log-reel."

For Reflection and Reasoning

• What difficulties did a sailor face when he sailed without knowledge of his exact location? What hazards were above the water and below the water? How did sailing require great faith?

• Demonstrate the use of a compass for identifying the direction you are moving.

• Devise a simple exercise for the students to practice using a compass. Example: Have them walk three paces north, ten paces west, five paces south, etc. Where do you arrive at the end of this exercise? The students would enjoy finding a treasure at the end. Have the students note that each person may not arrive at the same exact spot if their pace varies. Relate this discovery to the difficulty of sailing by dead reckoning.

• What is a mile? How do we use a mile measurement? How does it help us to find a specific location? Sailors measure distance with a *nautical mile*. Depending on the age and capacity of the students, the difference between the two types of miles may be explained.

• Reason with the students concerning the method of dead reckoning. What is a minute glass? A timer from a board game may be used to illustrate the minute glass.

• Why did the navigator need good mathematical skills? Why would dead reckoning perhaps not be accurate?

• If the students have the mathematical skills, have them calculate a distance using the formula *distance = rate x time*.

• Students who have previously studied Christopher Columbus may remember that Columbus kept a daily journal with his calculations of their travel based upon dead reckoning. They may also remember that he kept two records. Why? What he thought were the accurate measurements he knew would frighten the sailors, as they would know how far they were from home. Historians tell us that the record Columbus showed the sailors was actually closer to being correct.

Cultivating Student Mastery

1. How were the following part of Prince Henry's plan?
   • Establishing a school of navigation
   • Improving navigational instruments

2. Why did a navigator need good mathematical skills?

3. Why did sailors need faith in their navigator or captain?

Leading Idea

Prince Henry's dream required tools of navigation.

Student Text, page 44

• Webster described the *astrolabe* as "An instrument formerly used for taking the altitude of the sun or stars at sea." The quadrant is identified as "An instrument for taking the altitudes of the sun or stars, of great use in astronomy and navigation. Quadrants are variously made, but they all consist of the quarter of a circle whose limb is divided into ninety degrees..."

• "It was not possible to determine longitude at sea in the early days of transoceanic navigation, but it was quite easy to determine latitude. To go to a place of known latitude, the ship was sailed to that latitude and then sailed east or west along the latitude line until the place was reached. To find the latitude of the ship at sea, the noon altitude of the Sun was measured during the day or the altitude of a star of known declination was measured when it was on the meridian (due north or south) at night. The Sun's or star's declination for the date was looked up in an almanac. The latitude is then 90° - measured altitude + declination.

"A number of devices were used to measure the Sun's noon altitude. Among them were the quadrant, cross staff and, later, the back staff and the mariner's astrolabe. All these devices had a single use; to measure the altitude of a celestial body above the horizon."[29]

James E. Morrison

For Reflection and Reasoning

● Review: How did Prince Henry's school benefit sailors?

● For centuries people used the sun, moon, and stars to find the direction they wanted to travel. Why was travel on a ship, where land could not be seen, harder than travel on land?

● Using a globe or map, observe the latitude lines. What is the main line of latitude from which all others are measured?

● How could sailors determine the latitude line in the sea? What instruments did they use?

● *Student Activity Page 10-4.* Identify the pictures of the navigational instruments and discuss their use.

● Illustrate the use of the quadrant and the astrolabe. Students might enjoy building a model of an astrolabe.

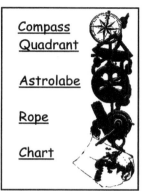

Compass
Quadrant

Astrolabe

Rope

Chart

Cultivating Student Mastery

1. In the 1400's, how did sailors stay on course? How well did this work?

2. How did improvements in navigational tools help sailors?

Leading Idea

In God's time, Prince Henry's dream was realized.

Student Text, pages 44-45

● "Bartholomew Diaz, or Dias, Portuguese navigator, flourished in the 15th century. His residence at the court of John II of Portugal brought him into contact with many scientific men, and, in 1487, the king gave him the command of three vessels to follow up the discoveries already made on the west coast of Africa. Driven by a violent storm, he sailed round the southern extremity of Africa and the Cape of Good Hope, without immediately realizing the fact, and discovered Algoa bay. The discontent of his crew compelled him to return, and he arrived in Lisbon, December 1488. He joined the expedition of Cabral, the discoverer of Brazil. In May 1500, he was lost in a storm off the great cape that he had discovered."[30]
Lincoln Library of Essential Information

● "Vasco da Gama, Portuguese navigator, was born about 1460 at Sines in Alemtejo. He early distinguished himself as an intrepid mariner and was selected by King Emanuel to discover the route to India around southern Africa. His expedition of four vessels with 168 men left Lisbon in July 1497, but was four months in reaching Saint Helena. After rounding the Cape of Good Hope, despite hurricanes and mutinies, he made Melinde early in the following year. Here he found a skillful Indian pilot, crossed the Indian Ocean, and arrived at Calicut in May 1498. The ruler of Calicut soon became actively hostile, and Da Gama had to fight his way out of the harbor. In September 1499, he arrived at Lisbon and was ennobled.

"Emanuel immediately dispatched a

fresh squadron of 13 ships under Cabral, who founded a factory at Calicut. But the Portuguese who had been left there were murdered, and, to avenge them, the king fitted out a squadron of 20 ships under Da Gama, 1502. The latter founded the colonies of Mozambique and Sofala, bombarded Calicut, and, late in 1503, reached the Tagus with 13 richly laden vessels. Twenty years later, Da Gama was again sent to India, this time as viceroy to reform abuses in the Portuguese administration there. Soon after his arrival, he died at Cochin, 1524."[31]

Lincoln Library of Essential Information

For Reflection and Reasoning

• Using a map or globe, locate the Cape of Good Hope. Imagine how long the voyage from Portugal to the eastern side of the continent would have taken. Why would this have been so frightening for the sailors?

• How did Dias's voyage accomplish part of Prince Henry's dream?

• Vasco da Gama achieved the dream of Prince Henry. How many years passed between the time Prince Henry set up his school and Vasco da Gama sailed around Africa to the Indies? Why did God not allow Prince Henry's dream to be realized until after Columbus made his voyage?

• Continue the timeline, *Student Activity Page 10-2*. Record "1487" and "Bartholomew Dias found the Cape of Good Hope." Record "1498" and "Vasco da Gama sailed from Portugal, around Africa, to the Indies."

Leading Idea

God used Prince Henry to help prepare the way for the discovery of the New World.

Student Text, pages 45-46

• "Columbus, disappearing from Italy in 1473, is next found in Portugal, and it is a natural inquiry why an active, adventurous spirit, having tested the exhilaration of the sea, should have made his way to that outpost of maritime ambition, bordering on the great waters, that had for many ages attracted and puzzled the discoverer and cosmographer. It is hardly to be doubted that the fame of the Portuguese voyaging out upon the vast deep, or following the western coast of Africa had for some time been a not unusual topic of talk among the seamen of the Mediterranean. . .

"Let us see how the great maritime questions stood in Portugal in 1473, and from what antecedents they had arisen.

"The Portuguese, at this time, had the reputation of being the most expert seamen in Europe . . . These hardy mariners had pushed boldly out, as early as we have any records, into the enticing and yet forbidding Sea of Darkness, not often perhaps willingly out of sight of land; but storms not infrequently gave them the experience of sea and sky, and nothing else. The great ocean was an untried waste for cartography. A few straggling beliefs in islands lying westward had come down from the ancients, and the fantastic notions of floating islands and steady lands, upon which the imagination of the Middle Ages thrived, were still rife. . .

"For centuries the Orient had been the dream of the philosopher and the goal of the merchant. Everything in the East was thought to be on a larger scale than in Europe, — metals were more abundant, pearls were rarer, spices were richer, plants were nobler, animals were statelier. Everything but man was more lordly. He had been fed there so luxuriously that he was believed to have dwindled in character. Europe was the world of active intelligence, the inheritor of Greek and Roman power, and its typical man belonged naturally with the grander externals of the East. There was a fitness in bringing the better man and the better nature into such relations that the one should sustain and enjoy the other.

"It was in the twelfth century, under the Mongol dynasty, that China became first generally known in Europe, under the name of Cathay, and then for the first time the Western nations received travelers' stories of the kingdom of the great Khan. . . . It was not, however, till Marco Polo returned from his visit to Kublai Khan, in the latter part of the thirteenth century, that a new enlargement of the ideas of Europe respecting the far Orient took place. The influence of his marvelous tales continued down to the days of Columbus, and when the great discoverer came on the scene it was to find the public mind occupied with the hopes of reaching these Eastern realms by way of the south. The experimental and accidental voyagings of the Portuguese on the Atlantic were held to be but preliminary to a steadier progression down the coast of Africa. . . .

"Within a few years after Henry's death — though some place it earlier — the explorations had been pushed to Sierra Leone and beyond Cape Mezurada. . . .

"This, then, was the condition of Portuguese seamanship and of its exploits when Columbus, some time, probably, in 1473, reached Portugal. He found that country so content with the rich product of the Guinea coast that it was some years later before the Portuguese began to push still farther to the south. The desire to extend the Christian faith to heathen, often on the lips of the discoverers of the fifteenth century, was never so powerful but that gold and pearls made them forget it."[32]

Justin Winsor, *Christopher Columbus*

For Reflection and Reasoning

• If the students have not studied the previous volumes in the series, *The Mighty Works of God,* the teacher may wish to expand the information included on Columbus.

• Review: Why were the people of Europe interested in finding a sea route to the Indies?

• What was Prince Henry's plan for sailing to the Indies? What was Columbus's plan?

• What does it mean — "God had an even greater plan"? What was God's plan?

• What was so important about Portugal that "Columbus knew God had brought him to Portugal"?

• How did God use Prince Henry as part of His plan for opening the path to the New World?

• Why did Columbus's men threaten him? Why were they afraid?

• *Student Activity Page 10-5.* Record *Suggested Student Notes* on map. Label: Portugal, Africa, Cape of Good Hope, Indies, and North America. Students may trace the route of Dias, da Gama, and Columbus with colored pencil or marker.

God Providentially led explorers and navigators to carry out His plan.

Leading Idea

God prepared the way for Christopher Columbus to be the link to the New World.

Student Text, page 46

For Reflection and Reasoning

● Complete *Student Activity Page 10-2.* Record "1492" and "Columbus found the New World."

● Review: What is history? What is a Providential view of history?

● What Providential events prepared the way for finding the New World? What was occurring in England? Who gave Columbus the plan for sailing west to find the Indies? Who did God use to help provide the knowledge that was needed for Columbus's voyage?

● What people was God preparing with His Word to develop a new nation? As they read the Bible, they were learning about self government. Why was that important for the beginning of the United States of America?

Cultivating Student Mastery

Students may prepare a short essay, considering the following topic:

1. How did God Providentially direct in the timing of Prince Henry's work and the exploration of Columbus?

PILGRIM
Seed of Our Christian Republic
Chapters 11-13
5-5½ Weeks

Chapter 11
Captain John Smith
Father of Virginia
8-10 Days

> **Leading Idea**
>
> *John Smith's character prepared him for his unique role as the Father of Virginia.*
>
> Student Text, pages 47-48

● History reveals that God prepares the way for each event of history. The Pilgrims' arrival in Plymouth in 1620 was preceded by many events which prepared the way.

First, the Bible in the hands of the people in England prepared a people who had learned to govern themselves, and, eventually their own church.

The settlement of Jamestown and the work of Captain John Smith were essential elements in the patchwork of events God would use to bring forth the nation of the United States of America.

● "A century had not elapsed after the discoveries of Columbus [1492], before a great social and political revolution had been effected in Europe. Commerce, hitherto confined to inland seas and along the coasts, was sending its ships across oceans. The art of printing had begun its wonderful work; and, through its instrumentality, intelligence had become generally diffused. Mind thus acting upon mind, in vastly multiplied opportunities, had awakened a great moral and intellectual power, whose presence and strength had not been suspected. The Protestant Reformation had weakened the bonds of spiritual dominion, and allowed the moral faculties fuller play; and the shadows of feudal institutions, so chilling to individual effort, were rapidly disappearing before the rising sun of the new era in the history of the world. Freedom of thought and action expanded the area of ideas, and gave birth to those tolerant principles which lead to brotherhood of feeling. The new impulse developed nobler motives for human action than the acquisition of wealth and power, and these soon engendered healthy schemes for founding industrial empires in the New World. . .

"Another event, favorable to the new impulse, now exerted a powerful influence. . . . Soldiers, an active, restless class in England, were deprived of employment, and would soon become dangerous to the public peace. While population and general prosperity had greatly increased, there was another large class, who, by idleness and dissipation, had squandered fortunes, and had become desperate men. The soldiers needed employment, either in their own art, or in equally exciting adventures; and the impoverished spendthrifts were ready for any thing which promised gain. Such were the men who stood ready to brave ocean perils and the greater dangers of the Western World, when such minds as those of Fernando Gorges, Bartholomew Gosnold, Chief Justice Popham, Richard Hakluyt, Captain John Smith, and others, devised new schemes for colonization. The weak and timid James the First, who desired and maintained peace with other nations during his reign, was glad to perceive a new field for restless and adventurous men to go to, and he readily granted a liberal patent [April 20, 1606] to the first company formed after his accession to the throne, for planting settlements in Virginia. The English then claimed dominion over a belt of territory extending from Cape Fear, in North Carolina, to Halifax, in Nova Scotia, and indefinitely westward. This was divided into two districts. One extended from the vicinity of New York city northward to the present southern boundary of Canada, including the whole of New England, and westward of it, and was called NORTH VIRGINIA. This territory was granted to a company of 'knights, gentlemen, and merchants' in the west of England, called the *Plymouth Company.* The other district extended from the mouth of the Potomac southward to Cape Fear, and was called SOUTH VIRGINIA. It was granted to a company of 'noblemen, gentlemen and merchants,' chiefly residents of London, called the *London Company.* . . ."[33]

Benson J. Lossing, *A Family History of the United States*

For Reflection and Reasoning

● *Student Activity Page 11-1.* Review the history of the Bible in English and its relationship to the history of exploration.

Record "Jamestown" for 1607. The *Student Activity Page* will be completed in a later lesson.

● What is a tenant? What is an apprentice?

● Locate England, Holland and Turkey on a map. On what sea was John Smith probably sailing?

● When John Smith was captured by the Turks, how was he treated? Why did he become angry?

● What is an unexplored wilderness? What does it mean that it is wild? What dangers might explorers and settlers face?

● What character qualities were seen in John Smith? Why were those character qualities needed to settle in the unexplored, wild wilderness of North America?

● *Student Activity Page 11-2.* Reason with the students to list the character qualities seen in the life of John Smith. Additional character qualities will be added in a future lesson. The student may then answer the question.

"Be not overcome of evil, but overcome evil with good."

Student Text, pages 48-49

● "The South Virginia, or London Company, sent Captain Christopher Newport, with three vessels and one hundred and five emigrants [Dec., 1606], to make a settlement upon Roanoke Island, where Raleigh's colony had perished almost twenty years before. . . . They possessed very poor materials for a colony. There was no *family* among them, and only 'twelve laborers and a few mechanics.' The remainder were 'gentlemen,' many of whom were vicious, dissolute men, totally unfit for such an enterprise, and quite unworthy to be actors in the glorious events anticipated by Gosnold and his enlightened associates at home. The voyage was a long and tedious one. Newport pursued the old route by the Canaries and the West Indies, and did not arrive upon the American coast until April, 1607, when a storm drove his vessels into Chesapeake Bay, where he found a good harbor. He named the capes at the entrance, *Charles* and *Henry*, in honor of the king's sons. A pleasant point of the Virginia peninsula, between the York and James Rivers, which they next landed upon and enjoyed repose, he named Point Comfort; and the noble Powhatan River which he soon afterward entered he called *James*. Sailing up the broad stream about fifty miles, the immigrants landed upon a beautiful, shaded peninsula, where they chose a site for the capital of the new empire, and called it JAMESTOWN.

"Ill feelings had been engendered before they reached the Canary Islands, and violent disputes had arisen during the long voyage. As the silly king had placed the names of the colonial council in a sealed box, with instructions not to open it until their arrival in Virginia, there was no competent authority on board to restore harmony. Captain Smith, who was the most able man among them, excited the envy of his companions; and being charged with a design to murder the council, usurp government, and proclaim himself king, he was placed in confinement. On opening the sealed box, it was discovered that Smith was one of the council. He was released from confinement; but, through the influence of Wingfield, an avaricious, unprincipled, but talented man, he was excluded from office. Smith demanded a trial upon the absurd charges. The accusation was withdrawn, and he took his seat in the council, over which Wingfield was chosen to preside."[34]
Benson J. Lossing, *A Family History of the United States*

● "(1.) '*Be not overcome of evil.* Let not the evil of any provocation that is given you have such a power over you, or make such an impression upon you, as to dispossess you of yourselves, to disturb your peace, to destroy your love, to ruffle and discompose your spirits, to transport you to any indecencies, or to bring you to study or attempt any revenge.' He that cannot quietly bear an injury is perfectly conquered by it. (2.) *But overcome evil with good,* with the good of patience and forbearance, nay, and of kindness and beneficence to those that wrong you. Learn to defeat their ill designs against you, and either to change them, or at least to preserve your own peace. He that hath this rule over his spirit is better than the mighty."

Matthew Henry, *Commentary*

● John Smith recorded more than one instance of the men trying to leave the colony in the Pinnace, and Smith's forcing them to stay:

"*Wingfield* and *Kendall* living in disgrace, seeing all things at randome in the absence of *Smith*. . . strengthened themselves with the sailers and other confederates, to regaine their former credit and authority, or at least such meanes abord the Pinnace, (being fitted to saile as *Smith* had appointed for trade) to alter her course and to goe for *England*.

"Smith unexpectedly returning had the plot discovered to him, much trouble he had to prevent it, till with store of sakre and musket shot he forced them stay or sinke in the river: which action cost the life of captaine *Kendall*.

"Now in *James* Towne they were all in combustion, the strongest preparing once more to run away with the Pinnace; which with the hazzard of his life, with Sakre falcon and musket shot, *Smith* forced now the third time to stay or sinke."[35]

John Smith, *The Settlement of Jamestown*

For Reflection and Reasoning

● Read Romans 12:21. What does it mean to be overcome? How could you be overcome with evil? How can you overcome evil with good?

● When Captain Smith was made a prisoner on his way to America, how did he respond? How had he previously responded to unjust imprisonment? John Smith had the choice of being overcome by evil or overcoming evil with good. Why was the court and a jury a better way to overcome the evil that was done against him? How does this event show a change in his character?

● The Student Text does not include the instructions for the government of the colony. The king had placed the names of the councilmen into a sealed box which was taken on board the ship. The box was not to be opened until the ship arrived in Virginia. What difficulties did this cause? For students who have studied *The Mighty Works of God: Liberty and Justice for All*, review the effect of the ar-

bitrary power held by a king. How did it affect the way the people of Jamestown were governed?

● What actions did Captain Smith take to help the colony? What is a deserter? Why did Captain Smith do something so drastic as to threaten to kill fellow settlers? What would have happened if the deserters had taken the only vessel? What type of men were they? How do you know?

● *Student Activity Page 11-3.* Students record Romans 12:21. Reason with the students to identify the evil actions of the settlers and the actions taken by Smith.

CAPTAIN JOHN SMITH	
Be not overcome with evil	But overcome evil with good. Romans 12:21
· Falsely accused of a plot to murder the chief men	· Asked for trial by jury
· Kept as prisoner in irons	· Gave the money he received to the settlement
	· Did everything he could for the sick
· Settlers took the only vessel and tried to leave Jamestown	· Kept the deserters from leaving

Leading Idea

Early settlers were unprepared for the many challenges of life in Virginia.

Student Text, pages 49-51

● "It was a happy hour for the Virginia settlers when Captain Smith took the reins of government. All was confusion; but he soon restored order; and by his courage and energy, inspired the Indians with awe, and compelled them to bring him supplies of food. In October, wild game became plentiful; and at the beginning of November, the abundant harvest of Indian corn was gathered by the natives, and they supplied the settlers with all they needed. Having established a degree of comfort and prosperity, Smith started, with some companions, to explore the surrounding country. He ascended the Chickahomminy River fifty miles from its mouth, and then, with two companions, penetrated the vast forest that covered the land. His companions were slain by the natives, and he was made a captive. After being exhibited in several villages, he was taken to Opechancanough, the eldest brother of Powhatan, who, regarding Smith as a superior being, spared his life, and conducted him to the emperor, then at Weroworomoco, on the York River. A solemn council decided that the captive must die, and Smith was prepared for execution. His head was placed upon a stone, and the heavy clubs of the executioners were raised to crush it, when Pocahontas, a child of 'ten or twelve years,' the favorite daughter of Powhatan,

rushed from her father's side, and casting herself upon the captive, besought the king to spare his life. Powhatan consented, and Smith was conducted in safety to Jamestown by a guard of twelve men, after an absence of seven weeks.

"God, in his providence, overrules every thing for good. It is seen in this event, for Smith's captivity was a public benefit. He had acquired a knowledge of the Indian character, and of the country and its resources, and also had formed friendly relations with the sachems and chiefs. Had his companions possessed half as much energy and honesty as Smith, all would have been well. But they were idle, improvident, and dissolute. As usual, he found every thing in disorder on his return from the forest. Only forty men were living, and a greater portion of them were on the point of escaping to the West Indies in the pinnace; but the courage and energy of Smith compelled them to remain. Conscious of the purity of their ruler and the wickedness of themselves, they hated him intensely, and from that time they plotted for his destruction, or the overthrow of his power."[36]

Benson J. Lossing, *A Family History of the United States*

For Reflection and Reasoning

• Review: If a nation is built upon self government, where must that self government begin? Why must the people have a Bible if they are to be self governed?

• What wrong idea did the settlers have about America? The Jamestown settlers were all men, they did not bring their families. Most of the men would have been known in England as "gentlemen". They were not used to hard, physical work. What did the new colony require of them for which they were not prepared?

• Did the Jamestown colonists try to make friends of the Indians? How do we know?

• When John Smith was captured by the Indians, how did the Indians treat their captive? Why?

• How was Pocahontas Providentially used to help John Smith and Jamestown?

• Reason with the students to identify the many efforts which John Smith made to preserve the colony. 1) He traded trinkets for corn when the people were nearly starving. 2) Tried to make friends of the Indians. The students may record these efforts in their notebook.

• *Student Activity Page 11-4.* Label Atlantic Ocean, Virginia, Chesapeake Bay, James River, and Jamestown.

Cultivating Student Mastery

1. In what ways were the Jamestown settlers foolish?

2. Why did so many settlers die?

3. How had John Smith been prepared to face such difficult circumstances?

Leading Idea

"He who will not work, shall not eat."

Student Text 51-52

● "Captain Newport arrived with supplies and one hundred and twenty immigrants, early in 1608. These were no better than the first adventurers. Instead of agriculturalists and mechanics, with families, they were idle 'gentlemen,' 'packed hither,' as Smith said, 'by their friends, to escape ill destinies.' There were also several unskillful goldsmiths, the very men least needed in the colony. Some glittering earth in the vicinity of Jamestown, was by them mistaken for gold; and in spite of the remonstrances of Smith, the whole industry of the colony was directed to the supposed treasure. 'There was no talk, no hope, no work, but dig gold, work gold, refine gold, load gold.' Newport loaded his vessel with the worthless earth, and returned to England, believing himself exceedingly rich; but science soon pronounced him miserably poor in useful knowledge and well-earned reputation.

"The gold-fever had taken strong hold upon the indolent dreamers, and Smith remonstrated against idleness and pleaded for industry, in vain. He implored the settlers to plow and sow, that they might reap and be happy. They refused to listen, and he turned from Jamestown with disgust. With a few sensible men, he went to explore the Chesapeake in an open boat, and every bay, inlet, and creek, received his attention. . .

Within three months he traveled full three thousand miles. It was one of the most wonderful of exploring expeditions, considered in all its aspects, ever recorded by the pen of history; and the map of the country, which Smith constructed on his return, is yet in existence in England, and is remarkable for its general accuracy."[37]

Benson J. Lossing, *A Family History of the United States*

● Although the setting of II Thessalonians 3:10 is not the same as the setting in which John Smith found himself in Jamestown, certainly the Biblical principle was the same. Matthew Henry comments on this Scripture: "For even when we were with you, this we commanded you, that if any would not work, neither should he eat." II Thessalonians 3:10. "(1.) There were some among them who were idle, *not working at all*, or doing nothing. It does not appear that they were gluttons or drunkards, but idle, and therefore disorderly people. It is not enough for any to say they do no hurt; for it is required of all persons that they do good in the places and relations in which Providence has placed them. . . . Industry in our particular callings as men is a duty required of us by our general calling as Christians."

For Reflection and Reasoning

● Review: What type of men came to Virginia? What did they think they would find, but did not?

● Why were the settlers so willing to start digging when they found *some glit-*

tering earth? Was that harder work or easier than tilling the soil, planting crops, and waiting for a harvest?

● Read II Thessalonians 3:10b. How did John Smith follow this Biblical instruction when he required the men to work? What types of jobs did Captain Smith give them? Were they important jobs? Why? How would they help meet the needs of the colony? Did his rule work in the colony? Why was it necessary for John Smith to make rules about working, and to force the settlers to do practical labor?

Cultivating Student Mastery

1. Was it right for John Smith to make the rule, "He who will not work shall not eat"? Why or why not?

2. How had the men shown that they needed John Smith to make rules for them?

3. Why was Captain Smith the best man to lead the colony?

Leading Idea — *The steadfastness and leadership of John Smith helped to preserve the Jamestown colony.*

Student Text, pages 52-53

● Webster defined *steadfastness* as "Firmness of mind or purpose; fixedness in principle; constancy; resolution. . ." He defines a *leader* as "One that leads or conducts; a guide; One who goes first."

● "Captain Smith returned to Jamestown on the 7th of September, 1608, and three days afterward he was formally made president of the settlement. Newport arrived soon afterward, with seventy immigrants, among whom were two females, the first English women ever seen upon the James River. To the soil they were compelled to look, chiefly, for their food,

and Smith exerted all his energies to turn the little industry of the settlers to agriculture. He succeeded, in a degree, but he had poor materials out of which to form a healthy, self-sustaining commonwealth. . . . Yet, with all his exertions, idleness and improvidence prevailed. At the end of two years from the first landing at Jamestown, and when the settlement numbered two hundred strong men, not more than forty acres were under cultivation. To the Indians the white people were compelled to look for their chief supply of food."[38]

Benson J. Lossing, *A Family History of the United States*

For Reflection and Reasoning

● Using a map of North America or a globe, locate the Chesapeake Bay. Note the distance to the Pacific Ocean. What false concept did the English have about the size of North America?

● Review the qualities of John Smith's character the students recorded on *Student Activity Page 11-2.* Were these qualities still seen in John Smith's life?

● Read I Corinthians 15:58. What does it mean to be steadfast? Was John Smith steadfast? What goals did he have? How did he try to reach his goals?

• What is a leader? When you play games, do you have a leader? What does the leader do?

Why did the Jamestown colony need a leader? Why was John Smith the right person to lead the colony? Identify exam-

ples of how his leadership protected the colony.

• *Student Activity Page 11-2.* Students may record additional qualities of character seen in John Smith's life.

• Complete *Student Activity Pages 11-5* and *11-6.*

Leading Idea

John Smith was resourceful in dealing with the Indians.

Student Text, pages 53-54

• William Penn gave vivid descriptions of the Indian character, including their ability to hide their true feelings. "They are great concealers of their own resentments, brought to it, I believe, by the revenge that hath been practised among them . . ." He also described their lack of understanding regarding ownership of personal property. "But in liberality they excel; nothing is too good for their friends: give them a fine gun, coat, or other thing, it may pass twenty hands before it sticks: light of heart, strong affections, but soon spent . . . Some kings have sold, others presented me with several parcels of land: the pay, or presents I

made them, were not hoarded by the particular owners, but the neighboring kings and their clans being present when the goods were brought out, the parties chiefly concerned consulted what, and to whom they should give them. . . . Then that king subdivideth it in like manner among his dependents, they hardly leaving themselves an equal share with one of their subjects . . . They care for little, because they want but little, and the reason is, a little contents them: in this they are sufficiently revenged on us; if they are ignorant of our pleasures, they are also free from our pains. . . ."[39]

William Penn, *Description of Pennsylvania*

For Reflection and Reasoning

• Review: What was the attitude of the Indians when the settlers arrived? The Indians were curious, but was there any fear? What were the Indians hoping to gain from the settlers? Was Powhatan an exception? Did the men of the Jamestown colony respect the Indians? Or were they

only interested in their own needs?

• How did John Smith, as the leader of the colony, treat the Indians? Were there times that he was kind? Were there times that he tricked them? Why did he do that?

• How did the Indians' ignorance of the

Englishmen's tools and equipment create problems?

• Why did Captain Smith return to England? Do you think his injury stopped him from further explorations? Why or why not?

John Smith—Explorer

Student Text, pages 54-56

• "The vast interior, now called NEW ENGLAND, was an unknown land, until Captain John Smith, with the mind of a philosopher and the courage of a hero, came, in 1614, and explored, not only the shores but the rivers which penetrated the wilderness. . . . With only eight men, Smith examined the region between Cape Cod and the Penobscot, constructed a map of the country, and after an absence of less than seven months, he returned to England, and laid a report before Prince Charles (afterward the unfortunate king who lost his head), the heir apparent to the throne. The prince, delighted with the whole account, confirmed the title which Smith had given to the territory delineated on the map, and it was named NEW ENGLAND. Crime, as usual, dimmed the luster of the discovery. Hunt, commander of one of the vessels of the expedition, kidnapped twenty-seven of the Indians, with Squanto, their chief, as soon as Smith had departed, took them to Spain and sold some of them into slavery."[40]

Benson J. Lossing, *A Family History of the United States*

For Reflection and Reasoning

• Review: How did John Smith aid the settlement at Jamestown? Whom did God provide to aid John Smith? Why did John Smith return to England?

• Once Smith recovered from his injury, what idea did he have?

• Discuss the life of an explorer. Why are there always risks for an explorer? When you or your family travel, are you traveling where others have traveled? Do you know where to expect difficulties? Why do you know? How do you know? When the first person explores a new land, do they know what dangers they will meet? In your reading or study of history, what explorers have you studied?

• As an explorer, Smith encountered many difficulties. What character qualities helped Smith overcome these difficulties? Identify the dangers Smith met in his explorations after he left Jamestown. How were his explorations a contribution for others?

Cultivating Student Mastery

1. What character must an explorer have? Why?

2. How did John Smith reflect the character of an explorer?

Leading Idea

John Smith — Father of Virginia

Student Text, pages 56

● As history unfolds, we see that God uses individuals to further His Story. John Smith provided an important link for the establishment of the Plymouth colony in 1620.

For Reflection and Reasoning

● Review the major links which have been studied in the movement of Christianity westward. How did each event and individual prepare the way for the next? How does this reveal God's Hand in history?

● Consider the contributions of John Smith to both Virginia and the Plymouth colony. Though the Jamestown settlement eventually did not survive, it was important to the beginning of the nation. Why was John Smith called the "Father of Virginia"? Would the Jamestown settlement have survived without John Smith's leadership?

Why was John Smith so important to the coming of the Pilgrims?

● *Student Activity Page 11-7.* Reasoning from the Student Text, identify the key contributions of John Smith as the Father of Virginia.

Cultivating Student Mastery

1. In your text it says that "John Smith is the most common of names, but this was the most uncommon of all the John

John Smith
Father of Virginia

"Captain John Smith was in Virginia less than three years, yet in that short time, he did a great deal."

1. <u>Saved the settlers from starving, by buying corn from the Indians</u>
2. <u>Saved them from Indian attacks</u>
3. <u>Taught them how to work</u>

God used the early settlement at Jamestown, under the leadership of John Smith, to open the way for settlement of the new land.

1. <u>Wrote two books on Virginia</u>
2. <u>Made maps of Virginia and New England</u>

Smiths." How was this John Smith "uncommon"?

2. Why did the settlers in Jamestown need a leader such as John Smith?

3. What quality of character do you admire most in John Smith? Why?

4. How did John Smith's work help in the establishment of the Plymouth colony?

Chapter 12
William Bradford

9-11 Days

Leading Idea

God prepares men and then He causes events.

Student Text, page 57

● "Among those devout people was our William Bradford, who was born *Anno* 1588 [9], in an obscure village called Austerfield, where the people were as unacquainted with the Bible, as the Jews do seem to have been with *part* of it in the days of Josiah; a most ignorant and licentious *people,* and *like unto their priest.* Hence, and in some other places, he had a comfortable inheritance left him of his honest parents, who died while he was yet a child, and cast him on the education, first of his grand parents, and then of his uncles, who devoted him, like his ancestors, unto the affairs of husbandry. Soon a long sickness kept him, as he would afterwards thankfully say, from the *vanities of youth,* and made him the fitter for what he was afterwards to undergo. When he was about a dozen years old, the reading of the Scriptures began to cause great impressions upon him. . . Nor could the wrath of his uncles, nor the scoff of his neighbours, now turned upon him, as one of the *Puritans,* divert him from his pious inclinations."[41]

Cotton Mather, *Lives of Bradford and Winthrop*

For Reflection and Reasoning

● Review: What is Divine Providence?

● Review the timeline, *Student Activity Page 11-1.* Note the relationship between the history of the English Bible, the developments in the fields of navigation and exploration, and the founding of Jamestown. Record "Plymouth" for 1620. How does the date of Bradford's birth relate to other events on the timeline?

● What is an orphan? William Bradford was orphaned when he was only one or two years old. With whom did William Bradford live? What occupation did his parents and other family members have? For what occupation was he trained?

● What are "vanities of youth"? Why did William Bradford think a long sickness was a blessing? What does that tell about his character? How did a long sickness prepare him for events later in life? Who arranged these events in Bradford's life?

● *Student Activity Page 12-1.* Outline and label England, Austerfield, and Scrooby. The small congregation of people from the north part of England eventually founded the colony in Plymouth, Massachusetts. See *Teacher Resource Page 12-1* for locations.

Cultivating Student Mastery

1. How did Bradford show his love for the Word of God?

2. How do the events from William Bradford's childhood illustrate the truth of Romans 8:28?

Leading Idea

The Word of God changed hearts, then lives, and then churches.

Student Text, pages 57-58

● "But that I may come more near my intendmente; when as by the travell & diligence of some godly & zealous preachers, & Gods blessing on their labours, as in other places of ye land, so in ye North parts, many became inlightened by ye word of God, and had their ignorance & sins discovered unto them, and begane by his grace to reforme their lives, and make conscience of their wayes, the worke of God was no sooner manifest in them, but presently they were both scoffed and scorned by ye prophane multitude, and ye ministers urged with ye yoak of subscription, or els must be silenced; and ye poore people were so vexed with apparators, & pursuants, & ye comissarie courts, as truly their affliction was not smale; which, notwithstanding, they bore sundrie years with much patience, till they were occasioned (by ye continuance & encrease of these troubles, and other means which ye Lord raised up in those days) to see further into things by the light of ye word of God. . . . So many therfore of these proffessors as saw ye evill of these things, in thes parts, and whose harts ye Lord had touched wth heavenly zeale for his trueth, they shooke of this yoake of antichristian bondage, and as ye Lords free people, joyned them selves (by a covenant of the Lord) into a church estate, in ye felowship of ye gospell, to walke in all his wayes, made known, or to be made known unto them, according to their best endeavours, whatsoever it should cost them, the Lord assisting them. And that it cost them something this ensewing historie will declare."[42]
William Bradford, *Of Plimoth Plantation*

● Webster defined a *separatist* as "One that withdraws from a church, or rather from an established church, to which he has belonged."

For Reflection and Reasoning

● Reason with the students concerning the changes which occurred in the lives of the Christians in the Scrooby congregation. Record and discuss the five steps of change on *Student Activity Page 12-2*.

1. They had the Bible to read.

Review the history of the Bible in English. Which Bibles were available to the Pilgrims? Was the King James Bible printed at the time William Bradford was a boy? The Geneva Bible was printed in 1559, and was probably used by the Scrooby congregation.

2. They saw they were sinners and had individual responsibility to God.

What Scripture verses might these Christians have read that would have taught them this idea? What does it mean to have individual responsibility to God?

3. They began to reform their lives.

What does it mean to reform their lives? Are there instructions in the Bible concerning how each Christian should live? What are some examples?

4. They learned to govern themselves.

What does it mean to govern oneself? What is self government? What guides the individual who is self governed?

Review: What is a Puritan? What did the Puritan want to have happen in the Church of England?

5. They separated from the Church of England and governed their own church.

What was a Separatist? How was a Separatist different from a Puritan? Was it easy to be a Separatist? William Bradford wrote in his history that "it cost them something." Why did the Church of England not want a congregation to be Separatists? Who was in control of the Church of England?

For students who have studied previous volumes in the series, *The Mighty Works of God*, these ideas should be a review.

• Would these changes in the lives of the people in the congregation at Scrooby have occurred if they had not had the Bible?

Note: This lesson will require two classtimes.

Leading Idea

Keeping a good conscience

Student Text, pages 58-59

• Webster defined the *conscience* as "Internal or self-knowledge, or judgment of right and wrong; or the faculty, power or principle within us, which decides on the lawfulness or unlawfulness of our own actions and affections, and instantly approves or condemns them."

For Reflection and Reasoning

• Review: What was a Puritan? What was a Separatist? In what ways were they the same? In what ways were they different?

• When Bradford chose to leave the Church of England and become part of the Separatist church at Scrooby, did he make that decision quickly and easily or with serious consideration? What had he done to be sure this was the right decision? What was most important to him?

• What is your conscience? How do you know what is right and wrong? What guides our conscience? Is it important that we study the Bible?

• When Bradford made his decision, his family did not want him to become a Separatist. In his writing, we can see that his family feared that certain things would happen to him. What were they?

Had Bradford previously cared well for his "estate"? What was his "estate"? What did he mean that he was desirous to augment what he had?

• See *Student Activity Page 12-3*. The students may record selected portions from William Bradford's statement which evidence his desire to keep a good conscience. Did Bradford's family think he was making a great sacrifice? Did Bradford think he was making a great sacrifice? Or did he feel honored that he could take these steps for the Lord? What does this tell about Bradford?

The students may record a summary statement about Bradford's character.

Cultivating Student Mastery

1. Why is it important to "keep a good conscience"?

2. How did William Bradford follow the Biblical principle found in Acts 24:16?

Leading Idea

Trusting in God's Providence

Student Text, pages 59-60

• "Having with a great company of Christians hired a ship to transport them for Holland, the master perfidiously betrayed them into hands of those persecutors, who rifled and ransacked their goods, and clapped their persons into prison at Boston, where they lay for a month together. But Mr. Bradford being a young man of about eighteen, was dismissed sooner than the rest, so that within a while he had opportunity with some others to get over to Zealand, through *perils,* both by *land* and *sea* not inconsiderable; where he was not long ashore ere a viper seized on his hand—that is, an officer—who carried him unto the magistrates, unto whom an envious passenger had accused him as having *fled* out of England. When the magistrates understood the true cause of his coming thither, they were well satisfied with him; and so he repaired joyfully unto his brethren at Amsterdam, where the difficulties to which he afterwards stooped in learning and serving of a Frenchman at the working of silks, were abundantly compensated by the delight wherewith he sat under the shadow of our Lord, in his purely dispensed ordinances. At the end of two years, he did, being of age to do it, convert his estate in England into money; but setting up for himself, he found some of his designs by the *providence* of God frowned upon, which he judged a *correction* bestowed by God upon him for certain decays of *internal piety,* whereinto he had fallen; the consumption of his *estate* he thought came to prevent a consumption in his *virtue.*"[43]

Cotton Mather, *Lives of Bradford and Winthrop*

• Webster defined *trust* as "Confidence; a reliance or resting of the mind on the integrity, veracity, justice, friendship or other sound principle of another person.

"He that putteth his *trust* in the Lord shall be safe. Prov. xxix."

• "The scope of these verses is to silence the fears, and encourage the faith, of the servants of God in their distresses. Perhaps it is intended, in the first place, for the support of God's Israel, in captivity; but all that faithfully serve God *through patience and comfort of this scripture may have hope. . . .*

"I. That they may depend upon his presence with them as their God, and a God all-sufficient for them in the worst of times. Observe with what tenderness God speaks, and how willing he is to let the heirs of promise know the immutability of his counsel, and how desirous to make them easy: '*Fear thou not, for I am with thee,* not only within call, but present with thee; *be not dismayed* at the power of those that are against thee, for *I am thy God,* and engaged for thee. Art thou weak? *I will strengthen thee.* Art thou destitute of friends? *I will help thee* in the time of need. Art thou ready to sink, ready to fall? *I will uphold thee with the right hand of my righteousness,* that right hand which is full of righteousness, in dispensing rewards and punishments,' Ps. xlviii. 10. . . ."

Matthew Henry, *Commentary*

For Reflection and Reasoning

• Review: What is Providence? What is a Separatist? What forced the Separatists to leave England?

• For students who have studied previous volumes in the series, *The Mighty*

Works of God, the events recorded in this section of the Student Text should be review. The emphasis of this lesson is to see William Bradford's constant trust in God's Providence.

● Read Isaiah 41:10, or other selected Scripture identifying God's protection. Even as a young man, Bradford trusted God to lead him. What helped Bradford through difficulties?

● What does it mean to trust someone? Does it mean we can depend on that person? Do you trust your friends? Do you trust your parents? Whom can we always trust? Did Bradford have parents who could guide him? What family did he have? Where did he put his trust?

● *Student Activity Page 12-4.* Answer the question regarding trusting in God's Providence. Using the Student Text, review the chronology of events leading to William Bradford's arrival in America. Emphasize the trust in God's Providence evidenced by the Separatists and particularly William Bradford.

1. The Separatists moved from England to Holland to worship in liberty.

What is liberty? What does it mean to worship in liberty?

When the Separatist congregation made their decision to leave Scrooby, Bradford chose to go with them. Did his family agree with his decision? Why did he choose to join them anyway? How did this action show his desire to keep a good conscience?

2. The master of the ship betrayed them and they were taken prisoner.

When Bradford and the other Separatists were put into prison, would it have been easy for Bradford to change his mind? Why did he continue on? Why was Bradford released from prison early?

3. In Holland, the Separatists found new ways to make a living. Bradford found a position dyeing silk.

In what occupation was Bradford trained? Since the Separatists came from the northern part of England, perhaps others were farmers as well. Might it have been hard to learn a new occupation?

4. When Bradford lost his money, he still trusted in God's Hand.

What is an estate? What does it mean to invest money? What sometimes happens when you invest money? Did Bradford blame anyone for this difficulty? Bradford believed God had a lesson for him. What does it mean to learn from difficult events?

● How are hardships an act of Providence?

Note: This lesson will require two class-times.

Leading Idea

A new colony established upon self government.

Student Text, pages 60-61

● ". . . After longe beating at sea they fell with that land which is called Cape Cod; the which being made & certainly knowne to be it, they were not a little joyfull. After some deliberation had amongst them selves & with ye mr. of ye ship, they tacked aboute and resolved to stande for ye southward (ye wind & weather being faire) to finde some place aboute Hudsons river for their habitation. But after they had sailed yt course aboute halfe ye day, they fell amongst deangerous shoulds and roring breakers, and they were so farr intangled ther with as they conceived them selves in great danger; & ye wind shrinking upon them withall, they resolved to bear up againe for the Cape, and thought them selves hapy to gett out of those dangers before night overtooke them, as by Gods providence they did. And ye next day they gott into ye Cape-harbor wher they ridd in saftie. . . .

"Being thus arrived in a good harbor and brought safe to land, they fell upon their knees & blessed ye God of heaven, who had brought them over ye vast & furious ocean, and delivered them from all ye periles & miseries therof, againe to set their feete on ye firme and stable earth, their proper elemente. . . ."[44]

William Bradford, *Of Plimoth Plantation*

● "But after he had resided in Holland about half a score years, he was one of those who bore a part in that hazardous and generous enterprise of removing into New-England, with part of the English church at Leyden, where, at their first landing, his dearest consort accidentally falling overboard, was drowned in the harbour; and the rest of his days were spent in the services, and temptations, of that American wilderness."[45]

Cotton Mather, *Lives of Bradford and Winthrop*

● "I shall a little returne backe and begine with a combination made by them before they came ashore, being ye first foundation of their govermente in this place; occasioned partly by ye discontented & mutinous speeches that some of the strangers amongst them had let fall from them in ye ship—That when they came a shore they would use their owne libertie; for none had power to comand them, the patente they had being for Virginia, and not for New-england, which belonged to an other Government, with which ye Virginia Company had nothing to doe. And partly that shuch an . . . acte by them done (This their condition considered) might be as firme as any patent, and in some respects more sure."[46]

William Bradford, *Of Plimoth Plantation*

● ". . . the winnowed remnant of the PILGRIMS who left Delft-Haven—crossed the stormy Atlantic. These were they who came to the New World to enjoy liberty of conscience and freedom of action, and to lay, broad and deep, a portion of the foundations of our happy Republic. . . Before proceeding to the shore, the PILGRIMS agreed upon a form of government, and committed it to writing. To that *first constitution of government* ever subscribed by a whole people, the forty-one affixed their names, and then elected John Carver to be their governor. In the cabin of the *May-Flower* the first republican government in America was solemnly inaugurated. That vessel thus became truly the cradle of liberty in America, rocked on the free waves of the ocean."[47]

Benson J. Lossing, *A Family History of the United States*

For Reflection and Reasoning

● Review: What is government? What is self government? What is civil government? How was Jamestown governed?

● What tragedy happened to Bradford shortly after the Pilgrims arrived at Cape Cod? How did he respond? How did this show his dependence on God's Providence?

● Why were the Pilgrims not governed by the King's patent?

Why must there be civil government? Do all people need civil government? Why? How much civil government do they need?

● The Mayflower Compact was a very important document. It was the first time a people set up their own civil government. The men all agreed to obey the rules of the Mayflower Compact.

• *Student Activity Page 12-5.* The students may enjoy reading the Mayflower Compact. Note that it is a very short document. In the Compact they agreed to set up laws and offices. What did they promise to do? Students may underline key phrases.

Further study will be given to the Mayflower Compact in a later year. The purpose of reading the document is to briefly introduce it to the students.

• Who was chosen as the first governor of Plymouth? What is a governor? Relate the definition of governor to the definition of government.

• Record *Suggested Student Notes* on *Student Activity Page 12-6.*

Suggested Student Notes

In the cabin of the Mayflower, the Pilgrims agreed upon a form of government based on self government. They put it into writing and all of the men signed their names.

Leading Idea

William Bradford provided Godly leadership for Plymouth Colony.

Student Text, pages 61-62

• "Here was Mr. Bradford, in the year 1621, unanimously chosen the governour of the plantation: the difficulties whereof were such, that if he had not been a person of more than ordinary piety, wisdom and courage, he must have sunk under them. He had, with a laudable industry, been laying up a treasure of experiences, and he had now occasion to use it: indeed, nothing but an *experienced* man could have been suitable to the necessities of the people. The potent nations of the Indians, into whose country they were come, would have cut them off, if the blessing of God upon *his* conduct had not quelled them; and if his prudence, justice and moderation had not overruled them, they had been ruined by their own distempers. . . .

"For two years together after the beginning of the colony, whereof he was now governour, the poor people had a great experiment of 'man's not living by bread alone;' for when they were left all together without one morsel of bread for many months one after another, still the good providence of God relieved them, and supplied them, and this for the most part out of the *sea.* In this low condition of affairs, there was no little exercise for the prudence and patience of the governour, who chearfully bore his part in all: and, that industry might not flag, he quickly set himself to settle *propriety* among the new-planters; forseeing that while the whole country laboured upon a common stock, the husbandry and business of the plantation could not flourish, as Plato and others long since dreamed that it would, if a *community* were established. Certain, if the spirit which dwelt in the old puritans, had not inspired these new-planters, they had sunk under the burden of these difficulties; but our Bradford had a double portion of that spirit. . . .

"The leader of a people in a wilderness had need to be a Moses; and if a Moses had not led the people of Plymouth Colony, when this worthy person was their governour, the people had never with so much unanimity and importunity still called him to lead them. . . . But as he found the providence of Heaven many ways recompensing his many acts of self-denial, so he gave this testimony to the faithfulness of the divine promises: 'That he had forsaken friends, houses and lands for the sake of the gospel, and the Lord gave them him again.' Here he prospered in his estate; and besides a worthy son which had by a former wife, he had also two sons and a daughter by another, whom he married in this land."[48]

Cotton Mather, *Lives of Bradford and Winthrop*

For Reflection and Reasoning

● Review: What document identified the civil government for Plymouth colony? Why was it written? How did this document show their understanding of self government? What is a governor? Who was the first governor of Plymouth Colony? How was the governor given his authority?

● What does it mean to be unanimously chosen? What does that tell about the attitude of the colonists toward William Bradford? How old was William Bradford when he was elected governor? What does this reveal about his character?

● Review: What is a leader? What made William Bradford a good leader?

● *Student Activity Page 12-7.* Consider the difficulties which the Pilgrims faced and the leadership Bradford gave to the colony. Discuss each event as it is identified. Record the leadership qualities of Bradford.

1. *Difficulties:* Lack of food; new arrivals

came without supplies.

Bradford: **Set up individual private property.**

Why were the people more willing to work once they owned their own land and all the crops from that land? Why would this have given them plenty?

2. *Difficulty:* Indians

Bradford: **The Pilgrims treated the Indians as they wanted to be treated. A peace treaty was made with the Indians.**

What difficulties had the Virginia colony had with the Indians? Why did the Plymouth colony not experience the same difficulties?

3. *Difficulty:* Busy life

Bradford: **Carefully recorded the history of Plymouth.**

How busy was William Bradford? When do you suppose he found time to record the history? What type of light would have been in his home? Would writing the history have been an easy task? Why do you think he did it?

Leading Idea

God prepared William Bradford to lead the Plymouth colony.

Student Text, pages 62-63

● "He was a person for study as well as action; and hence, notwithstanding the difficulties through which he passed in his youth, he attained unto a notable skill in languages: the Dutch tongue was become almost as vernacular to him as the English; the French tongue he could also manage; the Latin and the Greek he had mastered; but the Hebrew he most of all studied, 'Because,' he said, 'he would see with his own eyes the ancient oracles of God in their native beauty.' He was also skilled in History, in Antiquity, and in Philosophy . . . But the *crown* of all was his holy, prayerful, watchful, and fruitful walk with God, wherein he was very exemplary.

"At length he fell into an indisposition of body, which rendered him unhealthy for a whole winter; and as the spring advanced, his health yet more declined; yet he felt himself not what he counted sick, till one day; in the night after which, the God of heaven so filled his mind with ineffable consolations, that he seemed little short of Paul, rapt up unto the unutterable entertainments of Paradise. 'That the good Spirit of God had given him a pledge of his happiness in another world, and the first-fruits of his eternal glory;' and on the day following he died, May 9, 1657, in the 69th year of his age — lamented by all the colonies of New-England, as a common blessing and father to them all. . . .

 MEN are but FLOCKS:
 BRADFORD beheld their need,
  And long did them at once
   both rule and feed."[49]

Cotton Mather, *Lives of Bradford
and Winthrop*

For Reflection and Reasoning

● Review: What is a governor? How long was William Bradford governor of Plymouth Colony?

● Was William Bradford a busy man? What different responsibilities did he have? (Consider his responsibilities for both his family and the colony.) But, even when he was so busy, did he continue to learn? *Note:* We don't know at what age Bradford learned all of the languages, but we must assume that some of this study was after he was in America.

● What is Providence? How can you recognize God's Providence in your life? In your family's life? In your community? Throughout all of William Bradford's life, he recognized God's Hand protecting and guiding his own life and the life of the colony.

● Review: What difficulties in Bradford's early life did he recognize as Providential?

● In Bradford's *History*, he acknowledged God's Hand in giving long life to all those Pilgrims who survived the first winter. What is long life? Who is the oldest person you know? Do you have grandparents or great grandparents? Do you know how old they are? To what did Bradford credit the long life of the Pilgrims?

● What is a peril? Using the Student Text, review the perils which the Pilgrims had survived. If time permits, the students may look up the verses Bradford included in the history.

● Why did Bradford think it was important to record the perils which the Pilgrims endured? When we face a peril in our lives, does it help to know that God protected others in the same kind of peril or even something more difficult? Where did the Pilgrims look for encouragement?

Suggested Student Notes

**God Prepared William Bradford to lead
the Plymouth Colony**
1. **William Bradford learned Dutch, French, Latin, Greek, and Hebrew.**
2. **Bradford always recognized God's Providence in his life and in the life of the colony.**

Cultivating Student Mastery

1. How did difficulties strengthen Bradford's trust in Divine Providence?

Leading Idea

The Pilgrims were stepping stones of self government for others.

Student Text, page 63-64

● "Imperial bombast in James I had chuckled over this band of strong-souled ones. He had 'peppered them soundly,' as he loved to boast, and 'harried them' out of his land in the bitterness of their grief; but when their sturdy feet pressed Plymouth Rock they had a conscience void of offense toward Holland, England and God. An invisible hand had guided the helm of the *Mayflower* to a rock from which, in a wintry storm, a group of simple-hearted heroes, with bare heads, could proclaim a Church without a bishop and a State without a king."[50]

Thomas Armitage, *A History of the Baptists*

● "Our popular government lay in embryo on board the Mayflower, all-environed with its only possible preserva-

tives, popular intelligence and popular virtue. The idea born there, and embodied in a civil constitution . . . grew with the growth of the colonies, gradually expelling from the thoughts and affections of the people all other theories of civil government, until finally it enthroned itself in the national mind, and then embodied itself in our national government."[51]

J. W. Wellman, *The Church Polity of the Pilgrims*

● The Pilgrims identified Biblical principles of self and civil government. Those principles of government became the foundation for the nation, the United States of America.

For Reflection and Reasoning

● Review: What is government? What is self government? In what ways were the Pilgrims self governed?

● Why did the Pilgrims leave Holland and sail to America? To whom did they want to take the gospel of Christ? What is a stepping stone? What do stepping stones do? How can stepping stones lead a person to go in a particular direction?

● What ideas did the Pilgrims bring to America that would later be the ideas of the new nation, the United States of

America? How were these stepping stones? What was the basis or foundation of these stepping stones?

● *Student Activity Page 12-8.* Label the stepping stones: 1) Gospel of Jesus Christ; 2) Governed own family; 3) Governed own churches; 4) Governed own colony; and 5) United States of America.

The student may add illustrations to this page, i.e. a Pilgrim beside the first stepping stone and the United States flag by the last.

● How does Bradford's poem reflect his understanding of Divine Providence?

Chapter 13
Peter Stuyvesant
7-8 Days

Leading Idea

God Providentially directed people from many European countries to the New World.

Student Text, page 65

● "The State of New York commenced its political career when Peter Minuit, recently appointed Governor of New Netherland, arrived at New Amsterdam (as the germ of the present city of New York was called), in May, 1626. He immediately purchased of the Indians, for about twenty-four dollars, the whole of the island of Manhattan, on which the city of New York now stands, and began vigorously to perfect the founding of a State similar to those of Holland. . . . By conciliatory measures, he gained the confidence of the Indians; and he also opened a friendly correspondence with the Puritans at Plymouth. . . .

"For the purpose of encouraging emigration to New Netherland, the Dutch West India Company offered, in 1629, large tracts of land, and certain privileges, to those persons who should lead or send a given number of emigrants to occupy and till the soil. Directors of the company availed themselves of the privilege, and sent Wouter (Walter) Van Twiller to examine the country and select the lands. Immigrants came; and then were laid the foundations of the most noted of the manorial estates of New York. The proprietors were called *patroons* (patrons), and held a high political and social station in the New World. . . ."[52]

Benson J. Lossing, *A Family History of the United States*

For Reflection and Reasoning

● Locate the following places on a map: England, France, Holland, St. Lawrence River, Hudson River, Delaware River, Philadelphia, and Manhattan Island.

● Why did the settlers call their colony New Netherland? What is the name of New Netherland today? Why did they call their settlement New Amsterdam?

● Review: When the Separatists left England, to what country did they flee? Why did they go there? The Separatists fled to Holland in 1607. What language did the people of Holland speak? Why was this difficult for the Pilgrims?

● *Student Activity Page 11-1.* Add "New Netherland" to the timeline, under 1626.

● How many years passed between the arrival of the Pilgrims at Plymouth and the founding of New Netherland?

Leading Idea

Welcome to the new governor of New Amsterdam

Student Text, pages 65-66

● "Van Twiller. . . was succeeded in office, in May, 1638, by Sir William Keift. . . The people of New Netherland had already begun to murmur at Keift's course, and they charged the troubles with the Indians directly upon him. Unwilling to assume the entire responsibility of a war, himself, the governor called a meeting [Aug. 23, 1641] of the heads of families in New Amsterdam for consultation. They promptly chose 'twelve select men' [August 29], with DeVries at their head, to act for them; and this was the first representative assembly ever formed among Europeans on Manhattan Island. They did not agree with the governor's hostile views; and Keift finding them not only opposed to his war designs, but that they were also taking cognizance of alleged grievances of the people, dissolved them, in February 1642. . . ."[53]

Benson J. Lossing, *A Family History of the United States*

● "At length, in May, 1647, Peter Stuyvesant arrived, and the glee of the people sought expression in such profuse military salutes that nearly all the powder in the fort was used up. Stuyvesant's speech was brief and to the point, but it was not exactly that of a ruler who meant to be guided by public opinion rather than his own. 'I shall govern you as a father his children, for the advantage of the chartered West India Company, and these burghers, and this land;' in these words he summed up his view of the situation, and he summed it up correctly. In his mind the contrast between bad and good government was not the contrast between paternal and popular government, for the latter he would have ruled out as mere idiocy; it was the contrast between selfish and unselfish paternal government. If his rule was to be better than Van Twiller's and Keift's, it was because God had given him more honesty or more sense, or both. But he had no notion of resigning any of a ruler's prerogatives. He was first and always a man of masterful personality. . . .

". . . there is a fine portrait of him painted from life, and probably in Holland shortly before his coming to New Netherland, for the face is that of a man rather more than fifty years old. It is a strong face, such as might have belonged to one of Cromwell's sturdiest Ironsides. 'A valiant, weather-beaten, mettlesome, obstinate, leathern-sided, lion-hearted, generous-spirited old governor,' — such are the epithets applied to him by the admiring but judicious Knickerbocker. Years of military service had made him a rigid disciplinarian . . . When he formally assumed command at Fort Amsterdam, he sat with his hat on, as our informant tells us, 'quite like the Czar of Muscovy,' while a group of the principal inhabitants stood before him bareheaded and waited quite long enough before he condescended to take personal notice of them. He soon began issuing proclamations with as much zeal as Kieft had shown . . . Some said the new governor was not so much of a father, after all; some asked, with a sigh, if this was not just the sort of thing they had complained of in Director Kieft."[54]

John Fiske, *The Dutch and Quaker Colonies in America*

106

For Reflection and Reasoning

● What is a governor? The governor of New Netherland was appointed, not elected. If the governor did not please the colonists, the only thing they could do was to petition for a replacement. How was the method of choosing the New Netherland governor different from the method for choosing the governor in Plymouth?

● What "seed" of representative government was planted by Governor Kieft? What action did the Governor take when the representatives disagreed with him? How is this arbitrary rule or tyranny?

● What kind of governor do you think Peter Stuyvesant will be? The people were very excited when he arrived. Do you think they will be as excited after he has governed the colony for awhile? Why or why not?

● From the Student Text, identify the phrases which describe the power of government exercised by Peter Stuyvesant, i.e. "he should do exactly as he chose and that they must obey him."

How was this different from the power exercised by Governor Bradford in Plymouth?

● Have the students find phrases in the Student Text which describe Peter Stuyvesant's arrival. The students may enjoy drawing a picture of Peter Stuyvesant's arrival in New Amsterdam.

Life in New Amsterdam

Leading Idea

Student Text, pages 66-69

For Reflection and Reasoning

● What did the Dutch families like to use in building their houses? What is a tile? Where did they get the bricks for their homes?

● Discuss the design of their houses. How were their homes like our houses today? How were they different? Do you have a parlor in your house?

● Tulips were cultivated in Holland. The colonists in New Amsterdam loved tulips so much that they brought tulip bulbs with them from Holland, or had them sent by ship.

● Students may color the picture of New Amsterdam, *Student Activity Page 13-1.* The students may enjoy adding flowers to the picture.

Peter Stuyvesant, the last and best Dutch Governor

Leading Idea

Student Text, pages 69-70

● "Peter Stuyvesant was the last, and, like the renowned Wouter Van Twiller, the best of our ancient governors. Wouter having surpassed all who preceded him, and Peter, or Piet, as he was sociably called by the old Dutch burghers, who were ever prone to familiarize names, having never been equaled by any successor. He was in fact the very man fitted by nature to retrieve the desperate fortunes of her beloved province, had not the Fates, those most potent and unrelenting of all ancient spinsters, destined them to inextricable confusion."[55]

Washington Irving, *Knickerbocker's History of New York*

● "His [Peter Stuyvesant] treatment of the Indians was very kind and just, and they soon exhibited such friendship for the Dutch, that Stuyvesant was falsely charged with a design to employ them in murdering the English in New England. Long accustomed, as a military leader, to arbitrary rule, he was stern and inflexible, but he had the reputation of an honest man. He immediately commenced much needed reforms; and during his whole administration, which was ended by the subjugation of the Dutch by the English, in 1664, he was the faithful and energetic defender of the integrity of the province against its foes. By prudent management he avoided collisions with the English, and peaceably ended boundary disputes with them in the autumn of 1650. . ."[56]

Benson J. Lossing, *History of the United States*

● "External difficulties gave Stuyvesant little more trouble than a spirit opposed to his aristocratic views, which he saw manifested daily around him. While he had been judiciously removing all cause for ill-feeling with his neighbors, there was a power at work within his own domain which gave him great uneasiness. The democratic seed planted by the Twelve, in Keift's time, had begun to grow vigorously under the fostering care of a few enlightened Hollanders, and some Puritans who had settled in New Netherland. The latter, by their applause of English institutions, had diffused a desire among the people to partake of the blessings of English liberty, as they understood it, and as it appeared in New England. Stuyvesant was an aristocrat by birth, education, and pursuit, and vehemently opposed every semblance of democracy. At the beginning he found himself at variance with the people. At length an assembly of two deputies from each village in New Netherland, chosen by the inhabitants, convened at New Amsterdam [December, 1653], without the approbation of the governor. It was a spontaneous, and, in the eyes of the governor, a revolutionary movement. Their proceedings displeased him; and finding argument of no avail, he exercised his official prerogative, and commanded obedience to his will. The people grew bolder at every rebuff, and finally they not only resisted taxation, but openly expressed a willingness to bear English rule for the sake of enjoying English liberty."[57]

Benson J. Lossing, *A Family History of the United States*

For Reflection and Reasoning

● Consider the dress and life of the Dutch people in New York. How did both the Dutch dress and houses show their appreciation for beauty? How had New Amsterdam become a different place in 1664 than it had been in 1647?

● Review: What is government? What is self government?

● Peter Stuyvesant ruled as governor for seventeen years. Was he a good governor? Why?

Student Activity Page 13-2. List the qualities which characterized Stuyvesant's rule as governor. How did Peter Stuyvesant treat the Indians? How did it benefit the colony?

● Under the rule of Governor Stuyvesant, did the people have any opportunity for self government in their colony? What action of the people shows their interest in governing themselves? What example of self government was seen by the colonists in New Netherland?

Leading Idea

"I won't surrender."

Student Text, pages 70-71

● ". . . Charles II. had made up his mind to seize New Netherland by surprise. Some sovereigns would have waited for the next war, a few might have picked a quarrel on purpose, but Charles knew better. He preferred to take the almost certain chance of bringing on a war by seizing the coveted treasure in the first place. According to the English theory it was rightfully his already; surely he could expel intruders from his own territory without asking permission or notifying anybody! So Lord Stirling's claim upon Long Island was bought up for £3500, and then the island was granted to the king's worthy brother, James, Duke of York and Albany, with all the rights of a lord proprietary. Together with Long Island the grant included the mainland with its rivers west of the Connecticut River as far as the Delaware. This covered not only the whole of New Netherland, but half of the actual territory of Connecticut, to say nothing of Connecticut's extension to the Pacific Ocean. It was thus in flat violation of the charter granted two years before to Winthrop, but no Stuart king ever heeded such trifles as merely giving away to one man what he had already given away to another.

". . . a courier came spurring in wild haste to tell him that the English fleet had sailed from Boston and was hourly expected to show itself off Coney Island. . . The day after his arrival at Manhattan, the stately black frigates, with the red ensign of England flying at their mastheads, were seen coming up the Lower Bay, where they anchored just below the Narrows, and sent ashore a company of soldiers, who seized the blockhouse upon Staten Island.

"The situation was without a single ray of hope. Stuyvesant had at his command about 150 trained soldiers, besides 250 citizens capable of bearing arms, and among these there were many disaffected. Fort Amsterdam mounted 20 guns, with a very inadequate supply of powder; at the north was the Wall Street palisade, and both the river banks were completely defenceless against the approach of four frigates carrying not less than 120 guns, while the enemy's men, including New England volunteers, must have numbered nearly 1000. Yet Stuyvesant was determined to resist. On Saturday, August 30, Colonel Cartwright came up the bay with a summons to surrender the province of New Netherland, with an assurance that no harm should be done to life or property. It was found that Nicolls had forgotten to sign this paper, and while it was taken back for his signature, Stuyvesant consulted with the burgomasters and schepens, and found them strongly inclined to submission, but all the while all hands were kept bravely at work repairing the crazy fortificiations."[58]
John Fiske, *The Dutch and Quaker Colonies in America*

For Reflection and Reasoning

● Review: What gave England the right to claim the North American continent?

● Henry Hudson, from England, had explored the area which became New Netherland. However, he had carried on his explorations for Holland. What river was named for him?

• What startling news did Peter Stuyvesant receive? What effect would this have on the colony?

• Was New Amsterdam prepared to defend their city against the English? Why or why not?

• The street which ran along the crumbling wooden palisade was called Wall Street. In modern New York, businesses built their offices along Wall Street. The name Wall Street is used to refer to American business. A newspaper named *The Wall Street Journal* reports business and financial news which affects the whole nation.

• What was unusual about Peter Stuyvesant's leg? He had lost his leg many years before in a battle. When Peter Stuyvesant became angry, he would stomp his wooden leg. Do you think he stomped his leg the day the message came from King Charles?

• What does it mean to surrender?

• What had Peter Stuyvesant told the people about how he planned to rule

them? He had been a much better governor than the ones before him. However, Peter Stuyvesant was a very stubborn man and often demanded things of the people which they didn't want. How might this have affected their willingness to surrender?

• *Student Activity Page 13-3.* Using the Student Text, deduce the reasons that the citizens of New Amsterdam were willing to surrender to the English. Contrast the attitude of the citizens with the attitude of Peter Stuyvesant — "I won't surrender."

• What character was revealed in Peter Stuyvesant when the whole city was ready to surrender, but he refused?

Cultivating Student Mastery

1. Why did the citizens oppose Stuyvesant's refusal to surrender?

2. How was Peter Stuyvesant's power limited?

3. Why was it difficult for Stuyvesant to defend New Amsterdam?

Leading Idea

A time to surrender

Student Text, pages 71-72

• "On Tuesday morning a boat with a flag of truce rowed up to Whitehall, and Governor Winthrop, with half a dozen other gentlemen, came ashore. They were escorted to the parlour of the nearest tavern, where Stuyvesant and the city magistrates received them politely. Winthrop in his most kindly manner tried to persuade the gallant Director to accept the inevitable, but his arguments fell upon

deaf ears. Then Winthrop handed a letter to Stuyvesant, and the English gentlemen returned to their boat, while the Dutch dignitaries proceeded to the fort. The letter, addressed by Nicolls to Winthrop, was then read aloud by Stuyvesant: —

"MR. WINTHROP: As to those particulars you spoke to me, I do assure you that if the Manhadoes be delivered up to his

Majesty, I shall not hinder, but any people from the Netherlands may freely come and plant there or thereabouts; and such vessels of their own country may freely come thither, and any of them may as freely return home, in vessels of their own country; and this and much more is contained in the privilege of his Majesty's English subjects; and thus much you may, by what means you please, assure the Governor from, Sir, your very affectionate servant, RICHARD NICOLLS.'

"This wise and kindly document wrought a visible effect upon the burgomasters present, and they wished that it might be read to the citizens who were gathered in a vast crowd outside. But Stuyvesant, who did not wish to have any such effect produced, stoutly refused, and when the burgomasters insisted, he flew into a rage and tore the letter into small pieces. Thereupon several of the magistrates, gravely offended, left the room. The news was told to the throng of people, who received it with hisses and growls. Three prominent citizens came in where the Director was standing, and demanded the letter. Amid vociferous uproar Stuyvesant retreated into the council-chamber, while Nicholas Bayard, who had gathered up the fragments of the letter, pieced them together and made a true copy, which was read aloud to the people with marked and wholesome effect. There were many in the town who did not regard a surrender to England as the worst of misfortunes. They were weary of hard-headed Peter's arbitrary ways and disgusted with their High Mightinesses and the West India Company for leaving them unprotected; and in this mood they lent a willing ear to the offer of English liberties. Was it not better to surrender on favourable terms than to lose their lives in behalf of — what? their homes and families? No, indeed, but in behalf of a remote government which had done little or nothing for them! If they were lost to Holland, it was Holland's loss, not theirs. With such a temper the tact and moderation of Colonel Nicolls were likely to prevail.

"Meanwhile Stuyvesant wrote an elaborate argument to prove the justice and soundness of the Dutch title to New Netherland, and sent it by four trusty friends to Nicolls. The reply was what might have been expected. Nicolls was not there to argue the point. He stood upon no question of right; that was a matter for his Majesty and their High Mightinesses. He was only a soldier acting upon orders, and if his terms were refused he must attack. 'On Thursday,' quoth he, 'I shall speak with you at the Manhattans.' He was told that he would be welcome if he were to come as a friend. 'I shall come with ships and soldiers,' said Nicolls, 'hoist a white flag at the fort, and I may consider your proposals.'

"Accordingly on Thursday, September 4, two of the frigates came up and dropped anchor near Governor's Island, while Nicolls marched with three companies to the site of the Brooklyn end of Fulton Ferry, where he was joined by a large force from Connecticut and the English towns of Long Island. . . . 'Resistance is not soldiership,' said De Sille, 'it is sheer madness.' But Stuyvesant hesitated while the gunners, with lighted matches, awaited his order. Then Dominie Megapolensis laid his hand upon the veteran's shoulder, and mildly said, 'Of what avail are our poor guns against that broadside of more than sixty? It is wrong to shed blood to no purpose.' The order to fire was not given, and the frigates passed quietly into the North River. Leaving De Sille in command of the fort, the Director took 100 men and hurried up town to check any attempt of the enemy to land. He was met by a remonstrance signed by 93 leading citizens, among whose names he read that of his own son, Balthazar. Women and children flocked about the brave old man and added their tearful entreaties. 'Well, let it be so,' he said, 'I had rather be carried to my grave.' In a few moments the white flag fluttered over the ramparts of Fort Amsterdam, and so the rule of Holland in America came peacefully to an end."[59]

John Fiske, *The Dutch and Quaker Colonies in America*

For Reflection and Reasoning

● Review: What did the people of New Amsterdam want when the British came to take over the colony? Why? What did the governor want? Why? How much power did kings have in the 1600's?

● What were the terms of the letter that was sent from the English? Why did the governor not want to read it to the people? Continue the contrast chart, *Student Activity Page 13-3,* summarizing the actions of Stuyvesant and the people.

● What reasons did Stuyvesant give for why the colony should remain a Dutch colony? Was Stuyvesant brave? Was he willing to fight the enemy, even though they were greatly outnumbered? Would he have been likely to win? What event caused Stuyvesant to change his mind?

● Was Stuyvesant a representative of the people? Who had given Stuyvesant his authority? How was this event an example of arbitrary power?

● Why was the name changed from New Amsterdam to New York?

● The students would enjoy dramatizing the conflict between Stuyvesant and the colonists regarding the letter.

Cultivating Student Mastery

1. Prepare a simple timeline identifying the series of events from the startling message sent to Peter Stuyvesant to the surrender of New Amsterdam.

2. What forced Peter Stuyvesant to finally surrender?

Leading Idea

New York established local self government.

Student Text, page 72

● "Looked at merely with reference to its place in the chain of historic causation, the acquisition of New Netherland by the English was an event scarcely second in magnitude to the conquest of Canada in later days. . . . it brought the British frontier into direct and important contact with the French frontier, all the way from the headwaters of the Hudson River to those of the Ohio. It gave to the English the command of the commercial and military centre of the Atlantic coast of North America; and by bringing New England into closer relations with Virginia and Maryland, it prefigured and made possible a general union of Atlantic states.

"About a year after the surrender of New Amsterdam, the Director returned to Holland to make his report to the States General. His reception was at first rather a cold one. The directors of the West India Company were angry and wanted somebody to punish, and so the vials of their wrath were poured out upon poor Stuyvesant. But when he wrote to New York for testimony in justification of his conduct, it came in such plentiful amount and of such unimpeachable character that the good man was triumphantly vindicated, and the tongues of his detractors were silenced. He returned to New York in 1667 and passed the brief remainder of his life in peaceful retire-

112

ment on his bowery, which occupied the space now bounded by Fourth Avenue and the East River, and by Sixth and Seventeenth streets. His wooden house, of two stories with projecting rafters, stood at a point a little east of Third Avenue and just north of Tenth Street. The approach to it led through a garden, bright with Dutch flowers arranged in beds of geometrical pattern, after the stiff fashion that has generally prevailed in continental Europe. There the aged Stuyvesant spent in private life what were doubtless his happiest years. His city house, known as the Whitehall . . . became the official residence of his successor, Governor Nicolls. A warm friendship sprang up between the genial Englishman and the gallant old Dutchman, and many were the toothsome dinners, well salted with wit . . . of which Nicolls partook at the bowery. Stuyvesant was much interested in church affairs and in city improvements, and his venerable figure was one of the picturesque sights of the town. The long stormy day had a bright sunset. . . . Stuyvesant is one of the most picturesque figures of a strenuous and stirring time, none the less lovable and admirable because he stood for principles of government that have become discredited. He was a sterling gentleman of the old stripe, of whom there have been many that have deserved well of mankind, loyal and sound to the core, but without a particle of respect for popular liberty or for what in these latter days are known as the 'rights of man.' From such a standpoint the principles of Thomas Jefferson would have seemed fraught with ruin to the human race. This arbitrary theory of government has never flourished on the soil of the New World, and its career on Manhattan Island was one of its first and most significant failures."[60]

John Fiske, *The Dutch and Quaker Colonies in America*

● "Very soon after the conquest the people of New York perceived that a change of masters did not enhance their prosperity and happiness. They were disappointed in their hopes of a representative government; and their taxes, to support a government in which they had no voice, were increased. . . .

"At the close of 1683, Governor Andros returned to England, when the duke (who was a Roman Catholic) appointed Thomas Dongan, of the same faith, to succeed him. In the mean while, the duke had listened to the judicious advice of William Penn, and instructed Dongan to call an assembly of representatives. They met [October 17, 1683], and with the hearty concurrence of the governor, a CHARTER OF LIBERTIES was established, and the permanent foundation of a representative government was laid. The people rejoiced in the change, and were heartily engaged in the efforts to perfect a wise and liberal government, when the duke was elevated to the throne. . . As king, he refused to confirm the privileges which, as duke, he had granted . . ."[61]

Benson J. Lossing, *A Family History of the United States*

For Reflection and Reasoning

● Review: When Peter Stuyvesant first told the people of New Amsterdam that he would rule them "as a father rules his children," what did he mean? Did he plan to rule them by whatever he thought best? Did he consider what the people wanted? What kind of ruler was Peter Stuyvesant?

● The Student Text does not include the events which occurred after the surrender. For additional information, see Teacher Resource above. After Peter Stuyvesant surrendered to the English, how did he show that he loved his people as "a father"? How did the people show their love for Peter Stuyvesant in spite of his stubborn determination to have his own way?

● Review: How was the Plymouth colony governed? How was that different from the government in the New Netherland colony?

● Once the English controlled New York, the ideas of local self-government were established. What is local self-government? Review the flow of power and force as identified on *Student Activity Page 4-2.*

 **Leading Idea**

God used unique individuals and diverse colonies to produce the United States of America.

For Reflection and Reasoning

● *Student Activity Page 13-4.* Consider how God used unique individuals and the colonies of Jamestown, Plymouth, and New Netherland to produce the United States of America.

Supplemental Activities

● The student may enjoy additional reading. Suggestions:
  • *Peter Stuyvesant: Boy with Wooden Shoes,* the delightful children's biography by Mabel Cleland Widdemer, published by The Bobbs-Merrill Company, one of the *Childhood of Famous Americans* Series.
  • *The First Tulips in Holland,* by Phyllis Krasilovsky.

● The students may prepare a simple research project on the history of tulips, considering their country of origin, their development in Europe, and the effect upon the economics of Holland.

PATRIOT
First Christian Republic
Chapters 14-26
8-11 Weeks

Chapter 14
The Beginning of the Revolutionary War
4-5 Days

★ **Leading Idea**

No taxation without representation

Student Text, pages 73-74

• "The United Colonies contained a population, according to the estimate of Congress, of three millions; other estimates placed it lower. Pioneers had penetrated the forests west of the Alleghanies, and begun settlements that grew into great States; but the body of the people lived on the belt of land stretching from the Atlantic coast to the Gulf of Mexico. . . . This people—a new race, moulding their institutions under Christian influences—were fixed in the traits that characterize Americans. Without the infection of wild political or social theories, they were animated by a love of liberty and a spirit of personal independence unknown to the great body of the people of Europe, while at the same time recognizing the law which united the individual to the family and to the society in which he is appointed to live, to the municipality and the commonwealth which gave him protection, and to a great nation which met and satisfied the natural sentiment of country. The colonies had reached their development as thirteen distinct communities, each of which though claiming a common property in certain fundamental ideas, had modes of life, likes and dislikes, aims and ambitions, and an internal polity in many respects local and peculiar. They had attained the condition, in Milton's words, long wished for and spoken of, but never yet obtained, in which the people had justice in their own hands, and law executed full and finally in counties and precincts. . . .

"The people waited, in keen anxiety, to learn the effect produced in England by the fact of union, and the measures of the congress . . . As the sword suspended by a thread was about to fall, Lord North caused it to be made known to Franklin that the administration, for the sake of peace, might repeal the tax on tea and the Port Act, but 'that the Massachusetts Acts, being real amendments of their Constitution, must, for that reason, be continued, as well as to be a standing example of the power of Parliament.' This involved the subjection of the free municipalities of America—indeed, its whole internal polity—to the caprice of majorities to a legislative body three thousand miles away, in which they were not represented, and consequently the establishment of centralization in its worst form. Opposed to this assumption was the principle of local self-government. . . .

"The news of the reception of the petition to the king and of the address of both Houses of Parliament reached America when the popular party was in a state of great excitement. The numerous public meetings were demonstrations that one heart animated and one understanding governed this party. In Massachusetts, John Adams was urging in the public prints that all men were by nature equal, and that kings had but delegated authority, which the people might resume. . . ."[62]

Richard Frothingham, *The Rise of the Republic*

• Webster defined *militia* as "The body of soldiers in a state enrolled for discipline, but not engaged in actual service except in emergencies; as distinguished from regular troops whose sole occupation is war or military service. The militia of a country are the able bodied men organized into companies, regiments and brigades, with officers of all grades, and required by law to attend military exercises on certain days only, but at other times left to pursue their usual occupations."

For Reflection and Reasoning

• Review: What is civil government? What is local self government?

• The events of this chapter occurred in 1775. How many years had passed since the Pilgrims landed? How many colonies had been founded in America? How were these colonies governed? What is the relationship between local self government and liberty?

• Were the American colonists used to obeying laws? Whose laws? Why were they not willing to obey the laws of England in 1775? What are unjust laws? What made the laws unjust? What is tyranny?

• What are taxes? Why did the colonists want representation if they were going to be taxed?

• How did the colonists begin to prepare for war? Why were the soldiers called minute-men? Were these soldiers at a special base, prepared for war? Where were they? Why did the king think the Americans would not resist the British soldiers? What does it mean to resist?

• Locate Boston and Concord on a map.

• What is a goldsmith? An engraver? What important American leader was a goldsmith and engraver? Although this account identifies Paul Revere as a goldsmith, he was probably better known for his work as a silversmith.

• Why were Paul Revere and other American patriots watching the British troops? What did the British plan to do?

Cultivating Student Mastery

1. What is tyranny?

2. Why did the colonists believe that the king's taxes were a form of tyranny?

3. How did the colonists try to correct the difficulty with England?

4. How were their efforts rewarded?

Leading Idea

Paul Revere was "ready to ride and spread the alarm."

Student Text, pages 75-80

• "The Massachusetts militia, as before related, were organized, and the committee of safety were empowered to call them into the field whenever the attempt should be made to execute by force the Regulating Acts; while General Gage was instructed to disarm the inhabitants. As the news from England became more warlike, the committee of safety authorized the purchase of military stores, a portion of which were carried to Concord, a rural town about eighteen miles from Boston; and they organized express riders to summon the militia, in case the king's troops should take the field. In this preparatory work Joseph Warren was particularly active.

"The military stores deposited in Concord General Gage resolved to destroy, and for this purpose planned an expedition which he intended should be a secret one. A detachment left Boston stealthily on the evening of the 18th of April, and continued their march during the night. Warren, however, obtained intelligence of the movement in season to dispatch two expresses, by different route, into the country, with directions to call out the militia. The messengers mounted horses and spurred on from town to town on their eventful errand. 'The fate of a nation was riding that night'."[63]

Richard Frothingham, *The Rise of the Republic*

• Henry Wadsworth Longfellow's poem, *Paul Revere's Ride*, immortalized the event of the British attempt to surprise the Americans at Lexington and Concord.

For Reflection and Reasoning

• Review: Why were the colonists unhappy with England? What is tyranny? Why were British soldiers sent to America? How did the Americans prepare to defend their liberty? In what town did the British soldiers stay?

• How does representative government protect against tyranny?

• Locate Boston, Lexington, Concord, Roxbury, and Charlestown on a map.

• What was Paul Revere's responsibility on the night of April 18th? How was Paul Revere to know which way the British were marching?

• If Paul Revere had been caught by the British, he would have been punished as a traitor. What character was required for this responsibility?

• If desired, students may draw an illustration of the poem. Suggested title: God used Paul Revere to "ride and spread the alarm."

Leading Idea

"The shot heard round the world"

Student Text, pages 80-82

• " . . . when, at dawn, on the 19th of April. 1775—a day memorable in the annals of our Republic—Pitcairn, with the advanced guard, reached Lexington, a few miles from Concord, he found seventy determined men drawn up to oppose him. Pitcairn rode forward and shouted, 'Disperse! Disperse, you rebels! Down with your arms, and disperse!' They refused obedience, and he ordered his men to fire. That dreadful order was obeyed, and the FIRST BLOOD OF THE REVOLUTION flowed upon the tender grass on the Green at Lexington. Eight citizens were killed, several were wounded, and the remainder were dispersed. . . .

"Confident of full success, the British now pressed forward to Concord, and destroyed the stores. They were terribly annoyed by the minute-men on their way, who fired upon them from behind walls, trees, and buildings. Having accomplished their purpose, and killed several more patriots in a skirmish there, the royal troops hastily retreated to Lexington. The country was now thoroughly aroused, and minute-men were gathering by scores. Nothing but the timely arrival of Lord Percy with reinforcements, saved the eight hundred men from total destruction. The whole body now retreated. All the way back to Bunker's Hill, in Charlestown, the troops were terribly assailed by the patriots; and when, the following morning, they crossed over to Boston, they ascertained their loss to be, in killed and wounded, two hundred and seventy-three. The loss of the Americans in killed, wounded, and missing, was one hundred and three."[64]

Benson J. Lossing, *A Family History of the United States*

For Reflection and Reasoning

• Review: Why did the British want to attack Lexington and Concord? What key American leaders did the British hope to capture? Why? Using a map, review the location of Lexington, Concord, and Boston.

• What plan did the British have for their attack on Lexington? Did their plan succeed? Why or why not?

• What did the British think of the American militia and minute-men?

• Who were the regulars? Who were the rebels?

• What price did the Lexington minute-men pay for freedom on April 19? Why were they willing to pay such a price?

• What character was revealed by the Americans at Lexington and Concord? Note: The citizens of Lexington could stand in their houses and see the battle that day. How did this require great courage from every citizen, not just the militia?

● The stores the British were looking for were guns and gunpowder. Why did they want the stores? Why couldn't they find them?

● The Student Text does not describe where the colonists had hidden the stores. One ingenious farmer buried things in his field. When the British came looking, they couldn't find any supplies, just a farmer plowing his field. What character was required to continue working calmly in the face of the British army?

● Who had the most soldiers at Lexington? Who had the most at Concord?

● After a long exhausting day, the British were ready to return to Boston. Why were they so tired? How did the minute-men choose the best time to attack? How were the British surprised?

● Finally, the minute-men gained the victory over the British. Review the last stanzas from the poem. How did the minute-men and farmers fight "the American way"?

Cultivating Student Mastery

1. What were the plans of the British for Lexington and Concord?

2. What did the British accomplish?

3. How does this show God's Providence?

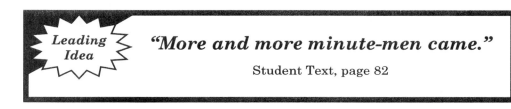

Leading Idea

"More and more minute-men came."

Student Text, page 82

● "The initial blow for freedom had now been struck. It was appalling to friend and foe. The news of this tragedy spread over the country like a blaze of lightning from a midnight cloud, and like the attendant thunder-peal, it aroused all hearts. From the hills and valleys of New England, the patriots went forth by hundreds, armed and unarmed; and before the close of the month [April, 1775], an army of twenty thousand men were forming camps and piling fortifications around Boston, from Roxbury to the river Mystic, determined to confine the fierce tiger of war, which had tasted their blood, upon that little peninsula."[65]
Benson J. Lossing, *A Family History of the United States*

● *Yankee Doodle* has been a popular song in America for over two hundred and fifty years. There have been many sets of verses written to fit the melody.

The tune of *Yankee Doodle* was well known in England, where it was used for children's games and songs. One legend says that when Oliver Cromwell rode his horse, he wore a hat with a large feather called a "macaroni." His enemies taunted him with a rhyme ending with "stuck a feather in his cap and called it macaroni."

The term "Yankee" quickly came to be a symbol of the fiercely independent Americans. The word probably originated from the Indians' mispronunciation of the word "English". "Doodle" was added by the British who were scornful of the American colonists. It may have come from "do little", and came to mean a simpleton, half-wit, or fool.

The song quickly became a favorite in the American colonies. Many variations to the words and the melody were quite popular, even before the American Revolution. The British used it to mock the untrained colonial army, and marched to it as they headed toward

Lexington and Concord in April of 1775. After the defeat of the British at Concord, the Colonial army sang it as they harried their enemy back toward Boston. Tradition says that at Cornwallis' surrender at Yorktown, in 1781, the British band played *The World Turned Upside Down.* The Americans responded with *Yankee Doodle*:

> It suits for peace, it suits for fun;
> And just as well for fighting.

For Reflection and Reasoning

● Review: Why did the colonists prepare to battle against England? How did they prepare? Who were the minute-men? Why did the British decide to attack Lexington and Concord? What happened?

● How do you think news of the British defeat was sent back to Boston? Consider: They did not have telephone, television, radio, or e-mail.

● How did the British reinforcements keep the American minute-men away from the British regulars?

● The minute men lived by this thought, "Never give up!" How did they put this into practice?

● It would seem that the British cannon should have been better than the minute-men's guns. Why? Why were the cannon difficult for the British to use?

● How many Americans died at Lexington and Concord? How many British died?

● The British expected to be successful at Lexington and Concord. The British thought they could quickly and easily defeat the Americans, whom they thought were foolish and unprepared.

● The battles of Lexington and Concord were just the beginning of a long, difficult struggle for liberty. Those who laid down their lives at Lexington and Concord inspired other American patriots to fight long and hard for liberty. Their example should inspire us today to work hard to protect liberty in our nation.

● Use *Student Activity Page 14-1* to enjoy learning the history of the song, *Yankee Doodle.* The students will enjoy singing the verses included. During the Revolutionary War, there were a variety of verses written to this song. During this study, the students may enjoy writing their own verses for Yankee Doodle.

● If desired, the students would enjoy building a diorama illustrating the battles of Lexington and Concord.

● How did the colonists show they believed that the Lord controlled the battle? What is "a day of fasting and prayer"? How did the timing of Connecticut's day of fasting and prayer reveal God's Hand?

Cultivating Student Mastery

1. The British planned to surprise the Americans. How did the Americans surprise the British instead?

Chapter 15
The Battle of Bunker Hill
2-3 Days

Leading Idea

A surprise for the British

Student Text, pages 83-88

● "Having repudiated royal authority, the people of Massachusetts were obedient to their chosen rulers, and efficient civil government was duly inaugurated. On the 19th of May [1775], the provincial Congress of Massachusetts clothed the Committee of Safety, sitting at Cambridge, with full powers to regulate the operations of the army. Artemas Ward was appointed commander-in-chief, Richard Gridley, chief engineer, and Israel Putnam, John Stark, and other veterans, who had served bravely in the French and Indian war, were appointed to important commands. The military genius developed in that old conflict, was not brought into requisition. Day by day the position of the British army became more perilous. Fortunately for its safety, large reinforcements, under those three experienced commanders, Generals Howe, Clinton, and Burgoyne, arrived on the 25th of May. It was timely: and then the whole British force in Boston amounted to about twelve thousand men, besides several well-manned vessels of war, under Admiral Graves. Gage now resolved to attack the Americans and penetrate the country.

"Preparatory to an invasion of the province, Gage issued a proclamation [June 10, 1775], declaring all Americans in arms to be rebels and traitors, and offering a free pardon to all who should return to their allegiance, except those arch-offenders, John Hancock and Samuel Adams. These he intended to seize and send to England to be hanged. The vigilant patriots, aware of Gage's hostile intentions, strengthened their intrenchments on Boston Neck, and on the evening of the 16th of June, General Ward sent Colonel Prescott with a detachment of one thousand men, to take possession of, and fortify, Bunker's Hill, in Charlestown, which commanded an important part of Boston and the surrounding water. By mistake they ascended Breed's Hill, within cannon shot of the city, and laboring with pick and spade all that night, they had cast up a strong redoubt of earth, on the summit of that eminence, before the British were aware of their presence. Gage and his officers were greatly astonished at the apparition of this military work, at the dawn of the 17th."[66]

Benson J. Lossing, *A Family History of the United States*

● "A redoubt is a small fortification generally composed of earth, and having very few features of a regular fort, except its arrangement for the use of cannons and muskets. They are often temporary structures, cast up in the progress of a siege, or a protracted battle."[67]

Benson J. Lossing, *A Family History of the United States*

● The Americans were bold in attempting to take a position of strength which would allow them to protect and defend the city of Boston. Boston held great influence throughout the colonies. Patriots such as John Hancock, Sam Adams, and others were energetically cultivating patriotic feelings.

For Reflection and Reasoning

• Review: Why were the Americans fighting the British?

• What reputation did the British generals have? How did this show that the British took the conflict in America seriously?

• In what way were the Americans much less prepared for battle than the British? In what way were they more prepared?

• Locate Bunker Hill, Breed's Hill, and Copp's Hill on the map in the Student Text. Consider: Where were the British? Where were the Americans?

• Why did the British want to occupy Bunker Hill? What advantage would this have given them? What plans did the Americans have for Bunker Hill? Why?

• When the Americans built their fort on Breed's Hill instead, it changed their threat against the British. Why was General Gage so concerned about having the Americans encamped on Breed's Hill?

• Using the map in the Student Text, review the events of the battle. Where were the troops? How did the British think the smoke from the fires in Charlestown would help them? What act of Providence overruled the British plan? How did the British burning of Charlestown affect the American soldiers?

Cultivating Student Mastery

1. What protection did the Americans build on Breed's Hill?

2. Why was it a surprise to the British?

3. How was it a threat to the British?

4. How did God's control of the weather benefit the Americans?

Leading Idea

Powder or not, we will stand.

Student Text, pages 88-90

• "The British generals were not only astonished, but alarmed, and at once perceived the necessity for driving the Americans from this commanding position, before they should plant a heavy battery there, for in that event, Boston must be evacuated before sunrise. The drums beat to arms and soon the city was in a great tumult. The imminent danger converted many Tories into professedly warm Whigs, for the days of British rule appeared to be closing. Every eminence and roof in Boston swarmed with people and at about sunrise [June 17, 1775], a heavy cannonade was opened upon the redoubt, from a battery on Copp's Hill, in Boston, and from the shipping in the harbor, but with very little effect. Hour after hour the patriots toiled on in the completion of their work, and at noon-day, their task was finished, and they laid aside their implements of labor for knapsacks and muskets. General Howe, with General Pigot, and three thousand men, crossed the Charles River at the same time, to Morton's Point, at the foot of the eastern slope of Breed's Hill, formed his troops into two columns, and marched slowly to attack the redoubt. Although the British commenced firing cannons soon after they began to ascend the hill, and the great guns of the ships, and the battery on Copp's Hill, poured an incessant storm upon the redoubt, the Americans kept perfect silence until they had approached within close musket shot. Hardly an American could be seen by the slowly approaching enemy, yet behind those rude mounds of earth, lay fifteen hundred determined men, ready to pour deadly volleys of musket-balls upon the foe, when their commanders should order them.

"It was now three o'clock in the afternoon. When the British column was within ten rods of the redoubt, Prescott shouted *Fire!* and instantly whole platoons of the assailants were prostrated by well-aimed bullets. The survivors fell back in great confusion, but were soon rallied for a second attack. They were again repulsed, with heavy loss, and while scattering in all directions, General Clinton arrived with a few followers, and joined Howe, as a volunteer. The fugitives were again rallied, and they rushed up to the redoubt in the face of a galling fire. For ten minutes the battle raged fearfully, and, in the mean while, Charlestown, at the foot of the eminence, having been fired by a carcass from Copp's Hill, sent up dense columns of

smoke, which completely enveloped the belligerents. The firing in the redoubt soon grew weaker, for the ammunition of the Americans had become exhausted. It ceased altogether, and then the British scaled the bank and compelled the Americans to retreat, while they fought fiercely with clubbed muskets. Overpowered, they fled across Charlestown Neck, gallantly covered by Putnam and a few brave men, and under that commander, they took position on Prospect Hill, and fortified it. The British took possession of Bunker's Hill, and erected a fortification there. There was absolutely no victory in the case. Completely exhausted, both parties sought rest, and hostilities ceased for a time. The Americans had lost, in killed, wounded, and prisoners, about four hundred and fifty men. The loss of the British from like causes, was almost eleven hundred. This was the first real *battle* of the Revolution, and lasted almost two hours.

"Terrible for the people of Boston and vicinity, were the events of that bright and cloudless, and truly beautiful June day. All the morning, as we have observed, and during the fierce conflict, roofs, steeples, and every high place, in and around the city, were filled with anxious spectators. Almost every family had a representative among the combatants; and in an agony of suspense, mothers, wives, sisters, and daughters, gazed upon the scene. Many a loved one perished; and there the country lost one of its most promising children, and freedom a devoted champion. Dr. Warren, who had just been appointed major-general, had crossed Charlestown Neck in the midst of flying balls from the British shipping, and reached the redoubt on Breed's Hill, at the moment when the enemy scaled its banks. He was killed by a musket ball, while retreating. Buried where he fell, near the redoubt, the tall Bunker Hill monument of today, standing on that spot, commemorates his death, as well as the patriotism of his countrymen."[68]

Benson J. Lossing, *A Family History of the United States*

For Reflection and Reasoning

● Review: What was the goal of the battle of Bunker Hill?

● What advantages did the British have in the battle against the Yankees on Breed's Hill?

● How did General Howe show good leadership for his men?

● *Student Activity Page 15-1.* What were the disadvantages for the American soldiers? How did they overcome the disadvantages?

● Why did Putnam have a difficult time bringing in new troops, called reinforcements?

● How did General Howe decide where to attack?

● Why was Dr. Joseph Warren the last American to leave the earthworks? How did Dr. Warren's death affect the Americans nearby? What American leaders were lost at Bunker Hill?

● Although the Americans lost the hill, why did they still rejoice?

Supplemental Activities

● Many memorials have been built to honor Americans who fought and died for our liberty.

Students may use books, the internet, or other resources to find pictures of the Bunker Hill monument. They may copy a picture or draw the monument for their notes, if desired.

Students may also record the answers to the following questions:
  • How does the Bunker Hill monument commemorate the patriotism of the men who fought and died there?
  • Why was the battle of Bunker Hill so important to the Americans?

Chapter 16
George Washington
Commander-in-Chief
3-4 Days

Leading Idea

> *The American troops accomplish more in one night than the British in a month.*

Student Text, pages 91-93

● " . . . the FIRST CONTINENTAL CONGRESS assembled in Carpenter's Hall, Philadelphia, on the 5th of September, 1774 . . . All but Georgia were represented. Peyton Randolph, of Virginia, was appointed President, and Charles Thomson of Pennsylvania, Secretary. The regular business of the Congress commenced on the morning of the 7th, after an impressive prayer for Divine guidance, uttered by the Rev. Jacob Duché, of Philadelphia. They remained in session until the 26th of October, during which time they matured measures for future action, which met with the general approbation of the American people. They prepared and put forth several State papers, marked by such signal ability and wisdom, as to draw from the earl of Chatham these words in the House of Lords: 'I must declare and avow, that in all my reading and study of history . . . that for solidity of reasoning, force of sagacity, and wisdom of conclusion, under such a complication of circumstances, no nation or body of men can stand in preference to the general Congress at Philadelphia.'"[69]

Benson J. Lossing, *A Family History of the United States*

● "While the whole country was excited by the rising rebellion, and on the very day [May 10] when Allen and Arnold took

Ticonderoga, the SECOND CONTINENTAL CONGRESS convened at Philadelphia. Notwithstanding New England was in a blaze of war, royal authority had virtually ceased in all the colonies, and the conflict for independence had actually begun, that august body held out to Great Britain a loyal, open hand of reconciliation. . . . Having resolved on armed resistance, they voted to raise an army of twenty thousand men; and two days before the battle of Bunker's Hill [June 15, 1775], they elected GEORGE WASHINGTON commander-in-chief of all the forces raised, or to be raised, for the defense of the colonies. That destined *Father of his Country,* was then forty-three years of age. They also adopted the incongruous mass of undisciplined troops at Boston, as a CONTINENTAL ARMY, and appointed general officers to assist Washington in its organization and future operations.

"General Washington took command of the army at Cambridge, on the 3d of July, and with the efficient aid of General Gates, who was doubtless the best disciplined soldier then in the field, order was soon brought out of great confusion, and the Americans were prepared to commence a regular siege of the British army in Boston. To the capture or expulsion of those troops, the efforts of Washington were mainly directed during the summer and autumn of 1775. Fortifications were built, a thorough organization of the army was effected, and all that industry and skill could do, with such material, in perfecting arrangements for a strong and fatal blow, was accomplished. . ."[70]

Benson J. Lossing, *A Family History of the United States*

For Reflection and Reasoning

• Review: What was the importance of the battles at Lexington, Concord, and Bunker Hill?

• What was the Continental Congress? Under whose authority did they meet?

• General George Washington was commander-in-chief of the American soldiers. What is a commander-in-chief? How did Washington carry out his duties? Who is commander-in-chief today in America? How does he carry out his duties?

• What does it mean that "the British were in a state of siege" in Boston?

• Once again, the British burned American towns. How did the Americans respond to these acts?

• How did the weather assist the Americans in their fight with the British? Who controls the weather?

• Locate Boston on a map. Note the position of the Americans and the British, and Washington's strategy to put Americans on either side of the British.

• How was Washington able to have the soldiers build forts without the British knowing what he was doing? What character does this show in Washington? What was General Howe's response when he observed the American forts? What did he plan to do? How were his plans Providentially foiled?

• At both Bunker Hill and Dorchester Heights, the Americans anticipated the plans of the British and worked to defeat them. How did Washington's efforts at Dorchester Heights give the Americans an advantage?

• Though the British troops had the best equipment and more training, what aided the Americans in their battle? Why were they fighting? If men are fighting for liberty, might they be willing to put forth more effort than if they are simply fighting to control others?

Cultivating Student Mastery

1. Students may write a brief essay, answering the following question: How did God Providentially aid in the Battle of Bunker Hill and at Dorchester Heights?

Leading Idea

God prepares men and then He causes events.

Student Text, pages 93-94

• Webster identified an *aide-de-camp* as "In *military affairs,* an officer whose duty is to receive and communicate the orders of a general officer."

• July, 1774 — "It has been kept in memory that on this occasion a young man from abroad, so small and delicate in his organization that he appeared to be much younger than perhaps he really was, took part in the debate before the crowd. They asked one another the name of the gifted stranger, who shone like a star first seen above a haze, of whose rising no one had taken note. He proved to be Alexander Hamilton, a West Indian. His mother, while he was yet a child, had left him an orphan and poor. A father's care he seems never to have known. The first written trace of his existence is in 1766, when his name occurs as witness to a legal paper executed in the Danish island of Santa Cruz. Three years later, when he had become 'a youth,' he 'contemned the groveling condition of a clerk,' fretted at the narrow bounds of his island cage, and to a friend of his own years confessed his ambition. 'I would willingly risk my life,' said he, 'though not my character, to exalt my station. I mean to prepare the way for futurity; we have seen such schemes successful when the projector is constant.' That way he prepared by integrity of conduct, diligence, and study. After an education as a merchant, during which he once at least conducted a voyage, and once had the charge of his employer's business, he found himself able to repair to New York, where he entered the college before the end of 1773. Trained from childhood to take care of himself, he possessed a manly self-reliance. His first sympathies in the contest had been on the British side against the Americans, but he soon changed his opinions; and in July, 1774, cosmopolitan New York, where he had neither father nor mother, nor sister nor brother, nor one person in whose veins ran the same blood as his own, adopted the volunteer from the tropics as its son."[71]

George Bancroft, *History of the United States of America, Volume IV*

● "Alexander Hamilton . . . joined the staff of the commander in chief in March, and thus obtained the precious opportunity of becoming familiar with the course of national affairs on the largest scale."[72]

George Bancroft, *History of the United States of America, Volume V*

For Reflection and Reasoning

● Using a map or globe, locate the island, Nevis, in the West Indies.

● What character qualities did Alexander Hamilton have at a very young age? Alexander was given much responsibility as a very young man. Do you know any boys who are put in charge of a store before they are sixteen years old? For what kinds of things would he have been responsible?

● Why was Alexander Hamilton called the "Little Lion"? How tall is your father? Hamilton was only five feet seven inches. Is that very tall for a man? His height would explain that he was called "Little." But why was he called a "Lion"?

● What was Hamilton's most important work for Washington?

● What is an aide-de-camp? Why was this such an important position? Why is it valuable for leaders to have wise advisors to assist them?

● *Student Activity Page 16-1.* List the character qualities Alexander Hamilton demonstrated at a young age. Take time to define any with which the students are not familiar:

Intelligent
Thoughtful
Loving
Responsible
Good business knowledge
Good habits of study and writing

● As a result of his character, Alexander Hamilton was given special opportunities. Answer question, *Student Activity Page 16-1.*

Cultivating Student Mastery

1. Why was Alexander Hamilton called the "Little Lion"?

2. How did God prepare Alexander Hamilton to take great responsibility later in life?

3. How did God use Hamilton's article about a storm to bring him to a new place where he could be well-educated?

Leading Idea

God prepared Alexander Hamilton for "just such a time as this".

Student Text, pages 94-96

• "The terms, WHIG and TORY, had long been used in England as titles of political parties. The former denoted the opposers of royalty; the latter indicated its supporters. These terms were introduced into America two or three years before the Revolution broke out, and became the distinctive titles of the *patriots* and *loyalists*."[73]

Benson J. Lossing, *A Family History of the United States*

For Reflection and Reasoning

• Review: What is a Tory? What events were taking place in America in 1774, when Hamilton arrived in Boston?

• Why were the Americans calling for a Congress?

• What part did Hamilton play in the Revolution?

• How did Hamilton's defense of Dr. Cooper show that he truly believed in free speech and free press?
    How did Hamilton act according to his conscience when Dr. Cooper was threatened?

• During his early years, Hamilton learned to write very well. How did he use his writing skills to help the patriot cause during the American Revolution? What is a political pamphlet?

• A person's external actions reveal his internal character. What actions of Hamilton reveal his persistence, diligence, and patience?

• *Student Activity Page 16-2.* Compare and contrast the life and character of Washington and Hamilton.

Supplemental Activities

• On January 1, 1776, the Continental Army, under General George Washington, unfurled the Union flag over the American camp at Cambridge. This was the first time the Americans had flown their own flag, representing the Union.
    Students may cut and glue construction paper strips and triangles to form a Union flag.

Blue

Red

Red

GRAND UNION FLAG
1775 - 1777

• For more advanced students, read *Warren's Address at Bunker Hill,* poem by John Pierpont.

Chapter 17
The Declaration of Independence
1-2 Days

Leading Idea

The American colonists counted the cost, and declared their independence from England.

Student Text, pages 97-98

● ". . . Thus the progress of the war brought to America independence in all but the name; she had her treasury, her army, the rudiments of a navy, incipient foreign relations, and a striving after free commerce with the world. She was self-existent, whether she would be so or not; through no other way would the king allow her to hope for rest.

"The declaration of independence was silently but steadily prepared in the convictions of all the people, just as every spire of grass is impearled by the dew, and reflects the morning sun. The many are more sagacious, more disinterested, more courageous, than the few. Language was their spontaneous creation; the science of ethics, as the word implies, is deduced from the inspirations of their conscience; law itself, as the greatest jurists have perceived, is necessarily moulded by their inward nature; the poet imbodies in words their oracles and their litanies; the philosopher draws ideal thought from the storehouse of their mind; the national heart is the great reservoir of noble resolutions and of high, enduring designs. It was the common people whose craving for the recognition of the unity of the universe and for a perfect mediator between themselves and the Infinite bore the Christian religion to its triumph over every worldly influence; it was the public faith that, in the days of the Reformation, sought abstract truth behind forms that had been abused, and outward acts that had lost their significance; and now the popular desire was once more the voice of the harbinger, crying in the wilderness. The people, whose spirit far outran conventions and congresses, had grown weary of atrophied institutions, and longed to fathom the mystery of the life of the public life. Instead of continuing a superstitious reverence for the scepter and the throne, as the symbols of order, they yearned for a nearer converse with the eternal rules of right, as the generative principles of social peace."[74]
George Bancroft, *History of the United States of America, Volume V*

For Reflection and Reasoning

● Review: Where was the first battle of the American Revolution fought? When? Why? What happened at the battles of Lexington and Concord? What happened at the battle of Bunker Hill?

● For students who have previously studied *The Mighty Works of God*, the information on the Declaration of Independence should be review.

● Why was it necessary for the American colonists to declare their independence from England?

● What God-given rights did the Declaration of Independence identify? Why is each of these so important?

● If desired, the teacher may read selective phrases from the Declaration identifying the acts of tyranny against the colonists. *Student Activity Page 17-1* is provided for supplemental use. Consider: What God-given rights did each of these acts violate?

● How did the colonists try to solve their problems with England? How did England respond?

● Upon what did the colonists depend for protection and guidance? How was Divine Providence seen in the battles which had already been fought? What cost were the colonists willing to pay for their independence?

● What promise did the colonists make in the Declaration? What did it mean to "mutually pledge"?

● *Student Activity Pages 17-2* and *3*. Record the following dates and events from the beginning of the American Revolution:

> **April 18, 1775 — Paul Revere's Ride**
> **April 19, 1775— Battles of Lexington and Concord.**
> **June 17, 1775 — Battle of Bunker Hill**
> **March 17, 1776 — British left Boston**
> **July 4, 1776 — Declaration of Independence**

Paste the pictures on timeline as indicated.

Suggested Student Notes

Record statement from Declaration of Independence included in the Student Text:

> **And for the support of this declaration, with a firm reliance on the protection of Divine Providence, we mutually pledge to each other our lives, our fortunes and our sacred honor.**

Chapter 18
The Battle of Long Island
3-4 Days

Leading Idea

Facing a strong enemy with bravery

Student Text, pages 99-102

● Webster defined *brave* as "To defy; to challenge; to encounter with courage and fortitude, or without being moved;" and *courage* as "that quality of mind which enables men to encounter danger and difficulties with firmness, or without fear or depression of spirits."

● " . . . If the American army had consisted of such veterans as Washington afterwards led at Monmouth, the disparity of numbers would still have told powerfully in favour of the British. As it was, in view of the crudeness of his material, Washington could hardly hope to do more with his army than to make it play the part of a detaining force. To keep the field in the face of overwhelming odds is one of the most arduous of military problems, and often calls for a higher order of intelligence than that which is displayed in the mere winning of battles. Upon this problem Washington was now to be employed for six months without respite, and it was not long before he gave evidence of military genius such as has seldom been surpassed in the history of modern warfare. At the outset the city of New York furnished the kernel of the problem. Without control of the water it would be well-nigh impossible to hold the city. Still there was a chance, and it was the part of a good general to take this chance, and cut out as much work as possible for the enemy. . . ."[75]

John Fiske, *The American Revolution*

For Reflection and Reasoning

● What does it mean to be brave? What was the situation for the Americans at Long Island? Why did the American troops need to show bravery, rather than just being confident of their strength?

● What did it mean for Washington to make the best use of the means that he had?

● What mistake did General Sullivan make? What price was paid for that mistake?

● What soldiers helped the British fight the Americans? Why did they participate in the war?

● What surprise did the Americans receive?

● How did Stirling show the courage of a leader when Lord Cornwallis tried to keep the Americans from escaping?

● *Student Activity Page 18-1.* Begin timeline identifying the action of the Battle of Long Island. Timeline will be completed in future lessons.

Battle of Long Island		
British	**Divine Providence**	**Americans**
July 2—General Howe landed on Staten Island with 9000 men		
Lord Howe arrived with ships of war and 20,000 men		Washington sent General Greene to Long Island to build earthworks
August 22—General Howe, with 15,000 troops, landed on Long Island		
		8,000 Americans camped in Brooklyn
Surrounded the Americans		Fought for four hours with skill and strength though surrounded
British tried to stop flight of Americans		American troops fled
	Rainstorm	
Rested in camp		Rested in camp
	August 29—Thick fog over New York Bay	
		Hidden by fog, 10,000 men stole away in boats to New York side
Woman sent servant to tell the British of the American's flight		
	Guard was German and could not understand the servant	
August 30—General Howe found the Americans were gone. Raised the British flag		
September 15—General Clinton arrived with 4,000 men		
		Americans fled without a shot
British took New York		

Leading Idea 1, Leading Idea 2, Leading Idea 3

Suggested Student Notes

Brave—To face danger with courage not with fear

Cultivating Student Mastery

1. How did the American soldiers show great bravery at the Battle of Long Island?

2. How did Stirling show great courage?

132

Leading Idea

God rules and overrules in the affairs of men.

Student Text, pages 102-104

● "Heavy as was the blow, however, General Howe's object was still but half attained. He had neither captured nor destroyed the American forces on Long Island, but had only driven them into their works. He was still confronted by 8,000 men on Brooklyn Heights, and the problem was how to dislodge them. In the evening Washington came over from New York, and made everything ready to resist a storm. To this end, on the next day, he brought over reinforcements, raising his total force within the works to 10,000 men. Under such circumstances, if the British had attempted a storm they would probably have been repulsed with great slaughter. But Howe had not forgotten Bunker Hill, and he thought it best to proceed by way of siege. As soon as Washington perceived this intention of his adversary, he saw that he must withdraw his army. He would have courted a storm, in which he was almost sure to be victorious, but he shrank from a siege, in which he was quite sure to lose his whole force. The British troops now invested him in a semicircle, and their ships might at any moment close in behind and cut off his only retreat. Accordingly, sending trusty messengers across the river, Washington collected every sloop, yacht, fishing-smack, yawl, scow, or row-boat that could be found in either water from the Battery to King's Bridge or Hell Gate; and after nightfall of the 29th, these craft were all assembled at the Brooklyn ferry, and wisely manned by the fishermen of Marblehead and Gloucester from Glover's Essex regiment, experts, every one of them, whether at oar or sail. All through the night the American troops were ferried across the broad river, as quietly as possible and in excellent order, while Washington superintended the details of the embarkation, and was himself the last man to leave the ground. At seven o'clock in the morning the whole American army had landed on the New York side, and had brought with them all their cannon, small arms, ammunition, tools, and horses, and all their larder besides, so that when the bewildered British climbed into the empty works they did not find so much as a biscuit or a glass of rum wherewith to console themselves.

"This retreat has always been regarded as one of the most brilliant incidents in Washington's career, and it would certainly be hard to find a more striking example of vigilance. Had Washington allowed himself to be cooped up on Brooklyn Heights he would have been forced to surrender . . . For this very reason it is hardly creditable to Howe that he should have let his adversary get away so easily. At daybreak, indeed, the Americans had been remarkably favoured by the sudden rise of a fog which covered the East river, but during the night the moon had shone brightly, and one can only wonder that the multitudinous plash of oars and the unavoidable murmur of ten thousand men embarking, with their heavy guns and stores, should not have attracted the attention of some wakeful sentinel, either on shore or on the fleet. A storming party of British, at the right moment, would at least have disturbed the proceedings. So rare a chance of ending the war at a blow was never again to be offered to the British commanders. . . ."[76]

John Fiske, *The American Revolution*

For Reflection and Reasoning

• Review: What is Providence?

• Why was Washington's mind "ill at ease"? How strong were the British troops? How strong were the American troops?

• What unexpected actions did Lord Howe take? How was this helpful?

• The Declaration of Independence said that the Americans had a firm reliance on the protection of Divine Providence. How did God overrule in the events on Long Island? Who controls the weather? Who sends the fog? Washington and the Americans saw the working of Divine Providence.

• When the woman sent her servant to notify the British of the flight of the Americans, how were her actions overruled?

• When the British troops realized that the Americans were gone, why did Washington have a smile on his face? What is "a calm and proud mien"?

• Why was George Washington in the last boat?

• The students may illustrate the flight of the American troops under Washington's leadership.

• Did the escape of the Americans stop General Howe? What did he do? What was his next plan?

• How did the Americans show they wanted to make peace? How did the English respond?

• Continue the timeline, *Student Activity Page 18-1*.

Cultivating Student Mastery

1. How did God control the events at the Battle of Long Island?

"Fear spread through the land and peace seemed a long way off."

Student Text, page 104

• Webster defined *fear* as "To feel a painful apprehension of some impending evil; to be afraid of . . ."

• " . . . For this once, however, out of personal regard for Lord Howe, and that nothing might be disdained which really looked toward a peaceful settlement, they would send a committee to Staten Island to confer with his lordship, who might regard this committee in whatever light he please. . . . The committee, consisting of Franklin, Rutledge, and John Adams, were hospitably entertained by Lord Howe, but their conference came to nothing, because the Americans now demanded a recognition of their independence as a condition which must precede all negotiation. There is no doubt that Lord Howe, who was a warm friend to the Americans and an energetic opponent of the king's policy, was bitterly grieved at this result. . . .

"Four days after this futile interview General Howe took possession of New York. After the loss of Brooklyn Heights,

Washington and Greene were already aware that the city could not be held. Its capture was very easily effected. Several ships-of-the-line ascended the Hudson . . . and while thus from either side these vessels swept the northern part of Manhattan with a searching fire, General Howe brought his army across from Brooklyn in boats and landed at Kipp's Bay, near the present site of East Thirty-Fourth Street. Washington came promptly down, with two New England brigades, to reinforce the men whom he had stationed at that point, and to hinder the landing of the enemy until Putnam should have time to evacuate the city. To Washington's wrath and disgust, these men were seized with panic, and suddenly turned and fled without firing a shot. . . .

"General Howe had thus got possession of the city of New York, but the conquest availed him little so long as the American army stood across the island, in the attitude of blockading him. . . ."[77]

John Fiske, *The American Revolution*

For Reflection and Reasoning

● What was a "ship-of-war"? How did such a ship create great danger for the American troops?

● Review the events of August 29 on Long Island. How were the American troops protected?

● What is fear? How much time had passed since the events on Long Island? Why should the American troops not have been afraid?

● Using the Student Text, list and discuss the reasons for the American soldiers' fear?
   - ships of war
   - ill-armed
   - worse clad
   - few tents
   - no pots or pans to cook their food

● How did their external circumstances affect the Americans' ability to fight?

● Was Washington afraid? How do you know? What might have been the reason for Washington's lack of fear?

● Complete the timeline, *Student Activity Page 18-1.*

● Review: What event took place on Christmas, 1776? See Chapter 1. The Battle of Trenton occurred after the Battle of Long Island. How was God's Hand seen in that battle?

Chapter 19
The Battle of Saratoga
5-6 Days

● "A chronology of the Battles of the War for Independence helps us understand the timing of this key event. Before the Battle of Saratoga, the main focus for both sides was on the Northern Colonies. Once the Americans were victorious at Saratoga, the North was secured to American hands and the struggle moved southward, finally culminating in the Battle of Yorktown.

"The geographical setting of the battle is the key to the British plan. They expected their superior war powers and advantages of position — being in control of Canada, the St. Lawrence River, the Great Lakes area and New York City on the Hudson River — to secure them an easy victory. They only had to make a clever plan, and co-ordinate their armies to consolidate power, and make a surprise attack. They would then establish a line of forts that reached from Canada to New York City. The Northern and Southern colonies would be forcibly divided and weakened.

"But the colonists' seeming disadvantages became their strength. Though they were unaware of the British plans, they surprised the British at Bennington and again at the battle site of Freeman's Farm. Their weaknesses were effectively turned around by the advantages of knowing their home territory, by the unity between the individual colonies and their commitment to protect their adjoining localities, and by early arrival at the battle site, at Freeman's Farm, allowing them to establish their campsite in a superior position."[78]

Penelope Paquette

● "Why was this one of the most decisive battles of history? The outcome determined the course of American history — the course of His Story of Christian liberty expressed in a form of external government.

"D.H. Montgomery in his volume, *The Leading Facts of American History*, states:

"'In the wars of over twenty centuries an eminent English writer finds only fifteen battles that have had a lasting influence on the world's history. The American victory at Saratoga, he says, was one of them. (*The Fifteen Decisive Battles of the World* by Sir Edward S. Creasy) It had two immense results:

1. It completely broke up the English plans for the war.

2. It secured for us the aid of England's old and powerful enemy, France.'"[79]

Penelope Paquette

Leading Idea

Praying for a "signal victory"

Student Text, pages 105-106

● "Military men, when considering the battle of Brandywine, have questioned the judgment of Washington in incurring the great risk incident to a disparity in numbers and discipline. The numbers engaged in the action have never been accurately ascertained. The British effective force, on the day of the battle, was probably not less than seventeen thousand men, while that of the Americans did not exceed eleven thousand, and many of these were raw militia. Washington was aware of the expectations of Congress and the whole country, and wisely considered that a defeat in battle would be less depressing upon the minds of the soldiers and the people, than permitting the enemy to march, without opposition, to the capture of Philadelphia, then the political metropolis of America. Influenced by these considerations, he resolved to fight the enemy; and had not conflicting intelligence perplexed and thwarted him in his plans, it is probable that victory would have crowned the American army. The result was disastrous, and many noble patriots slept their last sleep upon the battle-field that night."[80]

Benson J. Lossing, *Pictorial Field-Book of the Revolution*

• Webster defined *signal* as "Eminent; remarkable; memorable; distinguished from what is ordinary. . ."

• ". . . In great need, Washington prayed fervently for a 'signal stroke of Providence'.

"Others recognized the precarious position of the American cause. One Sunday in Sharon, Connecticut, Rev. Smith proclaimed that though a long night of disaster had been occurring, God would soon bring a signal victory for the American army. Before the service ended, a messenger arrived with news that British General Burgoyne had surrendered at Saratoga!"[81]

Mark A. Beliles & Stephen K. McDowell, *America's Providential History*

For Reflection and Reasoning

• Review: Who is the God of the battle? Name some battles in which God overruled men's plans.

• Why were the Americans discouraged by September, 1777?

• Contrast how well the British and American armies were prepared and equipped for battle.

• What is a "signal victory"?

• Why did the Americans need a "signal victory"? What did General Washington do? What did the pastors do? How did these actions show their trust in Divine Providence?

• Read selected verses, such as John 15:7, I John 3:22, and II Chronicles 7:14. Why did the colonists seek God's blessing on their battles?

Students may record one selected verse for notes. Cut and glue praying hands from *Student Activity Page 19-1* on *Student Notes*.

Leading Idea

Man proposes, God disposes

Student Text, pages 106-108

• ". . . In order to take possession of the whole state by one grand system of operations, it was decided that the invasion should be conducted by three distinct armies operating upon converging lines. A strong force from Canada was to take Ticonderoga, and proceed down the line of the Hudson to Albany. This force was now to be commanded by General Burgoyne, while his superior officer, General

Carleton, remained at Quebec. A second and much smaller force, under Colonel St. Leger, was to go up the St. Lawrence to Lake Ontario, land at Oswego, and, with the aid of Sir John Johnson and the Indians, reduce Fort Stanwix; after which he was to come down the Mohawk valley and unite his forces with those of Burgoyne. At the same time, Sir William Howe was to ascend the Hudson with the

138

main army, force the passes of the Highlands at Peekskill, and effect a junction with Burgoyne at Albany. The junction of the three armies was expected to complete the conquest of New York, and to insure the overthrow of American independence.

"Such was the plan of campaign prepared by the ministry. There can be no doubt that it was carefully studied, or that, if successful, it would have proved very disastrous to the Americans. . . .

"But whatever may be thought of the merits of Lord George's plan, there can be no doubt that its success was absolutely dependent upon the harmonious cooperation of all the forces involved in it. The ascent of the Hudson by Sir William Howe, with the main army, was as essential a part of the scheme as the descent of Burgoyne from the north; and as the two commanders could not easily communicate with each other, it was necessary that both should be strictly bound by their instructions. At this point, a fatal blunder was made. Burgoyne was expressly directed to follow the prescribed line down the Hudson, whatever might happen, until he should effect his junction with the main army. On the other hand, no such unconditional orders were received by Howe. He understood the plan of campaign, and knew that he was expected to ascend the river in force; but

he was left with the usual discretionary power, and we shall presently see what an imprudent use he made of it. The reasons for this inconsistency on the part of the ministry were for a long time unintelligible; but a memorandum of Lord Shelburne, lately brought to light by Lord Edmund Fitzmaurice, has solved the mystery. It seems that a dispatch, containing positive and explicit orders for Howe to ascend the Hudson, was duly drafted, and, with many other papers, awaited the minister's signature. Lord George Germain, being on his way to the country, called at his office to sign the dispatches; but when he came to the letter addressed to General Howe, he found it had not been 'fair copied.' Lord George, like the old gentleman who killed himself in defence of the great principle that crumpets are wholesome, never would be put out of his way by anything. Unwilling to lose his holiday he hurried off to the green meadows of Kent, intending to sign the letter on his return. But when he came back the matter had slipped from his mind. The document on which hung the fortunes of an army, and perhaps of a nation, got thrust unsigned into a pigeon-hole, where it was duly discovered some time after the disaster at Saratoga had become part of history."[82]

John Fiske, *The American Revolution*

For Reflection and Reasoning

● Who made the plans for the British Army? Why was this difficult for the British army?

● Why was it so important for the British to conquer and control New York? Consider the geographic location of New York.

● *Student Activity Page 19-2.* Label the locations identified in the Student Text. Using colored pencil or marker, identify the routes Burgoyne, St. Leger, and Howe were to follow. The map may be titled, "The British Plan".

● Why did the British plan not work?

● *Student Activity Pages 19-3* and *19-4,* record *Suggested Student Notes.* The *Student Activity Page* will be completed in later lessons.

Suggested Student Notes

British Army
• British Army planned to conquer and control all of New York.

Divine Providence
• Lord Germain did not sign the order for the British war plan.

Leading Idea

Though less prepared and poorly equipped, the Americans faced their enemy with boldness.

Student Text, pages 108-109

● "The American commander-in-chief continued his head quarters at Morristown until near the last of May. . . . his army had increased by recruits, to almost ten thousand men. He was prepared for action, offensive and defensive; but the movements of the British perplexed him. Burgoyne was assembling an army at St. John, on the Sorel, and vicinity, preparatory to an invasion of New York, by way of Lake Champlain, to achieve that darling object of the British ministry, the occupation of the country on the Hudson. But whether Howe was preparing to co-operate with Burgoyne, or to make another attempt to seize Philadelphia, Washington could not determine. He prepared for both events by stationing Arnold with a strong detachment on the west side of the Delaware, concentrating a large force on the Hudson, and moving the main body of his army to Middlebrook, within ten miles of the British camp at New Brunswick.

"Washington was not kept in suspense a great while. On the 12th of June [1777], Howe passed over from New York, where he made his head quarters during the winter, concentrated the main body of his army at New Brunswick, and tried to draw Washington into an engagement by a feigned movement [June 14] toward the Delaware. The chief, perceiving the meaning of this movement, and aware of his comparative strength, wisely remained in his strong position at Middlebrook until Howe suddenly retreated [June 19], sent some of his troops over to Staten Island [June 22], and appeared to be evacuating New Jersey. This movement perplexed Washington. He was fairly deceived; and ordering strong de-

tachments in pursuit, he advanced several miles in the same direction, with his whole army. Howe suddenly changed front [June 25], and attempted to gain the rear of the Americans; but, after Stirling's brigade had maintained a severe skirmish with a corps under Cornwallis [June 26], the Americans regained their camp without much loss. Five days afterward [June 30], the whole British army crossed over to Staten Island, and left New Jersey in the complete possession of the patriots.

"Washington now watched the movements of his enemy with great anxiety and the utmost vigilance. It was evident that some bold stroke was about to be attempted by the British. On the 12th of July, Burgoyne, who had been moving steadily up Lake Champlain, with a powerful army, consisting of about seven thousand British and German troops, and a large body of Canadians and Indians, took possession of Crown Point and Ticonderoga, and spread terror over the whole North. At the same time the British fleet at New York took such a position as induced the belief that it was about to pass up the Hudson and co-operate with the victorious invader. Finally, Howe left General Clinton in command at New York, and embarking on board the fleet with eighteen thousand troops [July 23], he sailed for the Delaware. When Washington comprehended this movement, he left a strong force on the Hudson, and with the main body of his troops pushed forward to Philadelphia. . . .

"The British fleet, with the army under Sir William Howe, did not go up the Delaware, as was anticipated, but ascended Chesapeake Bay, and at its head, near the village of Elkton, in Maryland, the land forces disembarked [Aug. 25], and marched toward Philadelphia. . . ."[83]

Benson J. Lossing, A History of the United States

● "During Burgoyne's approach, the Mohawk valley had become a scene of great confusion and alarm. Colonel St. Leger and his savages, joined by the Mohawk Indians, under Brant, and a body of Tories, under Johnson and Butler, had arrived from Oswego, and invested Fort Stanwix, on the 3d of August [1777]. The garrison was commanded by Colonel Gansevoort, and made a spirited defense. General Herkimer rallied the militia of his neighborhood; and while marching to the assistance of Gansevoort, he fell into an Indian ambuscade [Aug. 6] at Oriskany. His party was totally defeated, after a bloody conflict, and himself was mortally wounded. On the same day, a corps of the garrison, under Colonel Willet, made a successful sortie, and broke the power of the besiegers. Arnold, who

had been sent by Schuyler to the relief of the fort, soon afterward approached, when the besiegers fled [Aug. 22], and quiet was restored to the Mohawk valley."[84]

Benson J. Lossing, A History of the United States

● John Stark "was considered one of the ablest officers in the army; but he had lately gone home in disgust, for, like Arnold, he had been passed over by Congress in the list of promotions. Tired of sulking in his tent, no sooner did this rustic Achilles hear of the invaders' presence in New England than he forthwith sprang to arms, and in the twinkling of an eye 800 stout yeomen were marching under his orders. He refused to take instructions from any superior officer, but declared that he was acting under the sovereignty of New Hampshire alone, and would proceed upon his own responsibility in defending the common cause."[85]

John Fiske, The American Revolution

For Reflection and Reasoning

● Review: What was the British plan for New York?

● *Student Activity Page 19-2.* Label Fort Ticonderoga on the map.

● *Student Activity Pages 19-3* and *19-4.* Record *Suggested Student Notes. Student Activity Page* will be completed in later lessons.

● As the British troops began to move, how did the Americans respond? Though they did not have military training, how were they prepared? For what were they fighting? How did that make them more willing to join the battle?

● Review: What is the militia?

● Why had John Stark left the army and gone home? How did he show he still loved his country and wanted to defend it?

Suggested Student Notes

British Army
● Howe thought Burgoyne did not need help, so he moved south. He planned to join Burgoyne later.

● Colonel St. Leger was defeated.

Divine Providence
● Many Americans joined their local militia to fight the British.

Leading Idea

A signal victory

Student Text, pages 109-112

• "The disastrous events at Bennington and Fort Stanwix. . . greatly perplexed Burgoyne. To retreat, advance, or remain inactive, seemed equally perilous. With little hope of reaching Albany, where he had boasted he would eat his Christmas dinner, he crossed the Hudson and formed a fortified camp on the hills and plains of Saratoga. . . General Gates advanced to Bemis's Heights, about four miles north of Stillwater (and twenty-five from Albany), and also formed a fortified camp. Burgoyne perceived the necessity for immediate operations, and advancing toward the American camp, a severe but indecisive action ensued, on the 19th of September [1777]. Night terminated the conflict, and both parties claimed the victory. Burgoyne fell back to his camp, where he resolved to await the arrival of expected detachments from General Clinton, who was to attack the posts on the Hudson Highlands, and force his way to Albany. But after waiting a few days, and hearing nothing from Clinton, he prepared for another attempt upon the Americans, for the militia were flocking to Gates's camp, and Indian warriors of the SIX NATIONS were gathering there. His own force, on the contrary, was hourly diminishing. As his star, which arose so brightly at Ticonderoga, began to decline upon the Hudson, the Canadians and his Indian allies deserted him in great numbers. He was compelled to fight or flee. Again he advanced; and after a severe battle of several hours, on the 7th of October, and almost on the same ground occupied on the 19th of September, he was compelled to fall back to the heights of Saratoga, and leave the patri-ots in the possession of the field. Ten days afterward [October 17], finding only three days' provisions in his camp, hearing nothing of Clinton, and perceiving retreat impossible, he was compelled to surrender his whole army prisoners of war. Of necessity, the forts upon Lake Champlain now fell into the hands of the patriots."[86]

Benson J. Lossing, *A History of the United States*

• "On the 17th of October, accordingly, the articles were signed, exchanged, and put into execution. . . . At Burgoyne's earnest solicitation the American general consented that these proceedings should be styled a 'convention,' instead of a surrender . . .

"In carrying out the terms of the convention, both Gates and his soldiers showed praiseworthy delicacy. As the British marched off to a meadow by the river side and laid down their arms, the Americans remained within their lines, refusing to add to the humiliation of a gallant enemy by standing and looking on. As the disarmed soldiers then passed by the American lines, says. . . one of the captured officers, 'I did not observe the least disrespect or even a taunting look, but all was mute astonishment and pity.' Burgoyne stepped up and handed his sword to Gates, simply saying, 'The fortune of war, General Gates, has made me your prisoner.' The American general instantly returned the sword, replying, 'I shall always be ready to testify that it has not been through any fault of your excellency.' . . ."[87]

John Fiske, *The American Revolution*

For Reflection and Reasoning

• What character qualities were shown by the patriot leaders under General Gates? How was this character revealed in battle?

• In what way did Gates not show the

same character qualities as those under his command?

● How did Benedict Arnold demonstrate his bravery, even after he was ordered to stay behind?

● How was the American style of fighting different than that of the British? How had the American soldiers been prepared to fight? How did the American style of fighting give them an advantage?

● Why did Burgoyne resolve that he must surrender? Why did the British plan not work?

● Using the information given in the Teacher's Resource above, read or summarize the attitude of the American officers and soldiers at the surrender of General Burgoyne. How does this reveal Christian character?

● *Student Activity Pages 19-3* and *19-4.* Record Suggested Student Notes. *Student Activity Page* will be completed in later lessons.

● Using the key to the painting, assist the students in identifying the various individuals who participated in the Battle of Saratoga. Note that this is an artist's representation of the event. Some individuals included in the painting may not have actually been at the surrender of Burgoyne.

● Students may use toy soldiers to dramatize the events of the battles or students could act out the battles.

● It may be necessary to use two class-times for this lesson.

Suggested Student Notes

British Army
● **General Burgoyne surrendered.**

Divine Providence
● **God gave the "signal victory".**

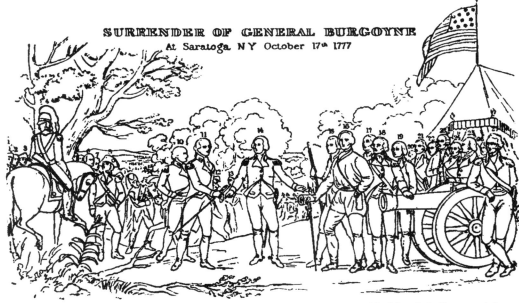

SURRENDER OF GENERAL BURGOYNE
At Saratoga N Y October 17th 1777

1. *Major Lithcow, Massachusetts*
2. *Colonel Cilly, New Hampshire*
3. *General Stark, New Hampshire*
4. *Captain Seymour, of Shelton's Horse*
5. *Major Hull, Massachusetts*
6. *Colonel Greaton, Massachusetts*
7. *Major Dearborne, New Hampshire*
8. *Colonel Scammell, New Hampshire*
9. *Colonel Lewis, quartermaster general, New Hampshire*
10. *Major General Phillips, British*
11. *Lieutenant General Burgoyne, British*
12. *General Baron Riedesel, German*
13. *Colonel Wilkinson, deputy adjutant general, American*
14. *General Gates*
15. *Colonel Prescott, Massachusetts Volunteers*
16. *Colonel Morgan, Virginia Riflemen*
17. *Brig. Gen. Rufus Putnam, Massachusetts*
18. *Lieut. Col. John Brooks, late Governor of Massachusetts*
19. *Rev. Mr. Hitchcock, chaplain, Rhode Island*
20. *Maj. Rob. Troup, aid-de-camp, New York*
21. *Major Haskell*
22. *Major Armstrong*
23. *Maj. Gen. Philip Schuyler, Albany*
24. *Brigadier General Glover, Massachusetts*
25. *Brigadier General Whipple, New Hampshire Militia*
26. *Maj. M. Clarkson, aid-de-camp, New York*
27. *Maj. Ebenezer Stevens, Massachusetts, Commanding the artillery*

Leading Idea

The effect of the signal victory

Student Text, page 112

• "... But when the capture of Burgoyne and his army. . . reached Versailles. . . Louis cast off all disguise, and informed the American commissioners... that the treaty of alliance and commerce, already negotiated, would be ratified, and 'that it was decided to acknowledge the independence of the United States.' ... War against England was to be made a common cause, and it was agreed that neither contracting party should conclude truce or peace with Great Britain without the formal consent of the other first obtained; and it was mutually covenanted not to lay down their arms until the independence of the United States should be formally or tacitly assured by the treaty or treaties that should terminate the war. Thus allied, by treaty, with the ancient and powerful French nation, the Americans felt certain of success."[88]

Benson J. Lossing, *The Pictorial Field-Book of the Revolution*

• "While these events were in progress at Saratoga, General Clinton was making hostile demonstrations upon the banks of the lower Hudson. He attempted the concerted co-operation with Burgoyne, but he was too late for success. He ascended the Hudson with a strong force, captured Forts Clinton and Montgomery, in the Highlands [October 6, 1777], and sent a marauding expedition above these mountain barriers, to devastate the country [October 13], and endeavor to draw off some of the patriot troops from Saratoga.... Informed of the surrender of Burgoyne, they hastily retreated, and Clinton and his army returned to New York. Some of Gates' troops now joined Washington at White Marsh, and Howe made several attempts to entice the chief from his encampment, but without success. Finally Washington moved from that position [December 11], and went into winter quarters at Valley Forge, where he might easier afford protection to Congress at York, and his stores at Reading. The events of that encampment at Valley Forge afford some of the gloomiest as well as some of the most brilliant scenes in the records of American patriotism."[89]

Benson J. Lossing, *A History of the United States*

For Reflection and Reasoning

• Review: What was the British plan for New York? How was their plan defeated?

• The surrender of Burgoyne was the "signal victory" for which the Americans had been seeking. How did Americans respond? What was the result of this victory in America? In England? In France?

• What does a "turning point" in a war mean?

• Did the victory at Saratoga mean that the rest of the war would be easy? The winter that followed Burgoyne's surrender was extremely difficult for the American army at Valley Forge.

• *Student Activity Pages 19-3* and *19-4.* Record *Suggested Student Notes.*

Suggested Student Notes

Divine Providence
• **The patriot spirit was revived.**

• **Some Englishmen supported American independence.**

• **France agreed to assist America.**

Chapter 20
A Winter at Valley Forge
2-3 Days

Leading Idea

> **The American soldiers paid a great price for liberty during the winter at Valley Forge.**

Student Text, pages 113-116

● "If there is a spot on the face of our broad land where patriotism should delight to pile its highest and most venerated monument, it should be in the bosom of that rugged gorge on the bank of the Schuylkill, twenty miles northwest from Philadelphia, known as Valley Forge, where the American army was encamped during the terrible winter of 1777-'78. In all the world's history, we have no record of purer devotion, holier sincerity, or more pious self-immolation, than was then and there exhibited in the camp of Washington. Many of the soldiers had marched thither from Whitemarsh, bare-footed, and left bloody footprints in the snow on their dreary journey. There in the midst of frost and snow, half-clad and scantily fed, they shivered in rude huts, while the British army was indulging in comforts and luxuries within a large city. Yet that freezing and starving army did not despair; nor did the commander-in-chief, who shared their privations and suffered injury at the hands of intriguing men, lose confidence in the patriotism of the people or his troops, or doubt the wisdom of Providence."[90]

Benson J. Lossing, *A Family History of the United States*

● As the men of the army suffered at Valley Forge, there were rumors which were critical of Washington. Washington wrote in response: "For the want of a two days' supply of provisions, an opportunity scarcely ever offered of taking an advantage of the enemy that has not been either totally obstructed or greatly impeded. Men are confined to hospitals, or in farmers' houses for want of shoes. We have this day no less than two thousand eight hundred and ninety-eight men in camp unfit for duty, because they are barefoot and otherwise naked. Our whole strength in continental troops amounts to no more than eight thousand two hundred in camp fit for duty. Since the fourth instant our numbers fit for duty from hardships and exposures have decreased nearly two thousand men. Numbers still are obliged to sit all night by fires. Gentlemen reprobate the going into winter-quarters as much as if they thought the soldiers were made of stocks or stones. I can assure those gentlemen that it is a much easier and less distressing thing to draw remonstrances in a comfortable room by a good fireside than to occupy a cold, bleak hill, and sleep under frost and snow without clothes or blankets. However, although they seem to have little feeling for the naked and distressed soldiers, I feel superabundantly for them, and from my soul I pity those miseries which it is neither in my power to relieve or prevent."

A committee was sent from congress to review the condition of the army. "Even so late as the eleventh of February, Dana, one of the committee, reported that men died for the want of straw or other bedding to raise them from the cold, damp earth. Inoculation was for a like reason delayed. Almost every species of camp-transportation was performed by men who, without a murmur, yoked themselves to little carriages of their own making, or loaded their fuel and provisions on their backs. Sometimes fuel was wanting, when for want of shoes and stockings they could not walk through the snow to cut it in the neighboring woods. Some brigades had been four days without meat. For days together the army was without bread. There was danger that the troops would perish from famine or disperse in search of food."[91]

George Bancroft, *History of the United States of America*

• Note Washington's concern for the men expressed in his letter to Governor George Clinton, February 16, 1778: "Dear Sir, It is with great reluctance, I trouble you on a subject, which does not fall within your province; but it is a subject that occasions me more distress, than I have felt, since the commencement of the war; and which loudly demands the most zealous exertions of every person of weight and authority, who is interested in the success of our affairs. I mean to present dreadful situation of the army for want of provisions, and the miserable prospects before us, with respect to futurity. It is more alarming that you will probably conceive, for, to form a just idea, it were necessary to be on the spot. For some days past, there has been little less, than a famine in camp. A part of the army has been a week, without any kind of flesh, and the rest for three or four days. Naked and starving as they are, we cannot enough admire the incomparable patience and fidelity of the soldiery, that they have not been ere this excited by their sufferings, to a general mutiny or dispersion. . . ."

This material is copyrighted by, and used with permission of, the Independence Hall Association. For further information, visit the Independence Hall Association's Home Page on the World Wide Web at http://www.ushistory.org.

• The sacrifices for liberty were commemorated on the one hundredth anniversary of the winter at Valley Forge. Henry Armitt Brown gave a moving oration. See *The Christian History of the American Revolution: Consider and Ponder*, pages 55-68.

For Reflection and Reasoning

• Why did the British want to take possession of Philadelphia? What did they not understand?

• Why did Washington choose to spend the winter at Valley Forge? What would have been easier?

• Using the Student Text, identify the hardships which the American soldiers endured during the winter at Valley Forge. Students may copy the list for notes, or, write a paragraph describing the difficult winter at Valley Forge.

Help the students to appreciate the sacrifice these men made for their liberty.

• Why couldn't the army afford to buy the needed food and clothes? How hard were the soldiers willing to work in order to get supplies? Why could the Congress not tax the states? Was there a national government, or just independent state governments? Each state had to make its own decision whether or not to provide for the army. How are American soldiers' housing, food, etc., paid today?

• Why did the soldiers not go home?

• How did Washington face the same difficulties as his men? How was he an encouragement to them? How did Washington prove himself to be a faithful leader?

• Besides the difficult life in Valley Forge, what other trouble did Washington have? What should the legislature have done for Washington?

• During the terrible winter at Valley Forge, upon whom did Washington depend for strength and provision? How do we know? Why was the Quaker, Isaac Potts, sure that the colonial army would be victorious?

• *Student Activity Page 20-1.* Label Philadelphia, Delaware River, and Valley Forge.

Leading Idea

God provided assistance in the American fight for liberty

Student Text, pages 116-118

• "There he [Washington] was saluted by a powerful ally, in the person of a stripling, less than twenty years of age. He was a wealthy French nobleman, who, several months before, while at a dinner with the Duke of Gloucester, first heard of the struggle of the Americans, their Declaration of Independence, and the preparations made to crush them. His young soul was fired with aspirations to give them his aid; and quitting the army, he hurried to Paris. Although he had just married a young and beautiful girl, and a bright career was opened for him in his own country, he left all, and hastened to America in a vessel fitted out at his own expense. He offered his services to the Continental Congress, and that body gave him the commission [July 31] of a major-general. Three days afterward [Aug. 3] he was introduced to Washington at a public dinner; and within less than forty days he was gallantly fighting [September 11], as a volunteer, for freedom in America, on the banks of the Brandywine. That young general was the Marquis de LA FAYETTE, whose name is forever linked with that of Washington and Liberty."[92]
Benson J. Lossing, *A Family History of the United States*

• "Among the foreign officers who came to America in 1777, was the Baron Steuben, who joined the Continental army at Valley Forge. He was a veteran from the armies of Frederic the Great of Prussia, and a skillful disciplinarian. He was made Inspector General of the army; and the vast advantages of his military instruction were seen on the field of Monmouth, and in subsequent conflicts."[93]
Benson J. Lossing, *A Family History of the United States*

• "The power of the British army was much weakened by indulgence, during that winter. Profligacy begat disease, crime, and insubordination. The evil effects produced upon the army led Dr. Franklin to say, 'Howe did not take Philadelphia—Philadelphia took Howe.'"[94]
Benson J. Lossing, *A Family History of the United States*

For Reflection and Reasoning

• Review: Why did Washington choose to camp at Valley Forge during the winter of 1777-1778? What difficulties did the American soldiers face during that winter? Why was Congress unable to help them?

• As God controls events, He also provides individuals to carry out His plan. How did the young Marquis de Lafayette help the American army? How had his heart been prepared to help defend liberty in America?

• Identify the background of Lafayette's life in France. How did he respond to the hard life at Valley Forge? What does that reveal about his character?

• How were the American soldiers Providentially encouraged at Valley Forge? How did they show their joy?

• When the French government learned about the character and needs of the American soldiers, who was Providentially chosen to help train the American army? Why was he chosen for this position?

• When the Baron arrived at Valley Forge and saw the conditions of the American soldiers, what did he say? Why? How did this reveal the soldiers' love and desire for liberty? How did it show the character of Washington as a leader?

• What is a bayonet? How were soldiers expected to use bayonets? How had the American soldiers used their bayonets?

• Baron Von Steuben was extremely pleased with the American soldiers. Why? How did he show his devotion and pride in the men? How did they respond?

• Why did the terrible winter at Valley Forge prove to be a benefit to the American army?

Suggested Student Notes

Identify the character of the American soldiers as seen at Valley Forge. Note their character and the military training they needed to defend their country.

Military Needs	Character of the American Soldiers
Lacked drill and discipline	Brave, patient, determined
Needed to be taught how to fight together	Splendid fighters
Ignorant in use of weapons	Quick and eager to learn

Cultivating Student Mastery

1. Describe the hardships faced during the winter at Valley Forge.

2. How can God's Providence be seen during the difficult winter?

Chapter 21
Battle of the Kegs
2-3 Days

The rebels "attack" Philadelphia

Student Text, pages 119-122

● "As soon as the British had taken possession of Philadelphia, they erected three batteries near the river, to protect the city against the American shipping. . . .

"During the occupation of the city, the enemy were annoyed by the patriots in various ways. In January [1778], some Whigs at Bordentown sent a number of kegs down the Delaware, which were filled with powder, and furnished with machinery, in such a manner that, on rubbing against any object in the stream, they would immediately explode. These torpedoes were the invention of Mr. Bushnell, of Connecticut, and will be noticed hereafter. They were intended for the destruction of the British shipping then lying in the river opposite Philadelphia. It so happened that, on the very night when these kegs were sent down, the vessels were hauled into the docks to avoid the effects of the ice then rapidly forming. They thus escaped mischief. One of these kegs exploded near the city, and spread general alarm. Not a stick or chip floated for twenty-four hours afterward but it was fired at by the British troops. This *battle of the kegs* furnished the theme for a facetious poem from the pen of Francis Hopkinson, Esq., one of the signers of the Declaration of Independence.

"Joseph Hopkinson, a son of Francis, was the author of 'Hail Columbia,' one of our most popular national songs."[95]

Benson J. Lossing, *The Pictorial Field-Book of the Revolution*

For Reflection and Reasoning

● What is a keg? Of what were they made? In colonial times, kegs were often used for storage and shipping. Many items were bought, sold, and stored in kegs, such as butter, crackers, and nails. On ships, kegs were used to carry fresh water for the sailors. Why?

● What did the British think was inside the kegs floating on the Delaware River? How did they react? How does the poem, *The Battle of the Kegs,* taunt the British about their great "bravery"?

● The poem, *The Battle of the Kegs,* may be sung to the tune of Yankee Doodle.

● Students may draw their own illustration of the Battle of the Kegs.

Chapter 22
George Rogers Clark
3-4 Days

Leading Idea → ***The struggle for the Western frontier***

Student Text, pages 123-124

• "During the years 1776 and 1777, Colonel Henry Hamilton, the British commander at Detroit, was busily engaged in preparing a general attack of Indian tribes upon the northwestern frontier. . . . While Hamilton was thus scheming and intriguing, a gallant young Virginian was preparing a most effective counter-stroke. In the late autumn of 1777, George Rogers Clark, then just twenty-five years old, was making his way back from Kentucky along the Wilderness Road, and heard with exultation the news of Burgoyne's surrender. Clark was a man of bold originality. He had been well educated by that excellent Scotch schoolmaster, Donald Robertson, among whose pupils was James Madison. In 1772, Clark was practicing the profession of a land surveyor upon the upper Ohio, and he rendered valuable service as a scout in the campaign of the Great Kanawha. For skill in woodcraft, as for indomitable perseverance and courage, he had few equals. He was a man of picturesque and stately presence, like an old Norse Viking, tall and massive, with ruddy cheeks, auburn hair, and piercing blue eyes sunk deep under thick yellow brows.

"When he heard of the 'convention' of Saratoga, Clark was meditating a stroke as momentous in the annals of the Mississippi valley as Burgoyne's overthrow in the annals of the Hudson. He had sent spies through the Illinois country, without giving them any inkling of his purpose, and from what he could gather from their reports he had made up his mind that by a bold and sudden movement the whole region could be secured and the British commander checkmated. On arriving in Virginia, he laid his scheme before Governor Patrick Henry; and Jefferson, Wythe, and Madison were also taken into his confidence. The plan met with warm approval; but as secrecy and dispatch were indispensable, it would not do to consult the legislature, and little could be done before authorizing the adventurous young man to raise a force of 350 men and collect material of war at Pittsburgh. People supposed that his object was merely to defend the Kentucky settlements. . . ."[96]

John Fiske, *The American Revolution*

For Reflection and Reasoning

• Using a map or globe, locate the Ohio River. What states border the Ohio River?

• The French had claimed the Ohio Valley, but when the British conquered Canada, they claimed the land north of the Ohio River. The American colonists had been settling in the wilderness lands of

Kentucky. Who had opened the Wilderness Road? For students who have studied *The Mighty Works of God: Self Government*, review the work of Daniel Boone. Boonesborough was settled in 1775.

● The British enlisted the Indians to fight the American colonists. What horrible actions did the Indians take against the settlers? How did the settlers respond? What character did they reveal?

● What was the attitude of the French concerning the Revolutionary War? Define backwoodsman. Why were the French afraid of the backwoodsmen?

● Patrick Henry was the Governor of Virginia when Clark proposed his plan for "defending the colonists." Why did Governor Henry want to keep the plan a secret? Was surprise important for success?

● *Student Activity Page 22-1.* Begin the chart on George Rogers Clark. Record the following under History: "Settler", "Surveyor" and under Character: "Courageous", "Good Fighter", and "Good Thinker."

● How would Clark's knowledge of the land assist him in his plan to protect the Western frontier?

● Why would each of these qualities be needed for his effort to protect the frontier?

● George Rogers Clark was the older brother of William Clark, who helped to lead the Lewis and Clark Expedition. For students who have studied *The Mights Works of God: Liberty and Justice for All*, review the contribution of the Lewis and Clark Expedition to the opening of the West.

Leading Idea

Victory without a battle

Student Text, pages 124-126

● "Clark had a hard winter's work in enlisting men, but at length in May, 1778, having collected a flotilla of boats and a few pieces of light artillery, he started from Pittsburgh with 180 picked riflemen, and rowed swiftly down the Ohio river a thousand miles to its junction with the Mississippi. The British garrison at Kaskaskia had been removed, to strengthen the posts at Detroit and Niagara, and the town was an easy prey. Hiding his boats in a creek, Clark marched across the prairie, and seized the place without resistance. The French inhabitants were not ill-disposed toward the change, especially when they heard of the new alliance between the United States and Louis XVI., and Clark showed consummate skill in playing upon their feelings. Cahokia and two other neighbouring villages were easily persuaded to submit, and the Catholic priest Gibault volunteered to carry Clark's proposals to Vincennes, on the Wabash; upon receiving the message this important post likewise submitted. As Clark had secured the friendship of the Spanish commandant at St. Louis, he felt secure from molestation for the present, and sent a party home to Virginia with the news of his bloodless conquest. The territory north of the Ohio was thus annexed to Virginia as the 'county' of Illinois, and a force of 500 men was raised for its defense."[97]

John Fiske, *The American Revolution*

For Reflection and Reasoning

• What was Clark's plan? Though the British had claimed the Ohio country, who was in control of the forts? Why? Why did Clark say, "There'll be no trouble with the French"?

• Locate the Ohio River and Kaskaskia on the map in Student Text, page 125. What difficulties did the men face as they traveled the fifty miles from the Ohio River to Kaskaskia?

• How did Clark and his soldiers gain a victory at Kaskaskia without a battle? Did the people at Kaskaskia expect the American soldiers?

• How had the King of France offered to help in the Revolution? What Frenchman had been helping the people before the King chose to help?

• *Student Activity Page 22-1.* Under character, record "Enthusiastic leader".

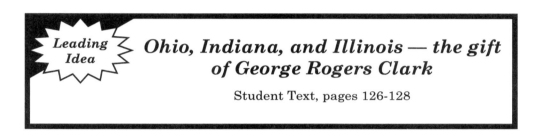

Leading Idea

Ohio, Indiana, and Illinois — the gift of George Rogers Clark

Student Text, pages 126-128

• "When these proceedings came to the ears of Colonel Hamilton at Detroit, he started out with a little army of about 500 men, regulars, Tories, and Indians, and after a march of seventy days through the primeval forest reached Vincennes, and took possession of it. He spent the winter intriguing with the Indian tribes, and threatened the Spanish governor at St. Louis with dire vengeance if he should lend aid or countenance to the nefarious proceedings of the American rebels. Meanwhile, the crafty Virginian was busily at work. Sending a few boats, with light artillery and provisions, to ascend the Ohio and Wabash, Clark started overland from Kaskaskia with 130 men; and after an arduous winter march of sixteen days across the drowned lands in what is now the state of Illinois, he appeared before Vincennes in time to pick up his boats and cannon. In the evening of February 23d the town surrendered, and the townspeople willingly assisted in the assault upon the fort. After a brisk cannonade and musket-fire for twenty hours, Hamilton surrendered at discretion, and British authority in this region was forever at an end. An expedition descending from Pittsburgh in boats had already captured Natchez and ousted the British from the lower Mississippi. Shortly after, the Cherokees and other Indians whom Hamilton had incited to take the war-path were overwhelmed by Colonel Shelby, and on the upper Ohio and Alleghany the Indian country was so thoroughly devastated by Colonel Brodhead that all along the frontier there reigned a profound peace, instead of the carnival of burning and scalping which the British commander had contemplated."[98]

John Fiske, *The American Revolution*

For Reflection and Reasoning

● Locate Kaskaskia, Vincennes, and the Wabash River on the map in the Student Text, page 125.

● Why were the American backwoodsmen able to surprise the British troops? What were the Americans willing to do that the British would not?

● How did Clark encourage his men to cross the cold, freezing rivers? How did he force them to finish the march? How did he show his care and concern for his men? How did God Providentially protect Clark and his men?

● Why can it be said that Ohio, Indiana, and Illinois are the gift of George Rogers Clark? Did he own them? How did he make them a gift? The territory later became the states of Ohio, Indiana, and Illinois.

● *Student Activity Page 22-1*. Record character: "Not afraid of difficulties", "Cared about his men". Contribution: "Captured the forts in the Ohio country." "Ohio, Indiana, Illinois became a territory of the United States."

● *Student Activity Page 22-2*. Label Ohio, Indiana, Illinois. Title: "The Gift of George Rogers Clark." Students may outline each state.

Chapter 23
A Traitor in the Camp
3-4 Days

Leading Idea

"For as he thinketh in his heart, so is he."

Student Text, pages 129-131

● "Benedict Arnold, born at Norwich, Conn., Jan. 3, 1741. As a boy he was bold, mischievous, and quarrelsome. Apprenticed to an apothecary, he ran away, enlisted as a soldier, but deserted. For four years (1763-67) he was a bookseller and druggist in New Haven, Conn., and was afterwards master and supercargo of a vessel trading to the West Indies. Immediately after the affair at Lexington, he raised a company of volunteers and marched to Cambridge. There he proposed to the Massachusetts Committee of Safety an expedition against Fort Ticonderoga, and was commissioned a colonel. Finding a small force, under Colonels Easton, Brown, and Allen, on the same errand when he reached Western Massachusetts, he joined them without command. Returning to Cambridge, he was placed at the head of an expedition for the capture of Quebec, which went by the way of the Kennebec, the Wilderness, and the Chaudiere River, and, after terrible sufferings, reached the St. Lawrence and boldly demanded the surrender of the city. He assisted Montgomery in the siege of Quebec, and was there severely wounded in the leg. Montgomery was killed, and Arnold was promoted to brigadier-general (Jan. 10, 1776) and took command of the remnant of the American troops in the vicinity of Quebec. . . . Arnold was deeply offended by the appointment, by Congress, early in 1777, of five of his juniors to the rank of major-general. He received the same appoint-

ment soon afterwards (Feb. 7, 1777), but the affront left an irritating thorn in his bosom, and he was continually in trouble with his fellow-officers, for his temper was violent and he was not upright in pecuniary transactions. General Schuyler admired him for his bravery, and was his abiding friend until his treason. He successfully went to the relief of Fort Schuyler on the upper Mohawk (August, 1777), with eight hundred volunteers; and in September and October following he was chiefly instrumental in the defeat of Burgoyne, in spite of General Gates. There he was again severely wounded in the same leg, and was disabled several months. When the British evacuated Philadelphia (June, 1778) Arnold was appointed commander at Philadelphia, where he married the beautiful young daughter of a leading Tory (Edward Shippen), lived extravagantly, became involved in debt, was accused of dishonest official conduct, plotted treason against his country, and, when his scheme had failed, fled to the British lines and obtained his promised reward. . . ."[99]
Benson J. Lossing, *Harpers' Popular Cyclopædia of United States History*

● Webster defined a *traitor* as "One who violates his allegiance and betrays his country; one guilty of treason . . . Or one who aids an enemy in conquering his country." He defined treason as "the highest crime of a civil nature of which a man can be guilty. . . . It is the offense of

Copyright © Ruth Smith

155

attempting to overthrow the government of the state to which the offender owes allegiance, or of betraying the state into the hands of a foreign power."

● Arnold was charged with misuse of public property and money. The charges were investigated and Arnold was acquitted of most of the charges. The matter was referred to the joint committee of Congress and the Assembly and Council of Pennsylvania, who referred the matter to a court-martial. The court martial ac-

quitted Arnold of all serious charges, but directed "that he should receive a public reprimand from the commander-in-chief for his imprudence in the use of wagons, and for hurriedly giving a pass in which all due forms were not attended to. The decision of the court-martial was promptly confirmed by Congress, and Washington had no alternative but to issue the reprimand, which he couched in words as delicate and gracious as possible."[100] However, the damage was already done in Arnold's heart.

For Reflection and Reasoning

● From the beginning of the war, how did Benedict Arnold help the Americans fight for Independence? How was he a good leader? How did he show great courage?

● Why did Arnold become angry toward his country?

● What is a Tory? The Tories remained loyal to the British during the Revolutionary War and hoped to remain under British rule. How was Benedict Arnold's marriage a compromise?

● What charges were made against Arnold? Was he guilty? Why did his hatred toward America increase?

● What is a traitor? Why is loyalty important in leadership?

● Review Proverbs 23:7 and *Student Activity Page 3-1*. What was the attitude in Arnold's heart when he led the American

soldiers to victory? What was in his heart when he decided to become a traitor? *Student Activity Page 23-1.*

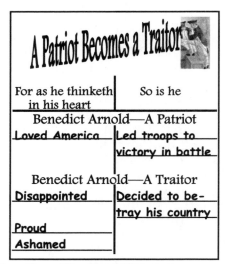

Cultivating Student Mastery

1. What is a traitor? How does a person first become a traitor?

2. What was a Tory?

Leading Idea

Benedict Arnold devised wicked plans.

Student Text, pages 131-132

● "A tribunal before which he [Arnold] was tried convicted him, but sentenced him to a reprimand only by the com-

mander-in-chief. Washington performed the duty with great delicacy, but the disgrace aroused in the bosom of Arnold a fierce spirit of revenge. He resolved to betray his country, and, making treasonable overtures to Sir Henry Clinton, kept up a correspondence on the subject for a long time with Major John André, the adjutant-general of the British army. This correspondence was carried on mutually under assumed names, and on the part of Arnold in a disguised hand. Feigning great patriotism and a desire to serve his country better, he asked for and, through the recommendation of General Schuyler and others, obtained the command of the important post of West Point. . . He arranged with Major André to surrender that post into the hands of a British force which Sir Henry might send up the Hudson. For this service he was to receive the commission of a brigadier in the British army and nearly $50,000 in gold. He made his headquarters at the house of Beverly Robinson, a Tory, opposite West Point, and the time chosen for the consummation of the treason was when Washington should be absent at a conference with Rochambeau at Hartford. Arnold and André had negotiated in writing; the former wished a personal interview, and arrangements were made for it. André went up the Hudson in the British sloop-of-war *Vulture* to Teller's (now Croton) Point, from which he was taken in the night in a small boat to a secluded spot near Haverstraw, on the west side of the river, where, in bushes, he met Arnold for the first time. Before they parted (Sept. 22, 1780) the whole matter was arranged: Clinton was to sail up the river with a strong force, and, after a show of resistance, Arnold was to surrender West Point and its dependencies into his hands. But all did not work well."[101]

Benson J. Lossing, *Harpers' Popular Cyclopædia of United States History*

For Reflection and Reasoning

• Review: What is a traitor? Why had Arnold changed from loving America to wanting to betray America?

• Using a map of New York, locate the Hudson River and West Point. Why was West Point important for the Americans?

• *Student Activity Page 23-2.* Reason from the Student Text to identify Arnold's plan: "Arnold planned to get command of West Point and then give it up to the British."

Reason from the Student Text to identify the steps which were taken by Arnold and André to complete Arnold's plan.

1. Wrote to Sir Henry Clinton
2. Asked for command of West Point
3. Wrote letters to André
4. Set a meeting with André to give maps and papers to the British
5. Chose September 25, 1780 to surrender the fort

• Read Psalm 37:12-13 and/or Proverbs 6:16-18. Reasoning from the verses, do you think God will bless Arnold's plan? Why or why not?

Leading Idea

Man proposes, God disposes

Student Text, pages 132-136

• "The *Vulture* was driven from her anchorage by some Americans with a cannon on Teller's Point, and when André, with Arnold, at Joshua H. Smith's house, above Haverstraw, looked for her in the early morning she had disappeared from sight. He had expected to return to the *Vulture* after the conference was over; now he was compelled to cross the river at King's Ferry, and return to New York by land. He left his uniform, and, disguised in citizen's dress, he crossed the river towards evening with a single attendant, passed through the Amercan works at Verplanck's Point without suspicion, spent the night not far from the Croton River, and the next morning journeyed over the Neutral Ground on horseback, with a full expectation of entering New York before night. Arnold had furnished him with papers revealing the condition of the highland stronghold."[102]

Benson J. Lossing, *Harpers' Popular Cyclopædia of United States History*

• "On the morning when André crossed Pine's Bridge, a little band of seven volunteers went out near Tarrytown to prevent cattle being driven to New York, and to arrest any suspicious characters who might travel that way. . . . The circumstances of the capture are minutely narrated in the testimony of Paulding and Williams, given at the trial of Smith, eleven days afterward. . . . 'Myself, Isaac Van Wart, and David Williams were lying by the side of the road about half a mile above Tarrytown, and about fifteen miles above Kingsbridge, on Saturday morning, between nine and ten o'clock, the 23d of September. We had lain there about an hour and a half, as near as I can recollect, and saw several persons we were acquainted with, whom we let pass. Presently, one of the young men who were with me said, "There comes a gentleman-like looking man, who appears to be well dressed, and has boots on, and whom you had better step out and stop, if you don't know him." On that I got up, and presented my firelock at the breast of the person, and told him to stand, and then I asked him which way he was going. "Gentlemen," said he, "I hope you belong to our party." I asked him what party. He said, "The Lower Party." Upon that I told him I did. Then he said, "I am a British officer, out in the country on particular business, and I

hope you will not detain me a minute," and, to show that he was a British officer, he pulled out his watch. Upon which I told him to dismount. He then said, "My God! I must do any thing to get along," and seemed to make a kind of laugh of it, and pulled out General Arnold's pass, which was to John Anderson, to pass all guards to White Plains and below. Upon that he dismounted. Said he, "Gentlemen, you had best let me go, or you will bring yourselves into trouble, for your stopping me will detain the general's business;" and said he was going to Dobbs's Ferry to meet a person there and get intelligence for General Arnold. . .'

"When further questioned, Paulding replied, that he asked the person his name, who told him it was John Anderson; and that, when Anderson produced General Arnold's pass, he should have let him go, if he had not before called himself a British officer. . . .

"'We took him into the bushes,' said Williams, 'and ordered him to pull off his clothes, which he did; but, on searching him narrowly, we could not find any sort of writings. We told him to pull off his boots, which he seemed to be indifferent about; but we got one boot off, and searched in that boot, and could find nothing. But we found there were some papers in the bottom of his stocking next to his foot; on which we made him pull his stocking off, and found three papers wrapped up. Mr. Paulding looked at the contents, and said he was a spy. We then made him pull off his other boot, and there we found three more papers at the bottom of his foot within his stocking."[103]

Benson J. Lossing, *Pictorial Field Book of the Revolution*

• ". . . The 24th was the day fixed upon for the ascent of the river by the British, and the surrender of West Point into the hands of the enemy. Yet, with all this guilt upon his soul, Arnold was composed, and the day on which his treason was to be consummated, no change was observed in his usual deportment.

"Washington returned from Hartford on the 24th. . . anxious to reach Arnold's quarters by breakfast time, and they had eighteen miles to ride. . . . When opposite West Point, the commander-in-chief turned his horse down a lane toward the river. La Fayette, perceiving it, said, 'General, you are going in a wrong direction; you know Mrs. Arnold is waiting breakfast for us, and that road will take us out of the way.' Washington answered, good-naturedly, 'Ah, I know you young men are all in love with Mrs. Arnold, and wish to get where she is as soon as possible. You may go and take your breakfast with her, and tell her not to wait for me, for I must ride down and examine the redoubts on this side of the river, and will be there in a short time.' The officers, however, did not leave him, except two aids-de-camp, who rode on, at the general's request to make known the cause of the delay.

"Breakfast was waiting when the officers arrived, and as soon as it was ascertained that the commander-in-chief and the other gentlemen would not be there, Arnold, his family, and the aids-de-camp sat down to breakfast. Arnold appeared somewhat moody. The enemy had not appeared according to arrangements, and Washington had returned at least two days sooner than he anticipated. While they were at table, Lieutenant Allen came with a letter for Arnold. The general broke the seal hastily, for he knew by the superscription that it was from Colonel Jameson, stationed at one of the outposts below. The letter was, indeed, from that officer; but, instead of conveying the expected intelligence that the enemy were moving up the river, it informed him that *Major André, of the British army, was a prisoner in his custody!* Arnold's presence of mind did not forsake him, and, although agitated, his emotion was not sufficiently manifest to excite the suspicion of those around him. He informed the aids-de-camp that his immediate attendance was required at West Point, and desired them to say to General Washington, when he arrived, that he was unexpectedly called over the river, and would soon return. He ordered a horse to be made ready, and then leaving the table, he went up to Mrs. Arnold's chamber, and sent for her. There was no

time to be lost, for another messenger might speedily arrive with evidence of his treason. In brief and hurried words he told her that they must instantly part, perhaps forever, for his life depended on reaching the enemy's lines without detection. Horror-stricken, the poor young creature, but one year a mother and not two a bride, swooned and sunk senseless upon the floor. Arnold dared not call for assistance, but kissing. . . his boy. . . he rushed from the room, mounted a horse belonging to one of the aids of Washington, and hastened toward the river. . . along a by-way down a steep hill, which is yet called *Arnold's Path*. At the dock he entered his barge, and directed the six oarsmen to push out into the middle of the stream, and pull for Teller's Point. . . .

"Washington arrived at Robinson's house shortly after Arnold had left. Informed that he had gone to West Point, the commander-in-chief took a hasty breakfast, and concluded not to wait, but go directly over and meet Arnold there. . . . While crossing the river in a barge, Washington expressed his expectation that they would be greeted with a salute, as General Arnold was at the Point; but, to his surprise, all was silent when they approached the landing-place. Colonel Lamb, the commanding officer, who came strolling down a winding path, was much confused when he saw the barge touch the shore. He apologized to Washington for the apparent neglect of courtesy, alleging his entire ignorance of his intended visit. The general was surprised, and said, 'Sir, is not General Arnold here?' 'No, sir,' replied Colonel Lamb, 'he has not been here these two days, nor have I heard from him within that time.' This awakened the suspicions of Washington. He proceeded, however, to inspect the several works at West Point, and at about noon returned to the Beverly Dock, from whence he had departed.

"While ascending from the river, Hamilton was seen approaching with hurried step and anxious countenance. He conversed with Washington in a low tone, and returned with him into the house, where he laid several papers, the damning evidence of Arnold's guilt, before him. These consisted of the documents . . . which Arnold had placed in André's hands. They were accompanied by a letter from Colonel Jameson, and one from André himself. . . .

"As soon as the contents of the papers were made known, Washington dispatched Hamilton on horseback to Verplanck's Point, that preparations might be made there to stop the traitor. But Arnold had got nearly six hours' the start of him . . . When Hamilton arrived at the Point, a flag of truce was approaching from the Vulture to that post. The bearer brought a letter from Arnold to Washing-ton, which Hamilton forwarded to the commander-in-chief, and then wrote to General Greene at Tappan, advising him to take precautionary measures to prevent any movement of the enemy in carrying out the traitor's projects. The failure of the plot was not known to Sir Henry Clinton until the arrival of the Vulture at New York the next morning, and then he had no disposition to venture an attack upon the Americans in the Highlands, now thoroughly awake to the danger that had threatened."[104]

Benson J. Lossing, *Pictorial Field Book of the Revolution*

For Reflection and Reasoning

• Review: Who controls battles? How did God control in each of the following battles: Long Island, Trenton, Vincennes?

• What did Arnold plan? How did God overrule and control the events Arnold had planned?

• *Student Activity Page 23-3.* Reasoning

from the Student Text, identify how God overruled the plans of Arnold.

• What price did André pay for his actions as a spy? What price did Arnold pay for his actions as a traitor? Why was Arnold's punishment worse than that of André? How was Arnold's punishment just?

Cultivating Student Mastery

Choose a topic for a brief essay:

1. God's Providence in the defeat of Benedict Arnold.

2. How was Arnold's punishment just?

3. Benedict Arnold — An example of Proverbs 6:16-19.

God Controls the Battle

ARNOLD'S PLAN	GOD'S PLAN
André planned to return to New York on the Vulture.	The Vulture was fired upon and moved away. André had to travel by land.
André believed the soldiers were British and declared himself an English officer.	The American soldiers found the papers from Arnold. André was taken prisoner.
Washington was to return to West Point on September 26.	Washington returned early, before Arnold could carry out his plan.

Chapter 24
The Swamp Fox
2-3 Days

 **Leading Idea**

Overcoming great difficulties with imagination and effort

Student Text, pages 137-138

• "Of all the picturesque characters of our Revolutionary period, there is perhaps no one. . . so closely associated with romantic adventure as Francis Marion. . . . He was now forty-seven years old, a man of few words and modest demeanor, small in stature and slight in frame, delicately organized, but endowed with wonderful nervous energy and sleepless intelligence. . . . The brightness of his fame was never sullied by an act of cruelty. . . . To distress the enemy in legitimate warfare was, on the other hand, a business in which few partisan commanders have excelled him. For swiftness and secrecy he was unequalled, and the boldness of his exploits seemed almost incredible, when compared with the meagerness of his resources. His force sometimes consisted of less than twenty men, and seldom exceeded seventy. To arm them, he was obliged to take the saws from sawmills and have them wrought into rude swords at the country forge, while pewter mugs and spoons were cast into bullets. With such equipment he would attack and overwhelm parties of more than two hundred Tories; or he would even swoop upon a column of British regulars on their march, throw them into disorder, set free their prisoners, slay and disarm a score or two, and plunge out of sight in the darkling forest as swiftly and mysteriously as he had come."[105]
John Fiske, *The American Revolution*

• Webster defined a *fox* as "A sly, cunning fellow."

For Reflection and Reasoning

• When the British were not gaining victory in the war, what new plan did they devise?

• *Student Activity Page 24-1.* Francis Marion brought together just a few men to do a great job. Using the Student Text, list what Marion's soldiers did not have. Explain the terms which the students do not understand.

List what Marion did have? What is wit? What is devotion? Why were these qualities so important for Marion's men?

• How did Marion and his men use what they had to make up for what they did not have? The students may write a paragraph or simply list how they overcame their difficulties. Possible answers:

· **They wore whatever they could get.**

· **The men carried anything that looked like a gun.**

The Swamp Fox	
Did Not Have	Did Have
Money	Horses that could
Uniforms	go like the wind
Guns	Keen wit
Swords	Muscles like steel
Bullets	Devotion to their
Food	country
Pay	
Blankets	

How did Marion and his men use what they did have to overcome what they did not have?

- Saws were made into weapons.
- Melted pewter dishes to make bullets.
- They ate what they could get.

● Why was Francis Marion called "The Swamp Fox"? How did his actions remind the enemy of a fox? Did he fight battles like other soldiers?

● Why would it have been easy for Francis Marion and his men not to fight? Why were they willing to fight the British?

"Every man will stand by you till death."

Student Test, pages 138-140

● Webster has defined *bold* as "Daring; courageous; brave; fearless."

For Reflection and Reasoning

● What does it mean to be bold? How were Marion and his men bold? How did their boldness make up for their lack of numbers?

● How did Marion use his imagination to win battles in the war?

● Review: What is a Tory?

● What was Marion's attitude toward the British? What was his attitude toward the Tories?

● How did the reputation of the "Swamp Fox" and his men help the bold soldier when he faced the whole Tory force? Why is a reputation so important?

● How were the men with Marion always ready? Why was it important to be "always ready"?

● Review: Who were the minute men? How were they "always ready"?

● How did Marion's men show they were as committed to the cause of liberty as their leader?

● When they faced the safe fort of the British, how did they conquer it?

● Why did Marion and his men make these wild raids? Was it simply for adventure? How were they a "torment" to their enemy? Why did they think this would encourage the patriots? Who were the patriots?

● Why did Marion's men promise, "Every man will stand by you till death"? How had they already shown their willingness to follow Marion anywhere, or to do anything he commanded? How had Marion proven himself a good leader?

● Older students would enjoy reading William Cullen Bryant's poem, *Student Activity Page 24-2.*

Suggested Student Notes

Marion and his men fought for—
    Patriotism
    Pure love of country
    Devotion to freedom

Cultivating Student Mastery

1. How did the imagination of Marion's men help them overcome difficulties?

2. How did Francis Marion fight like a fox?

3. Why did Marion and his men make their wild raids?

4. How did the Swamp Fox and his men help the patriot cause?

Chapter 25
The Close of the War
4-5 Days

 *Leading Idea*

"Man proposes, God disposes"

Student Text, pages 141-144

● "Cornwallis, confident that he could not maintain his position, determined to make a desperate effort at flight. His plan was to leave the sick and his baggage behind; cross over to Gloucester, and, with his detachment there, cut up or disperse the troops of DeChoisé, Weeden, and Lauzun; mount his infantry on horses taken from the duke's legion, and others that might be seized in the neighborhood; by rapid marches gain the forks of the Rappahannock and Potomac, and, forcing his way through Maryland, Pennsylvania, and New Jersey, form a junction with the army in New York. This was a most hazardous undertaking, but his only alternative was flight or capture. Boats were accordingly prepared, and at ten o'clock on the evening of the sixteenth a portion of his troops were conveyed across to Gloucester. So secretly was the whole movement performed, that the patriots did not perceive it; and had not a power mightier than man's interposed an obstacle, Cornwallis's desperate plan might have been successfully accomplished. The first body of troops had scarcely reached Gloucester Point, when a storm of wind and rain, almost as sudden and fierce as a summer tornado, made the passage of the river too hazardous to be again attempted. The storm continued with unabated violence until morning, and Cornwallis was obliged to abandon his design. The troops were brought back without much loss, and now

the last ray of hope began to fade from the vision of the earl.

"At daybreak, on the morning of the seventeenth, several new batteries in the second parallel were opened, and a more terrible storm of shells and round shot were poured upon the town than had yet been experienced by the enemy. Governor Nelson, who was at the head of the Virginia militia, commanded the first battery that opened upon the British works that morning. His fine stone mansion, the most commodious in the place, was a prominent object within the British lines. He knew that Cornwallis and his staff occupied it, and was probably in it when he began the cannonade. Regardless of the personal loss that must ensue, he pointed one of his heaviest guns directly toward his house, and ordered the gunner, and also a bombardier, to play upon it with the greatest vigor. The desired effect was accomplished. Upon the heights of Saratoga, Burgoyne found no place secure from the cannon-balls of the besiegers; in Yorktown there was like insecurity; and before ten o'clock in the morning, Cornwallis beat a parley, and proposed a cessation of hostilities. The house of Governor Nelson, I have already mentioned, still bears many scars received during the bombardment; and in the yard attached to the dwelling, I saw a huge unexploded bomb-shell which was cast there by order of the patriot owner."[106]
Benson J. Lossing, *Pictorial Field-book of the Revolution*

163

For Reflection and Reasoning

• Using a map of Virginia, locate Yorktown.

• How did the Americans gain an advantage over the British? Did the British expect Washington to arrive in Yorktown? How did the French help the Americans?

• Review: Who controls battles? How did God use the weather to guide the events at Bunker Hill, the siege of Boston, the Battle of Long Island, the Battle of Trenton?

• Cornwallis thought he still had a way of escape. What was his plan? How did God control the battle? Who controls the weather? Many historians describe this as an unusual and extremely violent storm.

• How did Governor Nelson show that liberty was more important than his own property?

• When Cornwallis surrendered, why did Washington not allow the soldiers to cheer? What does that reveal about George Washington's character and respect for the British?

• How was the news announced in Philadelphia? When the news of Cornwallis's surrender spread throughout the nation, how did the people celebrate?

Cultivating Student Mastery

1. How was God's Divine Providence shown in the events at Yorktown?

Leading Idea

"America proved her right to be the land of the free and the home of the brave."

For Reflection and Reasoning

• *Student Activity Page 25-1, 25-2,* and *25-3.* Use charts to review the events of the Revolutionary War, identifying the character, evidence of Divine Providence, and the historic importance of each event. This review will take a minimum of three days.

Note: See Chapter 1 for the Battle of Trenton.

"America proved her right to be the land of the free and the home of the brave." Part I				
Battle or Military Event	Individuals used by God	Character revealed	Divine Providence seen in the event	Historic Importance
British attacked Lexington & Concord, Massachusetts, April 19, 1775	Paul Revere Minute Men	<u>Ready</u> <u>Brave</u>	<u>Americans warned</u>	<u>American supplies &</u> <u>leaders protected</u>
British attacked Bunker Hill, near Boston and burned Charlestown June 17, 1775	American Soldiers	<u>Courage</u> <u>Determination</u>	<u>Americans ready</u> <u>A breeze revealed</u> <u>British troops</u>	<u>Americans driven back</u> <u>but encouraged</u>
Americans held the British under siege in Boston Spring, 1776	General Washington American Soldiers		<u>Fierce storm and</u> <u>ice stopped British</u> <u>attack</u>	<u>British fled Boston</u>
Declaration of Independence July 4, 1776				<u>United States declared</u> <u>free and Americans</u> <u>ready to defend liberty</u>

"America proved her right to be the land of the free and the home of the brave." Part II				
Battle or Military Event	Individuals used by God	Character revealed	Divine Providence seen in the event	Historic Importance
Battle of Long Island, New York August, 1776			<u>Great fog hid</u> <u>Americans</u>	British took over New York.
Battle of Tren- ton, New Jersey December, 1776	General Washington	<u>Brave</u> <u>Wise</u>	<u>Ice, snow, and</u> <u>sleet</u>	<u>American soldiers escaped</u> <u>across the river and held the</u> <u>town</u>
Battle of Saratoga September- October, 1777			British war plan never signed	<u>Turning point of war</u>
Winter at Valley Forge, Pennsylvania 1777-1778	American soldiers General Washington	<u>Brave</u> <u>Endured hardships</u> <u>Determined</u> <u>Trusted God</u>		The army was stronger and better prepared after the winter
	Lafayette	Paid his own expenses Never complained		<u>Encouraged and helped the</u> <u>Americans</u>
	Baron von Steuben	Admired and loved American soldiers		<u>Trained American soldiers</u>

| | | | "America proved her right to be the land of the free and the home of the brave." Part III | | |

Battle or Military Event	Individuals used by God	Character revealed	Divine Providence seen in the event	Historic Importance
The contest for liberty in the wilderness February, 1779	George Rogers Clark American soldiers	<u>Good fighter</u> <u>Good thinker</u> <u>Enthusiastic</u> <u>Brave</u>		<u>Western lands protected</u>
A traitor's attempt to betray the country to the British, September-October, 1780	Benedict Arnold	<u>Brave</u> <u>Turned against</u> <u>country</u>	<u>Washington arrived early</u> <u>Arnold's plot discovered</u>	<u>West Point preserved</u>
British turned to fighting in the South	Francis Marion "The Swamp Fox" Marion's men	<u>Clever</u> <u>Brave</u> <u>Loved country</u> <u>and freedom</u>		<u>Made enemy miserable and</u> <u>encouraged patriots</u>
Battle of Yorktown, Virginia October, 1781	General Washington		<u>Fierce storm</u>	<u>Cornwallis surrendered and</u> <u>the Americans won the</u> <u>War for Independence</u>

Supplemental Activities

● This volume includes selected individuals and key events of the Revolutionary War. To expand the study, additional individuals and events may be researched, including Betsy Ross and the flag, Ethan Allen, John Paul Jones, Nathan Hale, Patrick Henry, etc.

Chapter 26
Uniting the States
3-4 Days

Leading Idea

Thirteen independent States

Student Text, pages 145-147

• "The American Revolution would have been in vain if it had not resulted in true union and an adequate general — or federal — government of the thirteen newly free and sovereign states of America. Without a strong union and a well-structured over-all government, the independent states would have dissolved and disintegrated, either through gradual annihilation of one another or from attacks by preying and meddling foreign forces.

"Under the Articles of Confederation of 1782-1789, there were no provisions for the common defense nor were there enforceable laws for the common good with which to promote domestic tranquility and secure the blessings of liberty for which Americans had just paid dearly. It was a critical time when jealousy and self-interest of the states hindered voluntary union and effective cooperation for the good of the whole.

"But Providence worked by degrees to bring about timely issues that prompted a Constitutional Convention and a miraculous union bound by an American Christian Constitution—one government for a nation of diverse and independent states...."[107]
    Katherine Dang, *A Guide to American Christian Education for the Home and School*

• Webster defined *critical* as "Decisive; noting a time or state on which the issue of things depends; important, as regards the consequences; as a *critical* time or moment."

• Webster defined *constitution* as "The established form of government in a state, kingdom or country. . ."

• Webster also defined *union* as "The act of joining two or more things into one. . ."

For Reflection and Reasoning

• Review: What is civil government? What are the levels of civil government in America today?

• Review: What was the Declaration of Independence? Why was it so important in the history of the United States?

• When the thirteen states declared their independence from England, how were they governed? Since each state was independent and self governing without a national government, what difficulties arose during the Revolution? At Valley Forge, why did Washington's troops not have the supplies they needed? Why couldn't Congress force the states to pay?

• What were the Articles of Confederation?

Why didn't the Articles of Confederation work well? What was Hamilton's opinion concerning the Articles of Confederation? What did Hamilton do to try to improve the government?

• When the War ended, the soldiers went home, but many problems arose. How would trade be handled with other countries? Would agreements need to be made with each of the thirteen States, as separate countries? Would each state have its own money? Many difficult questions faced the leaders and people in each state.

Soon the people realized that something must change. The ten years following the American Revolution are called the "Critical Period" of American history. When is something critical?

• What is a representative? Why was it important that the Constitution was written by the *representatives* of the people?

• *Student Activity Page 26-1.* When the states faced the critical period in their history, they needed God's Hand to guide and direct the union of the nation. The events of the Revolution and the forming of the new nation inspired many new songs. The students may enjoy singing "God Save the Thirteen States," to the tune of "My Country 'Tis of Thee."

Cultivating Student Mastery

1. Before Americans could have strong self government in the nation, what did they need to have in their states, cities, homes, and individual lives? Why?

2. For what reason did wise men such as Washington, Madison, and Hamilton believe that there should be a convention?

3. Read the following verses: Joshua 24:15; Judges 6:1; Proverbs 4:23. Identify whether each verse describes the government of the individual, the family, or a nation. Does it show self government or a lack of self government?

Leading Idea

Uniting the states

Student Text, pages 147-148

For Reflection and Reasoning

• At the Convention in Philadelphia, a Constitution was written. The Constitution made all thirteen states part of one nation. Each state was still self governed, but there was to be a union of all thirteen states. What is a union?

• When a Convention finally met, Hamilton was one of the delegates from New York. What does it mean to be a delegate? How did Hamilton show his willingness to stand alone according to his own conscience?

• Why did Washington state that the Constitution had been "unanimously signed by eleven states and Colonel Hamilton from New York"? At that time, did the State of New York really approve the Constitution? Or, was it simply Alexander Hamilton's approval?

• What did it mean for the states to ratify the Constitution? How did the people approve the Constitution written by their representatives?

• Alexander Hamilton and James Madison approved of the ideas decided upon by the Convention. How were they used to convince the people to ratify the Constitution?

• What made the Constitution unique from the government of any other nation?

• Have you ever seen a stone wall or fence? What holds the stones together? Is there mortar or cement between each of the stones? Sometimes people illustrate the union of the United States as a stone wall. Each state is a separate, independent, self governing state. There is one national government that holds the states together. The students will be studying more of the Constitution in a later year.

• *Student Activity Page 26-2.* The students may label each of the "stones" with the names of the thirteen original states and color between the stones to represent the national government.

New Hampshire   Massachusetts
New York   Rhode Island
Connecticut   Pennsylvania
New Jersey   Maryland
Delaware   Virginia
North Carolina   South Carolina
Georgia

Title: "The United States of America."

• *Student Activity Page 26-3.* Discuss:
  • The states selected representatives to attend the Convention in Philadelphia. Color arrows from the states to the Convention. Record "States sent representatives to the Convention."
  • Those representatives wrote and signed the new Constitution. Record:"Representatives wrote the Constitution." Color the arrow from the Convention to the Constitution.
  • The Constitution was sent back to the states to be ratified by the people. Record: "Constitution sent to States to be ratified." Color the arrow from the Constitution to the states.
  • The people approved the Constitution, so they are governed by it.
  • What is civil government? How does this chart show a flow of power?

Note: This lesson will require two classtimes.

Cultivating Student Mastery

1. How did Alexander Hamilton act according to his own conscience? Would that have been difficult? Why or why not?

2. Since the Constitution had to be approved by the people in every state, who had the most power — the people or the delegates?

A government of the people and by the people

Student Text, pages 149-150

Leading Idea

• Webster defined *president* as "An officer appointed or elected to govern a province or territory, or to administer the government of a nation."

For Reflection and Reasoning

• Review: Who wrote the Constitution? Who approved the Constitution? Why was this so special? Had it ever been done before in the world? What had prepared them for writing a Constitution?

• In other countries, how were the laws written? In some countries, are the people ruled by laws? Are they ruled by the orders of one individual? Do you know of any countries like that in the world today?

• What is the President of the United States? Why did the people want George Washington to be their President? How did they honor him as he traveled to New York?

• What is a Vice President? Who was the first Vice President?

• *Student Activity Pages 26-4* and *26-5.* The students may identify the first four Presidents and their terms of office. Glue the pictures of the Presidents on the time-line. Discuss each President as the student completes the timeline.

• Why was George Washington willing to serve as President? Why did he not want a third term as President?

• Where was George Washington's home? He loved to be at Mount Vernon.

• Do you know the name of John Adams' wife? John and Abigail Adams were the first to live in the White House. Where is the White House? Who lives in the White House?

• Thomas Jefferson made many great contributions to America. What document did he write? What important purchase of land did he make for the United States? Under his direction, who traveled to the Pacific Ocean to identify the land west of the Mississippi? For students who have studied *The Mighty Works of God: Liberty and Justice for All*, this should be a review.

• John Adams and Thomas Jefferson died on the same day. Do you remember what the day was? On July 4, fifty years after the Declaration of Independence.

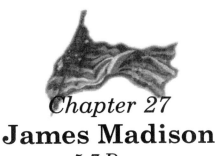

Chapter 27
James Madison
5-7 Days

> **Leading Idea**
>
> ## God prepared James Madison to seek a Constitution for the United States.
>
> Student Text, pages 151-152

● "The clarity of reasoning and the wide knowledge of political history, both ancient and modern, displayed in Madison's contribution to *The Federalist Papers* were surely a tribute to the excellent education he received and the efforts he made to build upon that education throughout his adult years. Not only did Madison receive a thorough education in the principles of government from Princeton's President, Dr. John Witherspoon, but he also gained a sound knowledge of economics from 'the old Doctor' and developed a sensitivity to fine literature and the arts. Madison's well rounded and thorough education—and its end results—should be thought-provoking for parents and teachers today. . . ."[108]

Mary-Elaine Swanson, *The Education of James Madison*

● "Dr. Witherspoon labored conscientiously to prepare his young men to take positions of leadership on the public scene — whether as pastors, planters, lawyers, merchants or statesmen. His emphasis on government and law in addition to divinity awakened Madison's interest in these subjects. Gaillard Hunt says that 'His favorite subjects at college were the history of the free states of antiquity and all subjects relating to government.'

"Therefore it is not surprising that Madison was anxious to participate in the great events that were beginning to unfold throughout the colonies. After his return to Virginia, he was elected in December of 1774 to the Orange County Committee of Safety to enforce the economic boycott of Britain. From this time on he became deeply concerned with Virginia politics. It was not until May, 1776, however, on the eve of Independence, that he made what he considered his *real* entry into public life. It was then that, as he proudly relates, 'I became a member of the convention in Virginia which instructed her delegates in Congress to propose the Declaration of Independence.'

"What a moment it must have been for this shy young scholar to enter the political arena. At age 25, he was one of the youngest members of the Virginia Convention and looked even younger than he was. He was only a little over five feet six inches tall and his pale face and thin frame gave him an air of frail health. But his face, says Hunt, 'was lighted up by a pair of hazel eyes which were ready to reflect a quiet humour.' His hair, light in color, he combed back into a queue tied with a plain ribbon. Indeed, as Hunt remarks, 'He was clothed so soberly that he looked more like a dissenting divine than the heir of a planter of a large estate, and before his election his neighbors declared he was more of a minister than a statesman.' . . ."[109]

Mary-Elaine Swanson, *The Education of James Madison*

For Reflection and Reasoning

• Review: What problem did the United States have after the Revolutionary War?

• In history, we see that God prepares men for each historic event. Name some of the men who were important in writing the Constitution.

• Using a map, locate the Potomac River and Chesapeake Bay. Why did Virginia and Maryland need an agreement for trade and navigation? What did Madison suggest?

• *Student Activity Pages 27-1 and 27-2.* Discuss how God prepared James Madison to seek a Constitution for the thirteen states. Complete the timeline, using the preprinted statements to glue in the appropriate boxes and have students record notes for the remaining statements.

Cultivating Student Mastery

1. Although James Madison did not fight during the Revolutionary War, how did he assist the states?

March 16, 1751	Born in Virginia
Age eighteen	Entered Princeton College
1772	Returned to Virginia, continued to study philosophy, theology, and law
Revolutionary War	Chairman of committee for public safety for Orange County, VA
1776	*Delegate to Virginia Convention—helped write the state constitution*
1779	*Delegate to Continental Congress*
1783	*Member of the State legislature*
1785	Planned a meeting at Mt. Vernon to reach an agreement about trade and navigation between Virginia and Maryland. All 13 states were invited.
1786	Convention held at Annapolis
1787	*Constitutional Convention in Philadelphia*

2. During and after college, James Madison studied law. How did that help him during 1776?

3. When the states did not agree about trade and navigation, how did Madison try to help?

Leading Idea

God prepared James Madison to understand a republican form of government.

Student Text, pages 152-154

• Webster defined *executive* as ". . . The body or person who carries the laws into effect, or superintends the enforcement of them, is *executive*."

• "At the Constitutional Convention, Madison's knowledge and experience were now well known and admired among his fellow delegates, and it will be remembered that Major William Pierce from Georgia, who wrote brief sketches of

his fellow delegates, remarked that 'every Person seems to acknowledge his greatness. He blends together the profound politician, with the Scholar.' Pierce also noted that Madison took the lead at the Convention in the discussion of every great question and showed himself to be 'the best informed Man of any point in debate.' He also remarked on Madison's 'remarkable sweet temper.' The latter quality was sometimes in short supply among the delegates during the debates that hot summer. Madison's calm, constructive style of debating must have come as a relief, particularly as he never spoke for more than 10 minutes at a time. Evidently he had learned the lesson Dr. Witherspoon had been at such pains to teach his pupils: Never to speak unless they had something to say and when they had said it to 'leave off.'"[110]

Mary-Elaine Swanson, *The Education of James Madison*

For Reflection and Reasoning

● Review: What is civil government? How was Madison prepared to seek a Constitution for the United States? How did he encourage the meeting to consider a government of all of the States? Why was such a government needed?

● What were Madison's ideas for the national government of the United States?
1. "States should join in a Republic." What is a Republic? Use *Student Activity Page 26-2* to review the idea of individual sovereign states and one national government.
2. "National government should have some power upon the states and some power upon individuals."
3. "The nation should have an executive." What is an executive?

● Madison's ideas became part of a plan written in Virginia, called the Virginia Plan. Why was the Virginia Plan called the "backbone" of the Constitution?

● What made Madison stand out from the other delegates at the Constitutional Convention? Was it his physical appearance? Or was it his character? How was it shown?

● Thomas Jefferson was in Paris at the time of the Constitutional Convention. How did he influence the men who wrote the Constitution? How did he help them understand ideas about laws and nations?

● Review the chart, Student Text, page 16. Who gives civil government the power to rule? How are representatives given power?

Suggested Student Notes

List James Madison's ideas for the national government of the United States.

Cultivating Student Mastery

1. Where did James Madison get his ideas for a new system of government?

2. What did James Madison do during the Convention to help himself? How did it help the whole country?

3. What character quality was shown by Madison's actions at the Convention?

4. Who gives civil government the power to rule?

Leading Idea

"Conscience is the most sacred of all property . . ."

Student Text, page 154

● Webster defined *property* as "The exclusive right of possessing, enjoying and disposing of a thing; ownership. . ."

● See definition of *conscience*, Teacher's Guide, page 97.

● In 1792, James Madison wrote on "Property": "Property. . . In the former sense, a man's land, or merchandise, or money, is called his property. In the latter sense, a man has a property of peculiar value in his religious opinions, and in the profession and practice dictated by them. . . He has an equal property in the free use of his faculties, and free choice of the objects on which to employ them. In a word, as a man is said to have a right to his property, he may be equally said to have a property in his rights. Where an excess of power prevails, property of no sort is duly respected. No man is safe in his opinions, his person, his faculties, or his possessions. Where there is an excess of liberty, the effect is the same . . . Government is instituted to protect property of every sort . . . This being the end of government . . . Conscience is the most sacred of all property . . ."[111]

For Reflection and Reasoning

● Do you have things which belong to you? Toys? Books? Clothes? Money? What does it mean that something "belongs to you"?

● What do your parents own? A car? A house? Furniture?

● What does it mean to own something? Noah Webster stated that something is our *property* when we have the right to decide how it is to be used or what should happen to it. We can decide who should be able to use it. If we want to throw it away, we can. What guides how we choose to use our property?

● What did James Madison believe about property? All of the property which we have discussed can be touched and seen. But Madison said that there is property which we can't see or touch. What kind of property is that?

● *Student Activity Page 27-3.* List the two kinds of property which Madison identified, Internal and External, and examples of each from the Student Text.

● What is your conscience? What does your conscience do? Why would it be the "most important"? Would our property of conscience decide how we will use all of the other property we have? What decides how you take care of your toys, books, or clothes? Or how you spend your money? Have your parents taught you certain rules? Does your conscience help you decide if you are obeying those rules or caring for your property as you should?

● What is the purpose of government? How does government protect property?

● Review: When the civil government of England did not allow the Separatists to have their own churches, what did they do? How did their actions show their understanding of the importance of conscience?

Leading Idea

God used Madison to bring about the ratification of the Constitution.

Student Text, pages 155-156

For Reflection and Reasoning

● Why was James Madison chosen to be on the Committee of Style and Arrangement? How had God prepared Madison for that work?

• After the Constitution was written and signed by the delegates at the Convention, what had to happen before it became law? Were all people in favor of the Constitution? What representative from New York helped the people understand the need for the Constitution? How did Hamilton work with James Madison and John Jay to reach that goal?

• The Teacher may show the students a copy of *The Federalist*.

• Review *Student Activity Page 26-3*. Who gave the representatives at the Convention their authority? When the Constitution was completed, how did the people again exercise their power? How does the ratification of the Constitution show that our civil government is "of the people, by the people, for the people"?

• Why was Madison called the "Father of the Constitution"?

Cultivating Student Mastery

The student may prepare a short essay, their own "Federalist Paper", on one of the following suggested topics:
* The Importance of Self Government
* The Purpose of Civil Government
* The Need for a National Constitution

James Madison — President

Student Text, pages 156-158

For Reflection and Reasoning

• Review: Use *Student Activity Page 26-4* to review the first four Presidents of the United States.

• Thomas Jefferson and James Madison were great friends. How had they encouraged each other in their work while Jefferson was in Paris?

• When Jefferson was President, what position did Madison hold?

• How did Dolley Madison help Jefferson in the White House?

• When Washington, D.C., was attacked by the British, how did Dolley Madison rescue an important artifact of American history?

• Describe the character for which James Madison was known. For what great writings is he remembered?

• *Student Activity Page 27-4*. Identify James Madison's contributions to America:

Father of the Constitution

An author of *The Federalist*

President of the United States

Supplemental Activities

● For additional reading, the students would enjoy the following biographies:
  • *Dolly Madison, Quaker Girl,* by Helen Albee Monsell, Childhood of Famous Americans Series, Bobbs-Merrill Company, 1944.
  • *Unfading Beauty, The Story of Dolley Madison,* by Tracy M. Leininger, His Seasons, 2000.
  • *James Madison, Father of the Constitution,* by Brent Kelley, Chelsea House Publishers, 2001.
  • *The Great Little Madison,* by Jean Fritz, G.T. Putnam Sons, 1989.

PIONEER
Westward Movement
Chapters 28-37
6-8 Weeks

Chapter 28
The War of 1812
3-4 Days

> **Leading Idea**
>
> ## *Though the enemy is strong, we must fight for liberty.*
>
> Student Text, page 159

- The War for Independence brought independence to the United States within the confines of land. However, England continued to claim the ocean.

    The United States carried on major shipping to Europe. The American ships were continually attacked by the British. As a result, war was declared to resolve America's independence at sea.

- "The real, final cause of the war, however, lay in the fact that England persisted in exercising her assumed 'right of search'. Her war ships stopped our merchant vessels, took American seamen out of them, and forcing them, under the sting of the lash, to enter her service and fight her battles. Her excuse was that she seized men who were British subjects and who had deserted and entered our service. This was true in some cases, but England made no discrimination, but took any able-bodied sailor she fancied. This was an outrage that we could no longer bear—thousands of our citizens had been kidnapped, but England refused to stop these acts of violence. For this reason Congress declared war in the summer of 1812. . . ."[112]

    D.H. Montgomery, *The Leading Facts of American History*

- ". . . in 1797, when war with that government seemed inevitable, Congress, on the urgent recommendation of President Adams, caused the frigates *United States, Constellation, and Constitution* to be completed, equipped, and sent to sea. This was the commencement of the American navy, which in after years, though weak in numbers, performed many brilliant exploits. From this time the navy became the cherished arm of the national defense; and chiefly through its instrumentality, the name and power of the United States began to be properly appreciated in Europe, at the beginning of the present century."[113]

Benson J. Lossing, *A Family History of the United States*

For Reflection and Reasoning

● Review: What is liberty? What war did Americans fight for their independence?

● Why did America and England go to war again in 1812? How were the British attacking American liberty?

● Why were the Americans not content to simply have liberty at home? Why did they need liberty at sea?

● Review: When the Revolutionary War began, who had the stronger, better-trained army? Why were the Americans not defeated?

● When America went to war with England in 1812, who had the stronger navy?

● *Student Activity Page 28-1.* Though the American navy was small and weak compared to the British navy, from the Student Text, deduce the ways in which the American navy was strong.

· **American ships were strongly built**
· **Officers had good experience**
· **Officers and men were not afraid of Britain**
· **Thought it was wrong for Britain to seize the men**

● Though the Americans did not have the stronger navy, what internal idea helped them to fight?

Cultivating Student Mastery

1. Complete *Student Activity Page 28-1.*

Leading Idea

"We have met the enemy and they are ours."

Student Text, pages 160-163

● ". . . During the summer of 1813, Commodore Oliver Hazzard Perry had prepared, on Lake Erie, an American squadron of nine vessels, mounting fifty-four guns, to co-operate with the Army of the West. The British had also fitted out a small squadron of six vessels, carrying sixty-three guns, commanded by Commodore Barclay. Perry's fleet was ready by the 2d of August, but some time was occupied in getting several of his vessels over the bar in the harbor of Lake Erie on the morning of the 10th of September, 1813, and a very severe battle ensued. The brave Perry managed with the skill of an old admiral, and the courage of the proudest soldier. His flag-ship, the *Lawrence*, had to bear the brunt of the battle, and very soon she became an unmanageable wreck, having all her crew, except four or five, killed or wounded. Perry then left her, in an open boat, and hoisted his flag on the *Niagara* at the moment when that of the *Lawrence* fell. With this vessel he passed through the enemy's line, pouring broadsides, right

178

and left, at half pistol-shot distance. The remainder of the squadron followed, with a fair wind, and the victory was soon decided. At four o'clock in the afternoon, every British vessel had surrendered to him; and before sunset, he had sent a messenger to General Harrison with the famous dispatch, '*We have met the enemy, and they are ours.*' This victory was hailed with unbounded demonstrations of joy. For a moment, party rancor was almost forgotten; and bonfires and illuminations lighted up the whole country."[114]

Benson J. Lossing, *A Family History of the United States*

● "Don't give up the ship." "These were the last words of Captain James Lawrence. . . when he fell mortally wounded in a battle. . . Perry had given Lawrence's name to his ship."[115]

D.H. Montgomery, *Leading Facts of American History*

For Reflection and Reasoning

● Using a map, locate Lake Erie. Why did both America and Great Britain want to control Lake Erie?

● When Perry arrived at Lake Erie, what problems did he find with the ship building? Why was there no more delay after he arrived? How long did it take to have the fleet ready after he took command?

● How did the sandbar provide protection to the Americans as they built the ships? How was it an obstacle to launching the ships? How was the obstacle overcome?

● Why did the British Captain Barclay plan to attack the American ships as they went across the sandbar? Why did he miss his opportunity?

● After Captain Barclay was not able to capture a ship, he slipped away and hid. Why?

● When Perry led his fleet with his flagship, the Lawrence, what was on his flag? What does that motto mean? When the Lawrence was destroyed, what did the British Captain expect Perry to do? What did Perry do? How was he following his own motto?

● Review: Who is in control of battles?

● How did God protect Perry and his men as they rowed to the Niagara?

● What happened to the British in their battle against Perry? Why was this unexpected?

● How much was Commander Perry willing to sacrifice to protect American control of Lake Erie?

● How did Perry describe the American victory against the British on Lake Erie?

● Review: How was the Northwest Territory protected during the Revolutionary War? What man did God use to protect that territory?

● How did Commander Perry's victory on Lake Erie protect the Northwest Territory? How was Perry honored for his victory?

● In what other ways did Perry defend his country?

● *Student Activity Page 28-2.* Label Lake Erie, Canada, New York, Pennsylvania, Ohio, Indiana, Michigan, Illinois.

● *Student Activity Page 28-3.* Identify Perry's character and God's Providence in the battle for Lake Erie.

WE HAVE MET THE ENEMY AND THEY ARE OURS.

	Perry's Character	Providence
"The young commander had taken charge of building a fleet before, and after he came there was no more delay."	Good commander	
"Unfortunately for Captain Barclay, he was invited to dinner on the other side of the lake, and accepted the invitation. Perry, too, had been watching. 'This is the time for me,' he said, . . ."	Well prepared	When Perry was ready, the British Captain was gone.
With great effort, Perry moved his ship over the sandbar.	Imagination	
"Upon his flagship he ran up a blue flag on which in clear white letters was [the] command, 'Don't give up the ship!'"	Courage	
"'Perry has lost his flagship,' thought the British, 'and he will soon surrender.' But Perry had no such intention."	Steadfastness	
"At first the smoke hid them from their enemies; then the British caught sight of them . . . Two bullets went through the boy's cap, but no one was injured . . ."		God protected Perry and his men.
" . . . in fifteen minutes after they left the Lawrence, Perry had run up his flag on the Niagara, and, with his new flagship, was all ready for another battle."	Steadfastness	
Then came the surrender of the British.		American victory

Leading Idea

Old Ironsides, a monument to American courage

Student Text, pages 164-166

• Webster defined *frigate* as "A ship of war, of a size larger than a sloop. . . having two decks and carrying from thirty to forty four guns. . . ."

• "England had been in the habit of treating America as though she owned the ocean from shore to shore. She had a magnificent navy of a thousand war ships. We had about a dozen! One of our twelve was the *Constitution* (44 guns), commanded by Captain Isaac Hull, a nephew of General William Hull. No braver officer ever trod a ship's deck. While cruising off the coast of Nova Scotia, Captain Hull fell in with the British man-of-war *Guerrièrre* (38 guns). The fight began (August 19, 1812). The *Constitution* carried more guns and more men than the British ship, and in twenty minutes the *Guerrière* surrendered, a shattered, helpless, sinking wreck. . . . this was only the beginning of our successes at sea, for out of fifteen such battles we won twelve. . . . The *Constitution*, almost unhurt, and henceforth known as *Old Ironsides*, was hailed with ringing cheers."[116]

D.H. Montgomery, *Leading Facts of American History*

• "While the army was suffering defeats, and became, in the mouths of the opponents of the administration, a staple rebuke, the little navy had acquitted itself nobly, and the national honor and prowess have been fully vindicated upon the ocean. . . . Nine of the American vessels were of a class less than frigates, and all of them could not well compare in appointments with those of the enemy. Yet the Americans were not dismayed by this disparity, but went out boldly in their ships to meet the war vessels of the proudest maritime nation upon the earth. . . ."[117]

Benson J. Lossing, *A Family History of the United States*

For Reflection and Reasoning

• Why was the frigate Constitution called "Old Ironsides"? Who commanded the Constitution in her first victory during the war? How long did the Constitution fight the British ship, Guerriere? What made this victory so special?

• Why did Captain Hull resign his ship?

• Using a map, locate the country of Brazil. Why were the Americans fighting so far away from home?

• For how long did the Constitution fight Java? What happened to the Java? How badly was the Constitution damaged?

• Who commanded the Constitution in 1815? For how long did the Constitution fight the Cyane and Lebane? How did the battle end?

• The Constitution, Old Ironsides, often faced stronger British ships, or several ships at a time. How did the bravery shown by her commanders and sailors equal the strength of the ship?

• Why is the Constitution a meaningful symbol of American liberty?

• Why did Americans not want the ship destroyed? Today "Old Ironsides" can still be seen in Boston.

• The students may draw a picture of Old Ironsides.

Cultivating Student Mastery

During the War of 1812, many men fought bravely to protect the liberty which had been won during the American Revolutionary War.

1. What character qualities were shown by the American navy commanders, and the captains of Old Ironsides?

2. How was their character the same or different from those who fought in the war for Independence?

3. In what way was the War of 1812 a war for Independence?

Chapter 29
The Star-Spangled Banner
3-4 Days

Leading Idea

The Star-Spangled Banner still waves.

Student Text, pages 167-170

• In 1814, a few weeks after the burning of Washington, the British moved from Canada by way of Lake Champlain to attack northern New York. "The next British attack was on Baltimore, by the same force and fleet that had taken Washington. That city was guarded by Fort McHenry. All day and all the following night (September 13, 1814) the enemy's ships hammered away with shot and shell at the fort. As the anxious hours of darkness slowly passed, the people of Baltimore asked each other, 'Can we possibly hold the fort?' When the sun rose the next morning the question was answered—'our flag was still there'; the British had given up the attack, and were sailing down Chesapeake Bay."[118]
D.H. Montgomery, *The Leading Facts of American History*

• The melody of our national anthem was borrowed from an English song of merriment and conviviality, titled "To Anacreon in Heaven," and was well-known in America long before Francis Scott Key's inspiring words were added in 1814.

The young Baltimore lawyer wrote his poem during the British naval bombardment of Fort McHenry, while he was on board one of the enemy ships, as an emissary to obtain the release of a friend. When the fierce shelling ceased and dawn came, he was elated to see that "our flag was still there." The song became popular immediately and was soon recognized as our national anthem; an act of Congress made this official in 1931.

For Reflection and Reasoning

• Review: America declared her independence from England in 1776, fought the War for Independence, wrote the Constitution in 1787, and began to prosper. By 1812, the United States was back at war with England, to protect her rights to sail her ocean vessels freely.

• Using a map, locate the setting of this event: Maryland, Chesapeake Bay, Annapolis, and Fort McHenry.

• Why was Francis Scott Key and his friend's place "the strangest place that could be imagined"? Why were they there?

● Why was Francis Scott Key so anxious to see the flag waving over the fort? What did it mean if the stars and stripes were still there?

● If we understand the history of when and why the Star Spangled Banner was written, how will it help us better understand the words? Will we love it even more?

● What does "national anthem" mean? An anthem is a hymn. *The Star-Spangled*

Banner is the *hymn* of our nation.

● Sing all stanzas of *The Star-Spangled Banner, Student Activity Page 29-1.*

Cultivating Student Mastery

1. In the attack on Baltimore, how were the British surprised?

2. What were the American patriots willing to sacrifice to protect our country's liberty?

> **Leading Idea**
>
> *"Tis the star-spangled banner, O! long may it wave"*
>
> Student Text, pages 170-171

For Reflection and Reasoning

● Use *Student Activity Page 29-1.* Read each stanza of *The Star-Spangled Banner* and discuss the ideas and unique vocabulary.

● Why did Francis Scott Key say "The dawn's early light" and "the twilight's last gleaming"? What question was he asking? Why?

● What is a banner?

● What was the author's hope or wish for the star-spangled banner?

● What danger did the country face? How did the banner still waving show triumph?

● What was Francis Scott Key's hope for

the future? What blessings are on this land? How did he recognize God's Hand? What should be our motto?

● Read the last two lines of each stanza. How are they alike? How are they different?

● Have the students underline the words and phrases Francis Scott Key used to describe the flag. How did his choice of words show his great love for America?

Cultivating Student Mastery

1. For what special occasions do we sing the national anthem?

2. Why do we often have fireworks at patriotic events?

Leading Idea

"The land of the free and the home of the brave"

Student Text, pages 171-172

● Noah Webster gave some key terms which define *free*: "Being at liberty, not enslaved, unconstrained, unrestrained, not obstructed, open."

● Webster defined *brave* as "To encounter with courage and fortitude, or without being moved."

● "The war, sometimes called 'the second war for independence,' had three chief results: 1. Though our military operations had generally been far from successful on land, yet we convinced Great Britain that we were able and determined to make our rights on the ocean respected. 2. The war showed foreign nations that any attempt to establish themselves on the territory of the United States was likely to end in disastrous failure. 3. By cutting off our foreign commerce for a number of years, the war caused us to build many cotton and woollen mills, thus making us to a much greater degree than before a manufacturing people — able to clothe ourselves, instead of having to depend on the looms of Great Britain for our calico and our broadcloth."[119]

D.H. Montgomery, *The Leading Facts of American History*

For Reflection and Reasoning

● Review: For what liberty was the War of 1812 fought?

● Review: What is a banner? How does our flag represent freedom?

● What does it mean to be free? What does it mean to have liberty?

● What liberty do we have in America? Do all other nations have this same liberty?

● Why do people from many countries want to come to America?

● What does it mean to be brave? What does it mean to have a "home of the brave"?

● If you are brave, do you stand up for what is right? If America is a "land of the free and the home of the brave", would that mean that Americans must be *brave* to stand up for what is right?

● If people are free, but do not stand up for what is right, what will happen to their freedom?

● America has had many brave men and women who had the courage to do what God led them to do. God has used them to protect and preserve the liberty in America. Name individuals from this year's study of history who showed great bravery to protect American liberty. If America is to stay free, it will take men and women who have the courage to stand for what is right today and in the future.

• When the War of 1812 ended, Americans had protected their freedom, not only on the land, but at sea. England realized that the people of the United States of America were determined to protect and preserve their liberty.

• *Student Activity Page 29-2.* Reason with the students to identify the type of character it takes to remain free — brave, courage, etc. Contrast with the character which will not remain free — timid, fear, etc.

• Read Deuteronomy 31:6. If we obey the Word of God, will God "go with us"? Will He guide us? Record all or a portion of the verse on *Student Activity Page 29-2.*

Supplemental Activities

• The original Star-Spangled Banner is on display at the Smithsonian Institution. Conduct online research to view pictures and additional information.

• Research and review proper flag etiquette.

• Students may enjoy further research and reading on the life of Francis Scott Key.

Chapter 30
Land of the Free
2-3 Days

"Land of the free"

Student Text, pages 173-174

● " . . . The stress in the United States always had been on 'useful knowledge'. . . Almost all the great and fruitful scientific ideas were hatched in Europe; but the widest applications of them to common life, or to destruction in war, were made in America. . . .

"The machine-tool industry with interchangeable parts was already entrenched in the Naugatuck valley of Connecticut by 1836, the year that Samuel Colt patented the revolving pistol, 'equalizer' of the frontier. Charles Goodyear in 1844 patented the vulcanization of rubber, which eventually enabled all America to roll or fly. Two years later, Elias Howe invented the sewing machine, which took the making of clothes out of the home and tailor's shop into the factory. Cyrus McCormick of Virginia in 1834 invented the reaper, which made possible prairie farming on a grand scale. More spectacular and far-reaching was Samuel F. B. Morse's invention of the electric telegraph in 1832. Morse worked it out while teaching painting and sculpture at New York University. His friends in Congress got him an appropriation of $30,000 in 1843 to establish between Baltimore and Washington the first telegraph line, built by Ezra Cornell who later founded Cornell University. The first message sent over this line in dots and dashes on 24 May 1844 between Morse himself and a friend in Baltimore, was 'What hath God wrought!'."[120]
Samuel Eliot Morison, *The Oxford History of the American People*

For Reflection and Reasoning

Note: If the students have not previously studied the Louisiana Purchase and the Lewis and Clark Expedition, the teacher may expand this lesson.

● Using a map, review how the Louisiana Purchase expanded the size of the nation. Why did families want to move West? See *Teacher Resource Page 30-1*.

● Use *Student Activity Page 7-5* to review: What is liberty? What is the source of liberty? What are the effects of liberty?

● Why is America called "the land of the free"?

● Why does civil liberty — "the land of the free" — make more inventions possible? What is the result when there is no civil liberty?

● Use *Student Activity Page 27-3* to review: What is property? What are the two kinds of property? Are a person's ideas his property? Do a person's ideas belong to him or the state? If a person has an idea for an invention, should he own that invention and be able to sell it to others?

● *Student Activity Pages 30-1* and *30-2.* Record the following early inventions :

- Eli Whitney—**Cotton Gin**
- Samuel F.B. Morse—**Telegraph**
- Cyrus McCormick—**Reaper**
- Alexander Graham Bell—**Telephone**
- Thomas Edison—**Lightbulb**

Cut and glue related pictures. The *Student Activity Page* will be completed in a later lesson.

● Why was transportation difficult? How does the size of the United States compare to the size of other countries? Great Britain? Spain? Mexico? Canada?

● If transportation improved, how would it improve communication?

Cultivating Student Mastery

1. *Student Activity Page 30-3.*

"So long as Americans are free they will continue to make our country ever more wonderful."

Student Text, page 174

For Reflection and Reasoning

● How is life in America today different from the 1800's or early 1900's? What inventions have changed daily life for the family? How has communication changed? How has transportation changed?

● Who was Laura Ingalls Wilder? Laura was born in 1867. During her childhood, how did people travel and communicate? Laura died in 1957. What inventions had been made during her lifetime?

● What did Laura Ingalls Wilder mean when she wrote, "But the real things haven't changed"?

● Do we have all the inventions we need today? What inventions might make life easier, communication better, or travel faster?

● Why is it important to protect the freedom we have in America?

● Record *Suggested Student Notes* on *Student Activity Page 30-4.*

Suggested Student Notes

"So long as Americans are free they will continue to make our country ever more wonderful."
Laura Ingalls Wilder

Supplemental Activities

The students may select one inventor for further research. Read a children's biography and write a biographical sketch of four or five paragraphs including the following:
- Basic history of the inventor.
- What influenced the inventor to develop his invention?
- When and where did he complete his invention?
- How did his invention improve the American way of life?
- What character qualities did he reveal in his life?

Chapter 31
Robert Fulton and the Steamboat
3-4 Days

Leading Idea

"Why not make it run a boat?"

Student Text, pages 175-176

• "James Watt, Scotch engineer and inventor, was born at Greenock on the Clyde, Scotland, January 19, 1736. He was educated mainly at the Greenock grammar school, which he was unable to attend regularly on account of poor health. He early showed an exceptional mechanical ingenuity and acquired skill in drawing and in carpentry.

"In 1755, Watt placed himself under a maker of mathematical instruments in London. He went to Glasgow in 1756 and was soon employed by the university there in fitting up the instruments in the Macfarlane observatory. His constant intercourse with the professors of the university and his ready access to books enabled him to acquire a considerable knowledge of science.

"During the winter of 1763-64, Watt repaired a working model of the Newcomen engine, kept for the use of the natural science class in the college. He was impressed with its contrivance, but he soon perceived its defects. It was worked by means of atmospheric pressure, steam being used only in producing, by its condensation, a vacuum in a cylinder into which a piston was forced by the pressure of the air. Watt found that about four-fifths of the steam, and consequently of the fuel, was wasted. At length, in 1765, he hit upon the expedient of the separate condenser. He did not rest content, but resolved to make steam his motive power. This done, he received a patent for his engine in 1769.

". . . By 1785, his engine had become available for the most delicate, as well as for the most laborious, forms of industry.

"Honors and affluence came to Watt as the inventor of the steam engine. He was made a fellow of the royal societies of Edinburgh and London in 1784 and 1785 respectively. The University of Glasgow gave him the degree of doctor of laws in 1806, and, in 1808, he was made a foreign member of the Institute of France. Died in Heathfield, England, August 25, 1819."[121]

Lincoln Library of Essential Information

For Reflection and Reasoning

• What is an inventor? What often happens with an inventor's first experiments? What character is necessary to continue working until an idea becomes a successful invention?

• James Watt is called a "Scotch" boy. From what country are the Scotch or

Scottish? Locate Scotland on a map or globe.

● Though James Watt was not strong physically, did it keep him from thinking up new ideas? What character quality is seen in Watt's life, even as a boy?

● Inventors build upon ideas of others. What ideas were used in the first experiments to make a steamboat?

● How was Johnny Fitch's steamboat different from the earlier ones? What was Johnny Fitch's prediction?

● On what river was Johnny Fitch's steamboat tested? In what year? What other great historic event occurred on that river? When did it happen? How much time passed between the two events?

● *Student Activity Page 31-1.* Record the inventions which prepared the way for the steamboat. The students may illus-

trate their idea of Rumsey and Fitch's boats. The section on Fulton will be completed in a later lesson.

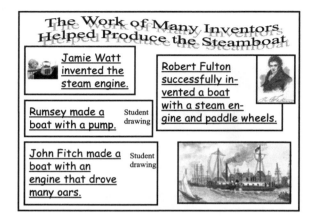

The Work of Many Inventors Helped Produce the Steamboat

Jamie Watt invented the steam engine.

Rumsey made a boat with a pump. *Student drawing*

John Fitch made a boat with an engine that drove many oars. *Student drawing*

Robert Fulton successfully invented a boat with a steam engine and paddle wheels.

Cultivating Student Mastery

1. How did James Watt become interested in the power of steam?

2. Why was Watt's steam engine better than the old-fashioned pumping engine?

Leading Idea

Harnessing the power of steam enriched life in the 19th century.

Student text, pages 176-178

● ". . . [1807] is remarkable in American history as the era of the commencement of successful steamboat navigation. Experiments in that direction had been made in this country many years before, but it was reserved for Robert Fulton to bear the honor of success. He spent a long time in France, partly in the pursuit of his profession as a portrait-painter, and in the study of the subject of steam navigation. Through the kindness of Joel Barlow, then [1797] in Paris (in whose family he remained seven years), he was enabled to study the natural sciences, modern languages, and to make experiments. There he became acquainted with Robert R. Livingston, and through his influence

and pecuniary aid, on his return to America, he was enabled to construct a steamboat, and to make a voyage on the Hudson from New York to Albany, 'against wind and tide,' in thirty-six hours. He took out his first patent in 1809. . . ."[122]
Benson J. Lossing, *A History of the United States*

● "Robert Fulton was born in Pennsylvania, in 1765, and was a student of West, the great painter, for several years. He had more genius for mechanics than the fine arts, and when he turned his efforts in that direction, he became very successful. He died in 1815, soon after launching a steamship of war, at the age of fifty years. At that time there were six steamboats afloat on the Hudson, and he was building a steamship, designed for a voyage to St. Petersburg, in Russia."[123]

Benson J. Lossing, A History of the United States

For Reflection and Reasoning

● Where was Robert Fulton born? Locate Pennsylvania on a map. Where did James Watt live? Look at the distance between the two places. Even though Robert Fulton and James Watt lived in different countries, how did James Watt's inventions benefit Fulton?

● How old was Robert Fulton when America declared her independence from England? How did he like to celebrate America's independence?

● How was Fulton's character similar to James Watt's?

● What is a miniature painter? Robert Fulton studied art under Benjamin West. Do you remember another inventor who studied art with Benjamin West? Students who have previously studied *The Mighty Works of God: Self Government* may remember that Samuel F.B. Morse studied with Benjamin West.

● Discuss Fulton's inventions which led to a steamboat. What caused the steamboat to move through the water?

● *Student Activity Page 30-1.* Add to the timeline of Inventions: "1807—Robert Fulton—Steamboat."

● What is a folly? Why might the people have thought the Clermont was a folly? How were they surprised?

● Locate New York and Albany on a map. On what river did the Clermont travel?

● Why were some people afraid of the steamboat?

● Complete *Student Activity Page 31-1.*

Leading Idea

Steamboats improved travel and shipping.

Student text, page 178

For Reflection and Reasoning

● What are rafts? Flat-boats? Barges? For what were they used on the Ohio River?

● How fast could the steamboat travel? Using the number of hours and total miles traveled, students may calculate the rate of speed.

● Before the invention of the steamboat, how much time was needed to ship goods from Pittsburgh to New Orleans? How did the steamboat make travel quicker? How did it make travel for pleasure easier? For business?

● Why did the arrival of the steamboat in Louisville create a "general alarm"?

● Although the steamboat greatly improved transportation, how was travel still limited? Could the steamboat travel on land? Using a map of the United States, locate the major rivers in the eastern and central regions of the country. How was travel to the West improved by the steamboat? How was it still limited?

● After reaching New Orleans, where might goods have been shipped?

● *Student Activity Page 31-2.* Label the Ohio and Mississippi Rivers, Pittsburgh, Louisville, Natchez, and New Orleans. Use a marker to trace the route of the steamboat from Pittsburgh to New Orleans.

Supplemental Activities

● The students may enjoy reading a biography of Robert Fulton. Suggested books:
   · *Robert Fulton: Boy Craftsman,* by Marguerite Henry, originally published by the Bobbs-Merrill Company in their Childhood of Famous Americans series.
   · *Robert Fulton and the Steamboat,* by Ralph Nading Hill, published by Random House.

192

Chapter 32
Path to the West
2-3 Days

Building roads for the nation to expand

Student Text, pages 179-181

• Daniel Webster recounted the development of roads and canals: "In my youth and early manhood I have traversed these mountains along all the roads or passes which lead through or over them. We are on Smith's River, which, while in college, I had occasion to swim. Even that could not always be done; and I have occasionally made a circuit of many rough and tedious miles to get over it. At that day, steam, as a motive power, acting on water and land, was thought of by nobody; nor were there good, practicable roads in this part of the State. At that day, one must have traversed this wilderness on horseback or on foot. So late as when I left college, there was no road from river to river for a carriage fit for the conveyance of persons. I well recollect the commencement of the system of turnpike roads. . . .

"I remember to have attended the first meeting of the proprietors of this turnpike at Andover. It was difficult to persuade men that it was possible to have a passable carriage road over these mountains. I was too young and too poor to be a subscriber, but I held the proxies of several absent subscribers, and what I lacked in knowledge and experience I made up in zeal. As far as I now remember, my first speech after I left college was in favor of what was then regarded as a great and almost impracticable internal improvement, to wit, the making

of a smooth, though hilly, road from Connecticut River, opposite the mouth of the White River, to the Merrimack River at the mouth of the Contoocook. Perhaps the most valuable result of making these and other turnpike roads was the diffusion of knowledge upon road-making among the people; for in a few years afterward, great numbers of the people went to church, to electoral and other meetings, in chaises and wagons, over very tolerable roads. The next step after turnpikes was canals.... This was thought to be a great and most useful achievement, and so indeed it was. But a vastly greater was now approaching, the era of steam. The application of steam to the moving of heavy bodies, on the water and on the land, towers above all other inventions of this or the preceding age. . ."[124]

Daniel Webster, *The Works of Daniel Webster*

• "In President Monroe's time the railway did not exist, and although the steamboat did, that could only go where some navigable river or lake opened the way. Look on the map of the United States . . . And you will see that the Allegheny Mountains shut out the East from the West. As the steamboat could not find a passage leading through those rough walls of rock, Congress resolved to build a wagon road over them. Such a road had already been begun (1811) at the head of navigation on the Potomac, at Cumberland, Maryland. This National Road was now (1825) gradually extending across the forest-covered mountains to Wheeling, on the Ohio River, where it connected with steamboats running to Cincinnati and to New Orleans.

"But that was not enough. There were millions of acres of fertile land in Ohio and the country beyond it, which emigrants wished to reach more directly than the steamboat could help them to do. Henry Clay, the 'Father of the National Road' urged its extension from Wheeling across Ohio, Indiana, and Illinois through to the Mississippi. President Monroe earnestly favored this enterprise, but he did not think that he had lawful power under the Constitution to spend the people's money for such purposes. Indirectly, however, he used every effort to help it forward. The road was extended nearly to the Mississippi, but by that time people had begun to build railways, so the National Road never got any farther. It was the first great work of the kind undertaken by the United States, costing, in the end, over $6,000,000. It stretched across the country for hundreds of miles, — broad, solid, smooth, — a true national highway.

"The traffic over the road was immense. Gayly painted stagecoaches ran through the more thickly settled parts. Beyond, toward the west, there was a constant stream of huge canvas-covered emigrant wagons, often so close together that the leaders of the teams could touch the wagon ahead of them with their noses. To see that procession of emigrant families going forward day after day showed how fast the people were settling that wild western country, which is now covered with cultivated farms, thriving towns, and busy cities."[125]

D.H. Montgomery, *The Leading Facts of American History*

● "Henry Clay was born in Virginia in 1777; died at Washington, 1852. He studied law, and in 1797 removed to Lexington, Kentucky. In 1799, when the people of Kentucky were adopting a state constitution, Clay urged them (but without success) to abolish slavery. He entered Congress in 1806, and continued in public life from that time until his death. He was a man of remarkable personal influence, a 'peacemaker' by temperament, and the greatest orator the Southwest ever possessed. Although ardently attached to his adopted state of Kentucky, yet he declared in 1850 that he owed his first allegiance to the Union, and a subordinate allegiance to his state. . . ."[126]

D.H. Montgomery, *The Leading Facts of American History*

For Reflection and Reasoning

● Why did families want to move West?

● Using a map, locate the Atlantic Ocean, Alleghany Mountains, Ohio River, Mississippi River, Ohio, Indiana, and Illinois. If there were no roads, no trains, and no airplanes, how could a person travel to the Mississippi River from the eastern United States?

● Review: How did steamboats make travel to the West easier? How was it still limited?

● What United States President traveled the Mississippi River on a barge during his youth? Where did he go? Why?

● Today, what material is used for the surface of roads? The first roads were simply trails or paths on which the horses and wagons traveled. After a heavy rain, what might happen to that type of road? With frequent use, the paths became hardened. Local paths were used, but there was no particular plan for the roads and good roads were not available to faraway places.

● What is an emigrant?

● Why did the people think a National Road should be constructed? Why was it called a National Road? How would the cost of the road be paid?

● *Student Activity Page 32-1.* Identify the states through which the National Road was built.

● Once people had automobiles, they wanted the roads to be smoother. What different types of material were used? Have you ever ridden on a brick road? A gravel road?

● Look at a road map of your state. If you want to visit someone who lives in another city, what route would you take? Identify different routes which you could take between your city/town and the nearest large city.

● Today, we have an Interstate Highway System. These highways were begun in 1956. How are interstate highways different from other highways?

● Students may draw a map of their neighborhood or the major roads of their city.

Cultivating Student Mastery

1. *Student Activity Page 32-1.*

Connecting the Great Lakes

Leading Idea

Student Text, pages 181-182

● Interest in developing canals existed for some time in the United States. In 1797, Robert Fulton and President George Washington communicated regarding canal navigation. Fulton sent Washington a copy of his *Treatise on Canal Navigation.*

● "At about this time a great work of internal improvement was completed. The Erie Canal, in the State of New York, was finished in 1825. It was the most important and stupendous public improvement ever undertaken in the United States; and, though it was the enterprise of the people of a single State, that originated and accomplished the labor of forming the channel of a river through a large extent of country, it has a character of nationality. Its earliest advocate was Jesse Hawley, who, in a series of articles published in 1807 and 1808, signed *Hercules,* set forth the feasibility and great importance of such a connection of the waters of Lake Erie and the Hudson River. His views were warmly seconded by Gouvernour Morris, Dewitt Clinton, and a few others, and its final accomplishment was the result, chiefly, of the untiring efforts, privately and officially, of the latter gentleman, while a member of the Legislature and governor of the State of New York. It is three hundred and sixty-three miles in length, and the first estimate of its cost was $5,000,000. Portions of it have since been enlarged, to meet the increasing demands of its commerce; and in 1853, the people of the State decided, by a general vote, to have it enlarged its entire length. . . ."[127]
　Benson J. Lossing, *A History of the United States*

● The Erie Canal was the engineering marvel of its day. The canal is 363 miles long, 40 feet wide, and 4 feet deep. There are 83 locks which deal with the difference of elevation between Lake Erie and the Hudson River. A towpath was built along the bank for the horses, mules, and oxen which were used to pull the boats.

• ". . . Before the canal was built, the charge for hauling a barrel of flour from Albany to Buffalo was ten dollars, and it took three weeks to get it there. After the canal was opened, a barrel of flour could be sent through in a week, at a cost of thirty cents! . . .

"The canal originally ran through a country in great part unsettled. It was the means of bringing in great numbers of emigrants from the East. On its banks arose scores of flourishing towns and rapidly growing cities. New York City gained immensely by the trade with the West, which began as soon as this water way was opened. Later, the canal was made free of toll, and from spring to the end of autumn a constant procession of boats laden with grain used to be seen going eastward day and night; while a similar procession, laden with merchandise, was seen going westward. This movement was a means of growth and a source of wealth to both sections of the country. On the one hand it made food cheaper all through the East; on the other, it made imported goods cheaper throughout the West."[128]

D.H. Montgomery, *The Leading Facts of American History*

For Reflection and Reasoning

• Review: Look at the student map, *Student Activity Page 31-2*. What was the route of the steamboat from Pittsburgh to New Orleans?

• As more and more families moved west, the rivers became very crowded. What types of boats traveled down the rivers?

• What is a canal? How is it different from a river?

• Sing the song, *The Erie Canal*.

• If a canal is built today, what equipment is used? How was the Erie Canal built?

• How did the boats move on the Erie Canal?

• Explain the system of locks which moved boats from one elevation to another between the Hudson River to Lake Erie.

• *Student Activity Page 32-2*. Label Erie Canal, Hudson River, the Great Lakes, New York City, Albany, Buffalo, Cleveland, Detroit, and Wisconsin. Trace the route from New York City to Wisconsin.

Cultivating Student Mastery

1. Complete *Student Activity Page 32-2*.

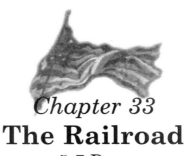

Chapter 33
The Railroad
5-7 Days

● Daniel Webster spoke at the opening of the Northern Railroad from Franklin to Grafton in New Hampshire, on the 28th of August, 1847: "Fellow-citizens, this railroad may be said to bring the sea to your doors. You cannot, indeed, snuff its salt water, but you will taste its best products, as fresh as those who live on its shores. I cannot conceive of any policy more useful to the great mass of the community than the policy which established these public improvements. Let me say, fellow-citizens, that in the history of human inventions there is hardly one so well calculated as that of railroads to equalize the condition of men. The richest must travel in the cars, for there they travel fastest; the poorest can travel in the cars, while they could not travel otherwise, because this mode of conveyance costs but little time or money. Probably there are in the multitude before me those who have friends at such distances that they could hardly have visited them, had not railroads come to their assistance to save them time and to save them expense. Men are thus brought together as neighbors and acquaintances, who live two hundred miles apart.

"We sometimes hear idle prejudices expressed against railroads because they are close corporations; but so from the necessity of the case they necessarily must be, because the track of a railway cannot be a road upon which every man may drive his own carriage. Sometimes, it is true, these railroads interrupt or annoy individuals in the enjoyment of their property . . . But I have observed, fellow-citizens, that railroad directors and railroad projectors are no enthusiastic lovers of landscape beauty; a handsome field or lawn, beautiful copses, and all the gorgeousness of forest scenery, pass for little in their eyes. Their business is to cut and to slash, to level or deface a finely rounded field, and fill up beautifully winding valleys. They are quite utilitarian in their creed and in their practice. Their business is to make a good road. They look upon a well-constructed embankment as an agreeable work of art; they behold with delight a long, deep cut through hard pan and rock, such as we have just passed; and if they can find a fair reason to run a tunnel under a deep mountain, they are half in raptures. To be serious, Gentlemen, I must say I admire the skill, the enterprise, and that rather bold defiance of expense, which have enabled the directors of this road to bring it with an easy ascent more than five hundred feet above the level of the Merrimac River. . . .

". . . But, fellow-citizens, health and industry, good morals and good government, have made your homes among these mountains prosperous and happy. This great improvement comes to your farther assistance. It will give you new facilities, connect you more readily with other portions of the State, and most assuredly, according to all experience, create new objects for the application of your enterprise and your labor. You do not yet begin to feel the benefits which it will confer on you. I rejoice most heartily that my native State has adopted a policy which has led to these results. I trust that policy may be steadily pursued, till internal improvement in some really and intrinsically useful form shall reach every glen and every mountain-side of the State. . . ."[129]
Daniel Webster, *The Works of Daniel Webster*

We need railroads!

Student Text, pages 183-184

For Reflection and Reasoning

• Why did Americans think that railroad travel was important? What transportation was available in America before the railroad?

• In a large country like America, how did railroads change what the people ate?

• Using a globe, compare the size of the United States and England. The Student Text says that America is "nearly forty times larger than England." Why are railroads even more helpful in a large country than in a smaller one?

• Discuss cars being drawn along the tracks by horses and mules before steam engines were used. Why were steam engines better?

• Enjoy the race between Peter Cooper's *Tom Thumb* and the horse-drawn car. Would you expect a horse-drawn car to outrace a locomotive?

• Why were railroads built near the rivers? How were most goods transported

before the railroad was built?

• Have you ever ridden on a railroad? Were you comfortable? What made the early railroads uncomfortable? Why was train travel dangerous?

• In spite of the discomfort, how was travel on the railroads of great benefit?

• *Student Activity Page 33-1*. Record student notes and color picture of train.

Suggested Student Notes

The railroad was of great benefit.
• **The train could carry large loads.**
• **The locomotive traveled at a great speed.**

Cultivating Student Mastery

1. How did the Tom Thumb race change people's minds about the locomotive?

2. How was transportation by train better than by horse and wagon?

A ride on the train with Charles Dickens

Student Text, pages 184-186

For Reflection and Reasoning

• What is an author? Have you ever

heard of the author, Charles Dickens? Do you know the titles of any books which he wrote? Charles Dickens wrote many books that were fiction, but his books told of life in England and Europe. He also wrote of many events in his life.

● An omnibus is "a large, usually four-wheeled, public passenger vehicle."

● What does Charles Dickens' description make you think? Was the train traveling fast? Why did Dickens say that though the American lakes are as broad as the English rivers, they seem very small? How does the size of America compare to the size of England?

● From Charles Dickens' description, how can you tell that the people in America were not used to the railroad? What did they do when it passed?

● Why did Dickens call the engine a "mad dragon" and a "thirsty monster"?

● Using Dickens' description, students may draw a picture of the train rushing through the American countryside or the interior of a passenger car. Details for the picture should be taken from the Student Text.

● *Student Activity Page 33-2.* The students may record words or phrases which describe the train.

Leading Idea

The north and south at war

Student Text, pages 186-187

● "By the time the Civil War started in 1861 — a war fought between a progressive industrial North and a conservative agricultural South — there were at least 200 operating railroads in America. The largest group of these ran in, around, and out of the Northeast. The second-largest congestion of rail lines was in the Midwest in a great ellipse formed by Chicago, St. Louis, Cincinnati, and Cleveland. There were a few lines in the South, and there was nothing but stagecoach service and the pony mail express in the Far West.

"As the Civil War raged on and bloodied the country, the railroads became a necessity of military life — and open targets. The North, with its vast network of tracks, used the rail lines to ship troops and supplies to the battle area. . . .

"Railroads came under increasing attack by both sides as the war spread west. Railroads, never before used as such, became war machines. Flatcars were used to haul heavy mortars into firing positions. Other cars towed high-flying observation balloons, used mostly by federal troops to spot Confederate positions. The trains delivered the troops, arms, and provisions for battle, as well as removing whole armies from war zones."[130]

Leonard Everett Fisher, *Tracks Across America*

● The Great Locomotive Chase was led by James J. Andrews. Lieutenant William Pittenger was from Company G of the 2d Ohio Volunteers. Several of the participants wrote of their adventure.

The newspaper, *Southern Confederacy*, Atlanta, Georgia, published an article on April 15, 1862, recounting the details of the great railroad chase. The article begins: "Since our last issue, we have obtained full particulars of the most thrilling railroad adventure that ever occurred on the American continent, as well as the mightiest and most important in its results, if successful, that has been conceived by the Lincoln Government since the commencement of this war. Nothing on so grand a scale has been attempted, and nothing within the range of possibility could be conceived, that would fall with such a tremendous, crushing force upon us, as the accomplishment of the plans which were concocted and dependent on the execution of the one whose history we now proceed to narrate. . . ."[131]

Lieut. William Pittenger, *Daring and Suffering: A History of The Great Railroad Adventure*

● *Teacher Resource Page 33-1* is an account of *The Great Locomotive Chase,* written by William Pittenger. This material may be used for expanding the details of the railroad chase for the students.

For Reflection and Reasoning

● The emphasis of this section is to consider the railroad and its effect on the Civil War. The study of the Civil War will be expanded in a later volume.

● What is a Civil War? Who were the "Union" soldiers? Who were the "Confederate" soldiers?

● How did the train change the method of battle in the Civil War?

● Discuss the location of telegraph wires along the railroad tracks. Why were railroad tracks and telegraph wires side by side? How would the use of the telegraph affect a war? This idea is not discussed in the Student Text, but students should be able to reason to a conclusion.

● How was the *Great Locomotive Chase* different than most battles? What plan did the Union soldiers have when they stole the General? What happened when

their plan was discovered? How did the *Great Locomotive Chase* end?

● *Student Activity Page 33-3.* Select two colors for the key to the map.
  · Label the cities through which Lincoln's funeral train traveled. Using the color key, draw railroad tracks to show the route of Lincoln's funeral train.
  · Label Chattanooga and Atlanta. Using the appropriate color from the key, draw railroad tracks depicting the Great Railroad Chase between the two cities.

Cultivating Student Mastery

1. During the American Civil War, how were railroads part of the battle?

2. How could the railroad help an army?

3. How could damaging the railroad be useful to an enemy?

Leading Idea

Joining the East and the West

Student Text, pages 188-189

● "Congress granted a tract of land in alternate sections, twenty miles wide, extending from Omaha to San Francisco in aid of this national enterprise. During the previous thirty-five years the government gave to road, canal, and railway corporations public lands nearly equal in area to that of the thirteen original states as they now stand."[132]

D.H. Montgomery, *The Leading Facts of American History*

For Reflection and Reasoning

● What does *transcontinental* mean?

● Without railroads, how did families or goods travel from California to the East or from the East to California?

● Locate Omaha, Nebraska, on a map. By the middle of the 19th Century, the railroads had been built to Omaha, Nebraska and railroad lines had been laid on the west coast. Note the great distance between Omaha and San Francisco. What geographic challenges did the railroads face?

● What difficulties were faced by the men who were hired to build the transcontinental railroad? What kind of character did these men need?

● What men were hired to build the railroad? Why were soldiers looking for work? What is an immigrant?

● What character quality in the Chinese workers made them effective on the railroads, in spite of their smaller size?

● What shows that the men working on the railroad had respect for God's law? How did they honor Sunday even though they probably could not attend church?

● Why did little towns spring up near the work sites along the tracks? What supplies did the railroad workers need? Who helped provide for them?

● Sing *I've Been Working on the Railroad.*

Leading Idea

Celebrating the joining of the East and West

Student Text, pages 189-190

● "A little more than two months after General Grant became President, the last spike of the last rail of the new road was driven at Ogden, Utah (1869). The blows of the sledge hammer which drove that spike—completing the greatest work of the kind then in the world—were telegraphed, as they fell, throughout the Union. . . .

"Between Omaha and San Francisco the railway crosses nine mountain ranges, including the Rockies and the Sierras, climbing, and then descending, over 8000 feet. In point of time, it is now no farther from New York to San Francisco than it was in the days of the Revolution from New York to Boston. Then it took our forefathers between five and six days to go by wagon somewhat less than 250 miles; now, in that time we can cross the entire continent.

"The result of this rapid means of travel is of the greatest importance to the republic. Once members of Congress laughed at the idea that California and Oregon would be added to the United States. They said that it would be practically impossible for such states, if added, to send representatives to the national capital, because it would take them the greater part of the year to get to Washington and back. For that reason they believed that the people who settled the Pacific coast would form a separate and independent republic. The railway and the telegraph have changed all that. They have connected the farthest extremities of the country so closely that they have made it possible for us to extend and maintain the Union from ocean to ocean."[133]

D.H. Montgomery, *The Leading Facts of American History*

For Reflection and Reasoning

• Throughout our nation's history, God has used men and events to unite individuals, states, and the nation. Sometimes that is a unity of ideas, sometimes it is a physical unity.

How did the American Revolution unite the colonies? How did the telegraph unite the nation? How was the civil war a test of the nation's unity? How did the transcontinental railroad unite the nation?

• Observe the details in the photograph of the trains coming together in Utah, Student Text, page 190.

• Using the information in the Teacher Resource above, consider the geographic challenges in building the railroad between Omaha and San Francisco. Compare the travel by wagon with travel by train and travel today.

• Enjoy the delightful poem by Bret Harte, *Student Activity Page 33-4.*

• *Student Activity Page 30-1.* Add to the timeline of Inventions: "1869—Transcontinental Railroad."

Suggested Student Notes

Record the words engraved on the gold spike and decorate the page with a drawing.

Supplemental Activities

• Plan a day for the students to wear railroading clothes. The students may dramatize the laying of the last track for the Transcontinental Railroad.

• The students would enjoy a field trip to visit a railroad museum.

Chapter 34
The Automobile
3-4 Days

> **Leading Idea**
>
> ### God prepares men with the interests and ideas to accomplish great tasks.
>
> Student Text, pages 191-193

● "The 'horseless carriage,' as the automobile was first called in America, was just that; a strongly built buggy with solid rubber tires and a one-cylinder gasoline engine geared to the rear axle by a bicycle chain. . . so motor vehicle designs changed slowly from those of carriages. First you had the 'runabout' steered by a tiller; then you added a 'tonneau' with a rear-opening door to make a 'touring car.' Better springs and pneumatic tires made the riding less rough; a canvas top and side-curtains protected passengers from rain; and by the end of World War I the average speed of cars had so increased that the public demanded a hardtop 'limousine,' 'sedan,' or 'cabriolet'.

"... In America... the automobile was an imported toy, a plaything of the rich, disliked because it was smelly, noisy, and frightened horses.... Theodore Roosevelt wrote in 1905 that he had taken but two 'auto rides' during his presidency and would take no more, because on the last one his chauffeur had been held up for speeding, which created undesirable publicity. Woodrow Wilson, president of Princeton in 1907, cautioned the students against indulging in the 'snobbery' of motoring. 'Nothing,' he said, 'has spread socialistic feelings in this country more' than this 'picture of the arrogance of wealth.'"[134]

Samuel Eliot Morison, *The Oxford History of the American People*

● "... from the time I saw that road engine as a boy of twelve right forward to today, my great interest has been in making a machine that would travel the roads. Driving to town I always had a pocket full of trinkets—nuts, washers, and odds and ends of machinery. Often I took a broken watch and tried to put it together. When I was thirteen I managed for the first time to put a watch together so that it would keep time. By the time I was fifteen I could do almost anything in watch repairing—although my tools were of the crudest. There is an immense amount to be learned simply by tinkering with things. It is not possible to learn from books how everything is made—and a real mechanic ought to know how nearly everything is made. Machines are to a mechanic what books are to a writer. He gets ideas from them, and if he has any brains he will apply these ideas.

"From the beginning I never could work up much interest in the labour of farming. I wanted to have some thing to do with machinery. My father was not entirely in sympathy with my bent toward mechanics. He thought that I ought to be a farmer. When I left school at seventeen and became an apprentice in the machine shop. . . I was all but given up for lost. . ."[135]

Henry Ford, *My Life and Work*

For Reflection and Reasoning

● What machines use electricity for their power? Steam? Gasoline?

● What did Henry Ford do to make his farm work easier? What character quality does that show?

● How old are you? Do you think you could take apart a watch and repair it?

● What inspired Henry to think about developing engines?

● What is an apprentice?

● What occupation did Henry Ford's father have? Did his father approve of Henry's interest in engines? Why did Henry feel he must work on engines, rather than farm? Who had given Henry his talent with engines?

Leading Idea

To be an inventor requires unique character qualities

Student Text, pages 193-195

● "My 'gasoline buggy' was the first and for a long time the only automobile in Detroit. It was considered to be something of a nuisance, for it made a racket and it scared horses. Also it blocked traffic. For if I stopped my machine anywhere in town a crowd was around it before I could start up again. If I left it alone even for a minute some inquisitive person always tried to run it. Finally, I had to carry a chain and chain it to a lamp post whenever I left it anywhere. . . ."[136]

Henry Ford, *My Life and Work*

● "No man exceeds Thomas A. Edison in broad vision and understanding. I met him first many years ago when I was with the Detroit Edison Company— probably about 1887 or thereabouts. . . . I was then working on my gasoline engine, and most people, including all of my associates in the electrical company, had taken pains to tell me that time spent on a gasoline engine was time wasted—that the power of the future was to be electricity. These criticisms had not made any impression on me. I was working ahead with all my might. But being in the same room with Edison suggested to me that it would be a good idea to find out if the master of electricity thought it was going to be the only power in the future. So, after Mr. Edison had finished his address, I managed to catch him alone for a moment. I told him what I was working on.

"At once he was interested. He is interested in every search for new knowledge. And then I asked him if he thought that there was a future for the internal combustion engine. He answered something in this fashion:

"'Yes, there is a big future for any light-weight engine that can develop a high horsepower and be self-contained. No one kind of motive power is ever going to do all the work of the country. We do not know what electricity can do, but I take for granted that it cannot do everything. Keep on with your engine. If you can get what you are after, I can see a great future.'

"That is characteristic of Edison. He was the central figure in the electrical industry, which was then young and enthusiastic. The rank and file of the electrical men could see nothing ahead but electricity, but their leader could see with crystal clearness that no one power could do all the work of the country. I suppose that is why he was the leader.

"Such was my first meeting with Edison. I did not see him again until many years after—until our motor had been developed and was in production.

He remembered perfectly our first meeting. Since then we have seen each other often. He is one of my closest friends, and we together have swapped many an idea."[137]

Henry Ford, *My Life and Work*

For Reflection and Reasoning

● Review: Why did Henry Ford not want to farm? What God-given interests did he have? How did his interests prepare him to become an inventor?

● What character does it take to be an inventor? How did Henry Ford display those characteristics?

● Why did Henry Ford want to work for the Edison Illuminating Company? Besides learning about electricity, why was the job important for his family?

● How did Clara Ford support her husband's efforts?

● Why were automobiles called "horseless carriages"? What does the prefix "quad" mean? Why did Henry Ford call his automobile a quadricycle? Did the early cars look more like bicycles than automobiles do today?

● Can you imagine streets without cars? How would they be different from the streets today?

● Why do you suppose Henry Ford's father would not ride in the quadricycle?

● Review: What great contribution did Thomas Edison make? Henry Ford and Thomas Edison became good friends. Why might this have happened?

● *Student Activity Page 34-1.* Students identify the character qualities needed by an inventor. Consider the following:
    Imaginative
    Steadfast
    Initiative
    Resourceful
    Enthusiastic
How did Henry Ford demonstrate each?

Cultivating Student Mastery

1. When did Henry Ford first become interested in making a machine which would travel on the road?

2. How did Henry Ford learn what was necessary to accomplish his goal?

3. How did Henry Ford reveal the character of an inventor?

Leading Idea

An automobile that every family could afford

Student Text, pages 195-196

● "Although there were cheap American cars before Ford's, there was no rugged, all-purpose car selling for less than

$1500, until Henry Ford brought out his Model T in 1908. Six years later he invented the assembly-line method of mass production; and a few months after that, to the astonishment of the world and the indignation of other employers, Ford announced a minimum wage of $5 a day for his workers. The Model T 'tin lizzie' or 'flivver,' as it was nicknamed sold over half a million in 1916, two million in 1923, and by 1927 when its production ceased (Ford having unwillingly substituted the slightly more sophisticated Model A), the staggering total of 15 million cars had been sold. . . .

"Model T was the car that revolutionized American life. The farmer now had a vehicle that he could use for pleasure, with a pickup truck attachment to carry crops to market; or, with rear wheel jacked up and a homemade attachment, saw wood, fill the silo, do everything (it was said) but wash the dishes. The skilled worker in town or city could live miles from his job and drive his family into the country after supper or on Sundays. . . ."[138]

Samuel Eliot Morison, *The Oxford History of the American People*

For Reflection and Reasoning

● The first automobiles were built one by one. This process took a long time. Why did it make the automobile expensive?

● What was Ford's dream? How could every family afford an automobile?

● Describe the process of mass production. Why is it called "mass production"? What are the benefits of this means of manufacturing? What are the disadvantages?

● How did the way people lived in America change when each family had their own automobile?

● *Student Activity Page 30-1.* Add to the timeline of Inventions: "1896—Henry Ford—Automobile."

Suggested Student Notes

Student Activity Page 34-2. In one paragraph, students may summarize the dream and accomplishments of Henry Ford. Or, students may record the following selected sentences from the *Student Text*:

> **"Ford's dream was to produce a car which could be the universal car. His idea was successful and soon Americans were driving their automobiles everywhere. Henry Ford's determination and his God-given talent for developing machines brought great change in America."**

Supplemental Activities

● A number of children's biographies are available on the life of Henry Ford. One delightful book is *Henry Ford, Young Man with Ideas*, originally published as part of the Childhood of Famous American Series by Bobbs-Merrill Co., and reprinted by Aladdin Books.

● A field trip to an automobile museum would help the students understand the automobile's development. The Henry Ford Museum in Dearborn, Michigan, would be of particular interest.

● Students may assemble a model of a Model T or Model A.

Chapter 35
A Dream to Fly
5-6 Days

Leading Idea

A family that encouraged learning and imagination

Student Text, pages 197-198

● "Orville was born in Dayton, Ohio, and Wilbur in Millville, Indiana, and their education was obtained in the public schools. They were sons of a bishop, himself an inventor, and grew up in a mentally-stimulating atmosphere. In 1896 the young men began their study of aeronautics, but did not allow these interests to interfere with the work in their bicycle shop in Dayton. Both men were reserved and modest and seldom spoke of their ambitions and plans, and consequently received little encouragement. . . ."[139]

The World Book

● ". . . we were lucky enough to grow up in a home environment where there was always much encouragement to children to pursue intellectual interests; to investigate whatever aroused curiosity. In a different kind of environment our curiosity might have been nipped long before it could have borne fruit."[140]

Orville Wright

● "Milton was a firm believer in the educational value of toys, and took genuine delight in selecting things that would stimulate the imagination of his children and inspire their curiosity. One such gift, purchased during the course of a church trip and presented to Wilbur, then eleven, and Orville, seven. . .would prove particularly significant. It was a toy helicopter designed by the French aeronautical experimenter Alphonse Penaud.

"Milton paid perhaps 50 cents for this variant of Europe's oldest mechanical toy — and the world's first powered flying machine. . . From the time of Leonardo, when portrait painters used the little helicopter to quiet fidgety young sitters, to that day in 1878 when Milton Wright presented the gadget to his sons, rotary-wing toys were to intrigue and inspire generations of children, a few of whom would, as adults, attempt to realize the dream of flight for themselves."[141]

Tom D. Crouch, *The Bishop's Boys: A Life of Wilbur and Orville Wright*

● "Both parents were great believers in formal and informal education alike. Their home was filled with books, and the children were encouraged to read at an early age."[142]

Tom D. Crouch, *The Bishop's Boys: A Life of Wilbur and Orville Wright*

For Reflection and Reasoning

● *Student Acitivity Page 35-1.* Label

Indiana, Millville, Ohio, and Dayton.

● Milton and Susan Wright described the

character of their sons, Wilbur and Orville. How did they describe each? What might it have been like to have brothers with those character qualities?

• Many fathers work at jobs close to their homes. What job did Milton Wright have? Why was he gone for long periods of time? How did he teach his children even while he was away? What did he try to teach them?

• Susan Wright was a very imaginative, skilled woman. How did she show her imagination? What did she do if she needed something that she did not have? What if she had a household tool that was broken? What special memory did Wilbur and Orville have of their mother?

• How did Father and Mother Wright work to make sure their children were well educated?

• Wilbur and Orville Wright were very creative with their chores and play. What imaginative things did they do to earn money? To make their chores easier?

• Orville and Wilbur Wright were born into a family that encouraged creativity, imagination, and hard work. All those character qualities would someday be needed for the task God wanted them to complete. How does their childhood reveal God's Providential preparation of these two brothers?

• *Student Activity Page 35-2.* Enter dates

The Development of Flying Machines and the Lives of Wilbur & Orville Wright	
The Development of Flight	**Wilbur and Orville Wright**
1480's — Leonardo da Vinci studied the flight of birds and designed many flying machines	
1783 — Montgolfier brothers constructed the first lighter-than air balloon	
1849 — Sir George Cayley designed a three-wing glider that lifted a person off the ground	
	April 16, 1867 — Wilbur Wright born
1884 — The first completely controllable airship was built by Charles Renard & Arthur Krebs	
	August 19, 1871 — Orville Wright born
1891 — Otto Lilienthal built the first practical glider for long flights	
	1892 — Wright Brothers bicycle shop opened
	1899 — First kite/glider experiments
1900 — Count Ferdinand Zeppelin's airship flies	1900 — First experiments at Kitty Hawk
	1901 — Glider experiments
	1902 — Successful glider experiments
1903 — Orville and Wilbur Wright developed the first self-propelled airplane that had a pilot, power, control, and could fly.	

for the birth of Wilbur and Orville Wright. This *Student Activity Page* will be completed in later lessons.

Cultivating Student Mastery

1. Father Wright believed that children should earn their own spending money. What inventive ways did Wilbur and Orville use to earn money as children?

2. God planned for Wilbur and Orville Wright to invent a wonderful machine. How did their childhood prepare them for that task?

Leading Idea

Two young men with a dream

Student Text, pages 198-200

● "Obviously a single toy cannot shape the course of a life. Still, the little helicopter that Milton Wright brought home to Cedar Rapids in the fall of 1878 made a very big impression on his two youngest sons. Orville described the result in court testimony offered in 1912: 'Our first interest [in flight] began when we were children. Father brought home to us a small toy actuated by a rubber spring which would lift itself into the air. We built a number of copies of this toy, which flew successfully . . . But when we undertook to build the toy on a much larger scale it failed to work so well.'"[143]

Tom D. Crouch, *The Bishop's Boys: A Life of Wilbur and Orville Wright*

● "Home was ever a magic circle for the brothers and contained the best company and most pleasing recreation. They did not see the use of visiting other homes, since they had one of their own that was entirely adequate."[144]

John R. McMahon, *The Wright Brothers: Fathers of Flight*

● ". . . Nightly after supper, at the dining room table, Wilbur and Orville toiled enthusiastically with the tools of carving and engraving. This was one of the activities which kept them at home evenings and the scene was a pattern of the family life. There was animated chat, considerable litter, a mother who glanced up from her knitting or darning to smile in sympathy on her children's efforts or to act as friendly umpire."[145]

John R. McMahon, *The Wright Brothers: Fathers of Flight*

● "The boyish indoor amusements were in effect part of a course in draftsmanship and woodworking that became a prime advantage in future creation. Thus they learned to draw plans to scale, and to execute them. . . This was a profitable home schooling which most of the predecessors in aerial experiment missed. A home workshop does not make every one an inventor yet it develops and edges wits."[146]

John R. McMahon, *The Wright Brothers: Fathers of Flight*

● Orville Wright spoke of his and his brother's early interest in flight, January 13, 1920: "In 1896 we read in the daily papers or in some of the magazines, of the experiments of Otto Lilienthal, who was making some gliding flights from the top of a small hill in Germany. . . . We began looking for books pertaining to flight."[147]

Orville Wright

For Reflection and Reasoning

• Review: What character qualities did Wilbur and Orville Wright learn in childhood?

• What sports did Wilbur and Orville enjoy? Why did they need strong minds and bodies to perform those games?

• How did the family show their love and concern for Wilbur after his accident? How did God use Wilbur's accident to help guide the two brothers toward their dream?

• What first interested Wilbur and Orville in flying machines?

• Wilbur and Orville supported themselves through their printing company. What new business did they try in 1892? Why were they so successful at their new work? What is a mechanic?

• Review the names and accomplishments of other men who worked to invent flying machines. Cut out the timeline, *Student Activity Page 35-3*, and glue it into the box on *Student Activity Page 35-2*. Discuss how God allowed other men to make discoveries and solve problems of flight at the same time as the Wright brothers. How did Orville and Wilbur learn from the work, successes, and failures of others?

• What problems did the brothers consider as they experimented with gliders?

Suggested Student Notes

Wilbur and Orville Wright had a dream to invent a flying machine.

God's Providence:
• **Family encouraged imagination**
• **Father gave them a flying toy**
• **Wilbur's illness provided time to read about other men's work on flight**

Leading Idea

Hard work and determination overcome many obstacles

Student Text, pages 200-202

• "Man Triumphs. It was in 1900 that Wilbur and Orville Wright began their experiments. So quietly did they work, down among the North Carolina sands, or near their home in Ohio, that four years after their first successful flight a year-book stated that 'the mere fact and but little description has ever been recorded.' In France, Santos-Dumont in 1906 flew 655 feet and Farman in 1907 covered 2,530 feet, yet the Wrights, who had stopped experiments in 1905 to give attention to their patents, were content with modestly announcing that in that year they had flown twenty-four miles! In their first secret flight, in 1903, they had traveled 852 feet, just nine days after the last spectacular failure of Langley's aerodrome."[148]

The World Book

• "Flying then was on a par with spiritism. It had no scientific basis or repute. The literature was meager, though inflated with words and cloudy guesses. Perhaps the lack of substance kept the brothers hungry for more; they tried to find something to put their teeth into, and they now took turns in reading the books aloud on winter evenings at home. After reading, they talked, argued, dreamed, and added cloudy guesses of their own to the fog-enveloped, illusory and haunting topic."[149]

John R. McMahon, *The Wright Brothers: Fathers of Flight*

● "Having set out with absolute faith in the existing scientific data, we were driven to doubt one thing after another

till, finally, after two years of experiments, we cast it aside, and decided to rely entirely on our own investigations."[150]

Wilbur Wright

● "These remarkable brothers have achieved their results entirely through their own work; their machine is built on data and formulae established by their own experiments, most of the text books being found to be so full of inaccuracies as to be practically useless to them."[151]

C. S. Rolls

For Reflection and Reasoning

● The Wright brothers began their experiments in flight by working with gliders. What is the difference between a glider and an airplane? What problems did the Wrights have to solve as they developed and improved their gliders?

● What place did Wilbur choose for their test flights in the gliders? Why did he choose it? How did he show diligence in choosing that location?

● *Student Activity Page 35-1.* Students may label North Carolina and Kitty Hawk on the map. Consider the distance between the Wrights' home in Dayton and their testing area in North Carolina. How did they travel? How did the distance between the two places make the tests and experiments more difficult?

● At the end of their glider testing in 1900, the young men were excited to continue their work. By the end of their flight tests in 1901, the two had faced so many problems that they were quite discouraged and almost gave up their experiments. What kept them working even when they faced so many difficulties?

● When the two brothers began to build their new glider in 1902, what challenging

tasks did they choose? Why? How did they become more excited as they did their work? Why were they happy?

● By the end of their glider testing in 1902, what had Wilbur and Orville proven? What were they ready to do?

● The Student Text refers to Wilbur and Orville "arguing". Often when the two brothers tried to solve some problem with their gliders or airplane, they would have two different ideas about how to solve the difficulty. Each would "argue" his point, trying to convince the other that his answer to the problem was the best. Both were so good at expressing themselves, that sometimes by the end of the discussion, they would find that they had actually switched sides in the "argument". All this arguing was very good-natured and thoroughly enjoyed by both men.

● How did Wilbur and Orville Wright show the following character traits as they worked to make their dream of a flying machine come true?
Imagination
Self-reliance
Determination

● *Student Activity Page 35-2.* Enter the events on the timeline for the years 1892-1902.

Cultivating Student Mastery

1. Students may prepare a short essay describing the character of Wilbur and Orville Wright. Consider the following questions:

- How was their character developed?
- How did their character help them reach their goals?
- How did their character help them overcome difficulties in their work?

Leading Idea

Success at last — The flying machine actually flew!

Student Text, pages 202-204

● Telegram from Orville Wright at Kitty Hawk, to Bishop Milton Wright, Dec. 17, 1903: "Success four flights Thursday morning all against twenty-one mile wind started from level with engine power alone average speed through air thirty-one miles longest 57 seconds inform press home Christmas."[152]

● "Man flew for the first time on Dec. 17, 1903, when Wilbur and Orville Wright launched themselves into the air at Kitty Hawk, North Carolina. They discovered the secret of flight and their principles are embodied in every practical airplane known in the world today. They are the immortal pioneers who lifted man from the earth and gave him another dimension to move in with freedom surpassing that of the birds."[153]
John R. McMahon, *The Wright Brothers: Fathers of Flight*

● Part of Wilbur Wright's statement to Associated Press, Jan. 5, 1904: "Only those who are acquainted with practical aeronautics can appreciate the difficulties of attempting the first trials of a flying machine in a twenty-five mile gale. As winter was already well set in, we should have postponed our trials to a more favorable season, but for the fact that we were determined, before returning home, to know whether the machine possessed sufficient power to fly, sufficient strength to withstand the shocks of landings, and sufficient capacity of control to make flight safe in boisterous winds, as well as in calm air. When these points had been definitely established, we at once packed our goods and returned home, knowing that the age of the flying machine had come at last."[154]

For Reflection and Reasoning

● Review: With what type of machine did Orville and Wilbur first experiment? How was it different from an airplane?

● What problems did the brothers have to solve to create an airplane that would fly?

● When Orville and Wilbur left for Kitty Hawk in September, 1903, how did they show their determination to make their dream come true?

● What new problems did the brothers have to face as they assembled the flying machine and prepared to test it?

● The Student Text does not describe the many difficulties which the men faced in their camp at Kitty Hawk, North

Carolina. One year the mosquito swarms forced them to stay covered with blankets at all times to avoid being severely bitten. Other times the cold was so extreme that they had to sleep covered with four or five blankets to keep from freezing. Several times, sandstorms swept across the island, covering everything with sand and stinging their eyes, faces, and any exposed skin with its force. Minor difficulties included a well which would not work and a fire that filled their sleeping tent with smoke. Yet, the two brothers endured all these difficulties and continued their work without discouragement.

• At the time of the first successful flight at Kitty Hawk, Orville set up his camera on a tripod, to take photographs of their test flights. In the excitement of the liftoff of the Flyer, one of the local men who had come to watch squeezed the shutter button. The picture which he captured on film that day has become famous as it recorded for all time the first successful flight of a flying machine. See Student Text, page 203.

• *Student Activity Page 35-2.* Record the final entry on the timeline.

The flying machine brought changes in the world.

Leading Idea

Student Text, page 204

• C. S. Rolls wrote after his flight of Oct. 8, 1908: ". . . after experience with every form of locomotion including cycle and motor racing, a voyage in a dirigible of the French Army and over 130 trips in an ordinary balloon there is nothing so fascinating as flying. It gives one an entirely new sense of life. The power of flight is as a fresh gift from the Creator, the greatest treasure yet given to Man and one, I believe, destined to work great changes in human life as we know it today."[155]

Russell Ash, *The Wright Brothers*

• C. S. Rolls' impression of the Wrights' achievement after flying with Wilbur in 1908: "Yet the work of these two men will, I believe, in time bring about one of the greatest changes the world has ever seen, perhaps about as great as the telegraph, the telephone or the railway train."[156]

Russell Ash, *The Wright Brothers*

• Major B. F. S. Baden-Powell, President of the Aeronautical Society of Great Britain wrote in the New York Herald, Oct. 6, 1908: "If only some of our people in England could see or imagine what Mr. Wright is now doing I am certain it would give them a terrible shock. A conquest of the air by any nation means more than the average man is willing to admit or even think about. That Wilbur Wright is the possessor of a power which controls the fate of nations is beyond dispute."[157]

Russell Ash, *The Wright Brothers*

For Reflection and Reasoning

• Review: What changes were made in communication across the nation by the

telegraph and telephone? Who invented each?

• Review: What changes were made in

transportation by the steamboat? Who made that invention? How did the railroad and automobile bring changes in transportation? How did these inventions unite the nation?

● Review: What dream did Wilbur and Orville Wright have? When did they accomplish their dream?

● *Student Activity Page 30-1.* Add to the timeline of Inventions: "1903—Wright Brothers—First Flight".

● Have you ever made a long trip by automobile? How much time did you spend driving? If you went the same distance by airplane, would it take less time? Why is flying a faster way to get from one place to another?

● What changes did the Wright brothers' success in flight bring about in the world?

How do we benefit from their work?

● What great accomplishments in flight have men made since the time of the Wright brothers?

● How do we know that Orville and Wilbur were not interested in the praise of men?

Cultivating Student Mastery

1. How long did Orville and Wilbur Wright work on their invention?

2. How much of the Wright Flyer did Orville and Wilbur make themselves? What does this show about their character?

3. How did Orville and Wilbur get the money for their invention?

Supplemental Activities

● Two poets recorded the excitement of the first successful flight by the Wright brothers. Students would enjoy reading one of those poems:
  · "Prelude to Icarus", written by John W. Andrews in 1936.
  · "The Wrights' Biplane", by Robert Frost.

● For additional reading on the Wright brothers, the younger students would enjoy the following biographies:
  · *Wilbur and Orville Wright: Boys with Wings,* by Augusta Stevenson, Childhood of Famous Americans Series, published by Bobbs-Merrill Company, 1959.
  · *The Sled The Brothers Made,* by Nancy Kelton, published by Raintree Editions, 1977.

● Recommended biographies for older students:
  · *The Wright Brothers at Kitty Hawk,* by Donald J. Sobol, published by Scholastic Inc., 1961.
  · *The Wright Brothers: Pioneers of American Aviation,* by Quentin Reynolds, published by Random House, 1950.

Chapter 36
The World at War
5-6 Days

● "The World at War" serves as a brief introduction to World War I and II. Further study will be given to the 20th Century in a later volume of *The Mighty Works of God.*

Leading Idea

The World at War

Student Text, pages 205-207

● Webster stated that *neutral* is "Not engaged on either side; not taking an active part with either of contending parties."

● "Of events in that quarter of the globe, [Europe] with which we have so much intercourse, and from which we derive our origin, we have always been anxious and interested spectators. The citizens of the United States cherish sentiments the most friendly, in favor of the liberty and happiness of their fellow men on that side of the Atlantic. In the wars of the European powers, in matters relating to themselves, we have never taken any part, nor does it comport with our policy so to do. It is only when our rights are invaded or seriously menaced, that we resent injuries, or make preparation for our defence. With the movements in this hemisphere, we are, of necessity, more immediately connected. . . ."

The Monroe Doctrine

● Webster defined *armistice* as "a truce".

For Reflection and Reasoning

● Review: What fruits of liberty were enjoyed by Americans? Use Chapters 30-35 to consider: How did liberty enable Americans to improve their way of living? What questions had been asked and answered? How were patience and diligence necessary for inventors?

● Review: What is government? What is God's plan for civil government?

● How did the war in Europe begin? What does it mean to "declare war" on another nation? What nations joined with Germany? Against what nations were they fighting? If the European nations could not defend their liberty, they would be controlled against their will.

● Note the path of the German army through Belgium and into France.

● What does it mean to be neutral during

a war? Who was the United States President during the war? Why did the United States want to stay neutral?

• In 1823, the United States adopted the Monroe Doctrine. It declared we would not take part in wars between European countries. It stated that the United States would only enter into conflict with nations from across the ocean if the United States was threatened. What actions against America caused the beginning of preparations for war?

• What event finally drew America into the war? Who were the Allies?

• What is an Armistice? November 11 was observed for many years as Armistice Day, in honor of the heroes of World War I. In 1953, this observance was changed to Veterans' Day to honor the soldiers of later wars.

• What is a relief effort? How did America show concern for families and children of Europe who suffered during the war?

• Herbert Hoover later became President of the United States. More of his life will be studied in a later volume of *The Mighty Works of God.*

• *Student Activity Page 36-1.* Label Germany, Italy, and Austria-Hungary and outline countries with one color. Label the Allied nations: France, Russia, and Great Britain. Outline them with a different color.

Cultivating Student Mastery

1. How were the Germans surprised when the United States entered the war?

2. How did the war change after the United States joined the Allies?

3. How long did the United States fight in World War I?

Leading Idea	*Americans taken by surprise*
	Student Text, pages 207-208

For Reflection and Reasoning

• Review: How did World War I end? Were all of the Germans pleased with the Armistice?

• Adolf Hitler was elected Chancellor by the people of Germany. What was Hitler's goal?

• How did the leaders of Germany, Japan, and Italy plan to control a great empire? How did they begin to work toward their goal?

• Why did Japan want to involve the United States in the war? How did they cause that to happen?

• Using a globe, locate Hawaii. Note the relationship of Japan, Hawaii, and the western shore of the United States. At the time of World War II, Hawaii was a U. S. territory, not a state. If an enemy could gain control of Hawaii, how would that put the mainland of the United States at risk?

• Note the picture of the bombing of the USS Shaw at Pearl Harbor, on page 208 of the Student Text. What losses did the United States suffer in the surprise attack at Pearl Harbor, December 7, 1941?

● Review: During the American Revolutionary War and the War of 1812, how did troops move? How did the army move supplies?

What invention changed the method of moving troops in the Civil War?

● In World War I, troops had moved and attacked only on land. What invention made World War II different? How?

● *Student Activity Page 36-2.* Title the page, "Remembering Pearl Harbor, December 7, 1941". The students may list the losses suffered at Pearl Harbor, or summarize how the Americans were taken by surprise.

● *Student Activity Page 36-3.* Label Pacific Ocean, Japan, Hawaii, and United States.

Cultivating Student Mastery

1. Why did the Japanese bomb the United States base at Pearl Harbor? Why did that attack force the United States to enter the war?

2. What inventions were important in World War II?

3. How did military leaders communicate? Why?

Anticipating the Enemy

Leading Idea

Student Text, pages 209-210

● "Less than six months after their victory at Pearl Harbor, the Japanese sent forth an enormous, combat-seasoned fleet of eighty-eight surface warships with the dual mission of capturing Midway atoll and luring the remains of the weakened U.S. Pacific Fleet to their destruction. . . .

"But events did not conform to the Japanese pattern. Forewarned through superior cryptanalysis and radio intelligence, American naval forces much inferior numerically to the Japanese. . . but superbly led and manned, sped past Midway and were waiting on the enemy's flank.

"The result was by no means a foregone conclusion. The Japanese spearhead held the veteran carriers *Akagi, Kaga, Hiryu,* and *Soryu,* under the command of Vice Admiral Chuichi Nagumo. This was the admiral and four of the six carriers which had attacked Pearl Harbor on December 7, and since then the Nagumo task force had scored one victory after another in the south Pacific and Indian Oceans."[158]

Gordon W. Prange, *Miracle at Midway*

For Reflection and Reasoning

● Review: Who controls the battle?

● Review: What European countries began World War II? Why?

● Review: What major event drew America into the war? Why did Japan attack Pearl Harbor?

● How did individual nations communicate with their military commanders? How did they protect their communications so the enemy would not know their plans?

● How did the Americans know that Japan was planning a major attack? What did they not know? How did they "trick" the Japanese into revealing their target?

● Why did Japan want to attack Hawaii or Midway?

● *Student Activity Page 36-4.* Write a summary of Japan's plan. Begin to list the Providential events which changed the results of the battle. The *Student Activity Page* will be completed in a later lesson.

Leading Idea

A miracle at Midway

Student Text, pages 210-212

● "Nagumo, his carrier captains, and his airmen fought skillfully and bravely at Midway as flight after flight of American bombers struck impotently. Then, suddenly, superb command decision, precision dive bombing and a pinch or two of luck all came together. When the battle ended, Japan had lost her four carriers, a heavy cruiser, and over 300 aircraft. Yet the battle could have gone the other way, and even so, the United States lost one carrier, *Yorktown,* and a destroyer, *Hammann.*

"Events at Midway cast serious doubt upon the popular contention that, had the Japanese not achieved surprise at Pearl Harbor, they would have been open to almost certain defeat. This time the U.S. Pacific Fleet knew the Japanese were coming, almost to the minute when they would strike, where and in what strength. American ships were in the open sea, free to maneuver and with the advantage of surprise. Nevertheless, the results were such a narrow squeak that we believe the title *Miracle at Midway* is not so much alliterative as exactly factual. Land-based bombing proved totally ineffectual and carrier-based efforts equally so until the last-minute linking up and successful marksmanship of the dive bombers. In view of the fact that six months of war had passed since Pearl Harbor, with consequent combat seasoning on the part of commanders, ships and crews, one cannot help but suspect that, had the U.S. Pacific Fleet sortied to meet Nagumo's task force on December 7, results might have been just as bad if not worse. This was the opinion of Admiral Nimitz, who frankly considered it 'God's mercy' that Admiral Husband E. Kimmel's ships were at their moorings instead of on the deep Pacific.

"In some ways, Midway was the reverse image of Pearl Harbor. This time the story was one of Japanese overconfidence, careless planning, slipshod training and contempt for the enemy; of American cool-headedness, ingenuity, and intelligence well acted upon. At the time, the nation rejoiced that Pearl Harbor had been at least partially avenged. Yet Midway was much more than that; it is generally conceded to have been the turning point in the Pacific war. . . ."[159]
Gordon W. Prange, *Miracle at Midway*

For Reflection and Reasoning

● Review: What was Japan's plan? How had the Americans learned of the plan?

● How did the American ships keep the Japanese from knowing of their preparations? Could this be accomplished in a war today? Why?

• The Japanese had three brand new battleships. Why did Commander Yamamoto decide not to use them in the battle of Midway?

• Instead of surprising the Americans at Midway when the Japanese began their attack — what happened?

• What change of plans did Nagumo make when the Japanese pilots spotted the American fleet? How did this change of plans help the Americans? Taking the time to load a different type of bomb delayed the planes from leaving the carriers and provided better targets.

• On *Student Activity Page 36-4*, continue to identify the Providential events which changed the results of the battle.

• Review: See *Student Activity Page 19-3*. Note how a series of small events were used by God to bring forth the turning point in the Revolutionary War.

• As in the Revolutionary War, how did a series of small events produce a turning point in World War II? How is this an example of Divine Providence?

Supplemental Activities

• *Student Activity Page 36-5*. Students may decode the message.

• Armistice Day, later called Veterans Day, has been a special time of honoring the soldiers who have fought to preserve liberty in America. The Unknown Soldier was buried in the Tomb at Arlington Cemetery November 11, 1921. Students might enjoy researching the history of the Tomb of the Unknown Soldier at Arlington Cemetery.

Chapter 37
"In God We Trust"
1-2 Days

● *Motto* is defined as: "1. A sentence, phrase, or word inscribed on something as appropriate to or indicative of its character or use. 2. A short expression of a guiding principle."[160]

For Reflection and Reasoning

● Review: When was the *Star-Spangled Banner* written? By whom?

● Sing the national anthem. See *Student Activity Page 29-1.*

● In the last stanza of the Star-Spangled Banner, what did Francis Scott Key state as our nation's motto? What is a motto? During his lifetime, upon Whom did the American people depend? How did they show their dependence upon God?

● In 1956, what motto did Congress approve for the United States?

● Look at some coins or currency to see the motto.

● Answer the questions from the Student Text:
   · What does it mean to say, "In God We Trust"?
   · Who controls and directs the events of history?
   · Who decides the victor in the battles?
   · Who protects and provides for this nation?

● What do many Americans today not understand? What must America do?

● What questions must we ask ourselves? What answer can you give?

● How does the study of Divine Providence in our nation's history help us to say, "In God we trust"?

● Sing *My Country 'tis of Thee*, particularly noting the words of the first and last verses.

● *Student Activity Page 37-1.* Students may copy the final phrases of the second verse of the Star-Spangled Banner and color the flag and motto.

    'Tis the star-spangled banner;
    Oh, long may it wave
    O'er the land of the free,
    And the home of the brave.

Cultivating Student Mastery

Students may answer the questions found in the third paragraph of the Student Text.

Conclusion

1-2 Days

Leading Idea	*Divine Providence*

● As God is timing all events, the individual must learn to trust in His Divine Providence, recognizing God's Hand in all events — past, present, and future. History reveals countless examples of individuals who rested in His Divine Providence. History also reveals countless examples of individuals who sought to fulfill their own plans, not recognizing that God directs and controls the events of history. Whose plan overrules in the affairs of men and nations?

The American Christian has great liberty to learn of Divine Providence and see the evidence of His Hand working in the lives of men and nations. With that liberty comes a great responsibility to remember His mighty works and acknowledge Him.

For Reflection and Reasoning

● Read Psalm 33:12 and Proverbs 14:34. What do these verses teach about nations? What is righteousness? In order for a nation to be blessed, who or what must be righteous?

The United States is a representative republic. How does the character of the leaders reflect the character of the people? If the United States is to have righteous leaders, who must first be righteous? If the laws are to be righteous, who must first be righteous? For God to bless the United States of America, the people and the leaders must turn their hearts to His Word and be willing to be guided by the Scriptures.

● What is the responsibility of civil government? See Chapter 4. If the civil government is to fulfill its Biblical responsi-

bility, then who must know what the Bible teaches concerning what is good and what is evil? Should it be the leaders? The people? Both? How can each person in America take his responsibility?

● Read Psalm 105:5a. How do God's marvelous works show His Providence? Why is this history series called *The Mighty Works of God*? Why is it important to remember God's works?

● Review: What is Providence? Review page 1 of the Student Text. Why is this book called *Divine Providence*? Review the student notebook to remember individuals and events which reveal God's care, God's control, God's plan, God's timing.

● If we believe that God has a plan for our nation, will it make a difference in

223

our lives? If we believe that God directs and controls events in our lives, how will it affect our actions?

• Sing songs which the students have enjoyed during the year.

• *Student Activity Page 37-2.* The students may identify key words which relate to Divine Providence.

Clues:
1. What does God command us to remember? (Psalm 78:7)
2. What do we call God's working throughout history?

Clues:
3. (Across) God has a _____ for every individual.
3. (Down) What God gives us is His

_____.
4. God gives _____ to men and nations who obey Him. (See SAP 1-1)

Part IV

APPENDIX

Endnotes

[1] Emma Willard, *History of the United States, or Republic of America,* 1845, in *The Christian History of the Constitution of the United States of America: Christian Self-Government* (San Francisco: Foundation for American Christian Education, 1966), page 405.

[2] Rev. S. W. Foljambe, "The Hand of God in American History", 1876, in *The Christian History of the American Revolution: Consider and Ponder* (San Francisco: Foundation for American Christian Education, 1976), page 47.

[3] Ibid., page 46.

[4] Verna M. Hall, *The Christian History of the Constitution of the United States of America: Christian Self-Government* (San Francisco: Foundation for American Christian Education, 1966), page 6A.

[5] Katherine Dang, "Geography: An American Christian Approach", in *A Guide to American Christian Education for the Home and School* (Camarillo: American Christian History Institute, 1987), page 272.

[6] Foljambe, page 47.

[7] Katherine Dang, *Universal History, Volume I: Ancient History—Law Without Liberty* (Oakland: Katherine Dang, 2000), pages 6-7.

[8] Washington Irving, *Life of George Washington, Volume 2.* (New York: G. P. Putnam & Co., 1855), pages 476-487.

[9] Ibid., pages 500-506.

[10] James Madison, "Property", 1792, in *The Christian History of the Constitution of the United States of America: Christian Self-Government* (San Francisco: Foundation for American Christian Education, 1966), page 248A.

[11] Verna M. Hall, *The Christian History of the American Revolution: Consider and Ponder* (San Francisco: Foundation for American Christian Education, 1975), page xxvi.

[12] Emma Willard, *Universal History.* (New York: A. S. Barnes & Co., 1848), pages 36, 38.

[13] John Frost, *Pictorial History of the World.* (Hartford: O. D. Case & Co., 1855), page 21.

[14] James B. Rose, *Spiritual Liberty is Causative to Religious and Civil Liberty,* A Tract on America's Christian History and Government. (Granger: Pilgrim Institute and American Christian History Institute).

[15] *Lincoln Library of Essential Information, Volume I,* p. 789.

[16] Newton Marshall Hall and Irving Francis Wood, *The Book of Life, Volume 7* (Chicago: John Rudin & Company, Inc., 1953), page 47.

[17] William Bradford, *Of Plimoth Plantation* (Boston: Wright & Potter Printing Co., 1901), pages 11-13.

[18] Daniel Neal, *The History of the Puritans, Volume I* (New York: Harper & Brothers, 1843), pages 227-232.

[19] H. W. Hoare, *The Evolution of the English Bible* (New York: E.P. Dutton & Co., 1901), page 219.

[20] Ibid., pages 222-223.

[21] Ibid., page 226.

[22] Frank Charles Thompson, "Comprehensive Bible Helps", in *The Thompson Chain Reference Bible.* (Indianapolis: B. B. Kirkbride Bible Co., Inc., 1982), page 181.

[23] Verna M. Hall, *The Christian History of the American Revolution* (San Francisco: Foundation for American Christian Education, 1976), page xxv.

24 *Lincoln Library of Essential Information, Volume II* (Buffalo: The Frontier Press Company, 1926) page 1853.

25 Justin Winsor, *Christopher Columbus* (Boston and New York: Houghton, Mifflin and Company, 1892), pages 91-97.

26 *Encyclopedia Brittanica, Volume XI* (Chicago: The Werner Company, 1893), page 673.

27 *Webster's Seventh New Collegiate Dictionary.* (Springfield: G & C Merriam Company, 1965), page 128.

28 Darold Booton, Jr., *Nathaniel Bowditch — Mathematician and Navigator*, Part II (Mishawaka: Pilgrim Institute) page 1.

29 James E. Morrison, "The Mariner's Astrolabe." Janus. http://www.astrolabes.org/mariner.htm (June 5, 2002).

30 *Lincoln Library of Essential Information, Volume II.* (Buffalo: The Frontier Press Company, 1926) page 1788.

31 Ibid., page 1820.

32 Winsor, pages 85-102.

33 Benson J. Lossing, *A Family History of the United States* (Providence: Murphy & McCarthy, 1881), pages 62-64.

34 Ibid., page 64-65.

35 John Smith, *The Settlement of Jamestown. Old South Leaflets,* No. 167 (Boston: Old South Meeting House), page 9.

36 Lossing, pages 65-67.

37 Ibid., page 67.

38 Ibid., pages 67-68.

39 William Penn, *A Letter from William Penn,* 1683, pages 5-6.

40 Lossing, page 74.

41 Cotton Mather, *Lives of Bradford and Winthrop. Old South Leaflet,* No. 77 (Boston: The Old South Association), page 3.

42 Bradford, pages 11-13.

43 Mather, pages 4-5.

44 Bradford, pages 93-94.

45 Mather, page 5.

46 Bradford, page 109.

47 Lossing, page 78.

48 Mather, pages 5-8.

49 Ibid. page 8.

50 Thomas Armitage, *A History of the Baptists, Volume II,* 1800 (Reprint Watertown: Maranatha Baptist Press, 1976), p. 619.

51 J. W. Wellman, *The Church Polity of the Pilgrims,* 1857 in *The Christian History of the Constitution of the United States of America*, page 147.

52 Lossing, 139-141

53 Ibid., pages 140-141.

54 John Fiske, *The Dutch and Quaker Colonies in America, Volume I* (Boston: Houston, Mifflin and Company, 1899), pages 198-201.

55 Washington Irving, *Knickerbocker's History of New York* in *The Works of Washington Irving, Volume I* (New York: P.F. Collier), page 488.

56 Lossing, pages 141-142.

57 Ibid., page 143

58 Fiske, pages 283-287.

59 Ibid., pages 287-291.

60 Ibid., pages 291-294.

61 Lossing, page 144

62 Richard Frothingham, "The Rise of the Republic", 1890, in *The Christian History of the Constitution of the United States of America: Christian Self-Government* (San Francisco: Foundation for American Christian Education, 1966), pages 344-345.

63 Ibid., page 345.

64 Lossing, pages 232-233.

65 Ibid., page 233.

66 Ibid., pages 234-235.

67 Ibid., pages 234-235.

68 Ibid., pages 235-237.

69 Ibid., pages 227-228.

70 Ibid., pages 237-238.

71 George Bancroft, *History of the United States of America, Volume IV* (Boston: Little, Brown, and Company, 1879), pages 355-356.

72 George Bancroft, *History of the United States of America, Volume V* (Boston: Little, Brown, and Company, 1879), page 553.

73 Lossing, page 226.

74 George Bancroft, *History of the United States of America, Volume V*, pages 165-166.

75 John Fiske, *The American Revolution, Volume I* (Boston and New York: Houghton, Mifflin and Company, 1891), page 205.

76 Ibid., pages 210-212.

77 Ibid., pages 213-215.

78 Penelope Paquette, *The Battle of Saratoga* (unpublished).

79 Ibid.

80 Benson J. Lossing, *The Pictorial Field-Book of the Revolution, Volume I* (New York: Harper & Brothers, Publishers, 1859), page 178.

81 Mark A. Beliles & Stephen K. McDowell, *America's Providential History* (Charlottesville: Providence Foundation, 1992), page 162.

82 Fiske, *The American Revolution, Volume I*, pages 262-268.

83 Benson J. Lossing, *A History of the United States* (New York: James Sheehy, Pub-

lisher, 1881), pages 271-273.

[84] Ibid., page 278.

[85] Fiske, *The American Revolution, Volume I,* pages 281-282.

[86] Lossing, *A History of the United States,* pages 278-279.

[87] Fiske, *The American Revolution, Volume I,* pages 336-337.

[88] Lossing, *The Pictorial Field-Book of the Revolution, Volume I,* pages 86-87.

[89] Lossing, *A History of the United States,* pages 283-284.

[90] Lossing, *A Family History of the United States,* pages 284-285.

[91] Bancroft, *History of the United States of America, Volume V,* pages 213 and 217.

[92] Lossing, *A Family History of the United States,* pages 272-273.

[93] Ibid., page 291.

[94] Ibid., page 285.

[95] Lossing, *The Pictorial Field-Book of The Revolution, Volume II,* page 104.

[96] John Fiske, *The American Revolution, Volume II* (Boston and New York: Houston, Mifflin and Company, 1899), pages 103-105.

[97] Ibid., pages 105-106.

[98] Ibid., pages 106-107.

[99] Benson J. Lossing, *Harpers' Popular Cyclopædia of United States History, Volume I* (New York: Harper & Brothers, Publishers, 1892), pages 68-69.

[100] Fiske, *The American Revolution, Volume II,* page 214.

[101] Lossing, *Harpers' Popular Cyclopædia of United States History, Volume II,* pages 1409-1410.

[102] Benson J. Lossing, *Harpers' Popular Cyclo-pædia of United States History, Volume II* (New York: Harper & Brothers, Publishers, 1893) , pages 1409-1410.

[103] Lossing, *The Pictorial Field-Book of the Revolution, Volume I,* pages 755-756.

[104] Ibid., pages 725-728.

[105] Fiske, *The American Revolution, Volume II,* pages 183-184.

[106] Lossing, *The Pictorial Field-Book of the Revolution, Volume II,* pages 314-315.

[107] Katherine Dang, "American Christian History Curriculum for Senior High School", in *A Guide to American Christian Education for the Home and School* (Camarillo: American Christian History Institute, 1987), page 298.

[108] Mary-Elaine Swanson, *The Education of James Madison: A Model for Today* (Montgomery: The Hoffman Education Center for the Family, 1992), pages 15-16.

[109] Ibid., pages 110-111.

[110] Ibid., page 193.

[111] Madison, page 248A.

[112] D.H. Montgomery, *The Leading Facts of American History* (Boston: Ginn and Company, 1910), page 201.

[113] Lossing, *A Family History of the United States,* page 382.

[114] Ibid., pages 422-423.

[115] Montgomery, page 204.

[116] D.H. Montgomery, *The Leading Facts of American History* (New York: Ginn & Company, 1899), page 204.

[117] Lossing, *A Family History of the United States,* pages 414-415.

[118] Montgomery, pages 206-207.

[119] Ibid., page 224.

[120] Samuel Eliot Morison, *The Oxford History of the American People* (New York: Oxford University Press, 1965), pages 534-535.

[121] *Lincoln Library of Essential Information, Volume II,* page 1999.

[122] Lossing, *A History of the United States,* page 399.

[123] Ibid., page 399.

[124] Daniel Webster, *The Works of Daniel Webster, Volume II* (Boston: Little, Brown and Company, 1856), pages 409-410.

[125] Montgomery, pages 215-216.

[126] Ibid., page 213.

[127] Lossing, *A History of the United States,* pages 456-457.

[128] Montgomery, pages 221-222.

[129] Webster, pages 411-413.

[130] Leonard Everett Fisher, *Tracks Across America* (New York: Holiday House, 1992), pages 48 and 52.

[131] Lieut. William Pittenger, *Daring and Suffer-ing: A History of The Great Railroad Adven-ture* (Philadelphia: J. W. Daughaday, Pub-lisher, 1863), page 72.

[132] Montgomery, pages 336-337.

[133] Ibid., pages 336-337.

[134] Morison, pages 888-889.

[135] Henry Ford, *My Life and Work* (New York: Doubleday, Page Company, 1924), pages 23-24.

[136] Ibid., page 33.

[137] Ibid., pages 234-235.

[138] Morison, pages 889-890.

[139] *The World Book, Volume 10* (Chicago: W. F. Quarrie & Company, 1928) page 6363.

[140] Orville Wright in *The Wright Brothers* (Sussex: Wayland Publishers Limited, 1974), page 10.

[141] Tom D. Crouch, *The Bishop's Boys: A Life of Wilbur and Orville Wright.* (New York: W. W. Norton & Company, 1989), page 56.

142 Ibid., page 57.
143 Ibid., page 57.
144 John R. McMahon, *The Wright Brothers: Fathers of Flight* (Boston: Little, Brown, and Company, 1930), page 41.
145 Ibid., page 47.
146 Ibid., page 48.
147 Orville Wright in *The Wright Brothers,* page 19.
148 *The World Book, Volume 4,* pages 2237-2238.
149 McMahon, page 63.
150 Wilbur Wright in *The Wright Brothers,* page 41.
151 C. S. Rolls, 1908, in *The Wright Brothers,* page 83.
152 McMahon, page 146.

153 Ibid., page 4.
154 Wilbur Wright in *The Wright Brothers,* page 47.
155 Russell Ash, *The Wright Brothers* (East Sussex: Wayland Publishers Limited, 1974), page 68.
156 Rolls, page 83.
157 Major B. F. S. Baden-Powell in *The Wright Brothers,* page 69.
158 Gordon W. Prange, *Miracle at Midway* (New York: Penguin Books, 1982), page xi.
159 Ibid., pages xii-xiii.
160 *Webster's New Collegiate Dictionary* (Springfield: G & C Merriam Company, 1976), page 752.

Bibliography

Armitage, Thomas. *A History of the Baptists,* Volume II, 1800. Reprint Watertown: Maranatha Baptist Press, 1976.

Ash, Russell. *The Wright Brothers.* East Sussex: Wayland Publishers Limited, 1974.

Bancroft, George. *History of the United States of America, Volume IV and V.* Boston: Little, Brown, and Company, 1879.

Beliles, Mark A. and Stephen K. McDowell. *America's Providential History.* Charlottesville: Providence Foundation, 1992.

Booton, Darold, Jr. *Nathaniel Bowditch — Mathematician and Navigator.* Mishawaka: Pilgrim Institute.

Bradford, William. *Of Plimoth Plantation.* Boston: Wright & Potter Printing Co., 1901.

Crouch, Tom D. *The Bishop's Boys: A Life of Wilbur and Orville Wright.* New York: W. W. Norton & Company, 1989

Curtis, George Ticknor. *The Constitution of the United States, and its History,* in *Narrative and Critical History of America, Volume VII.* Boston and New York: Houghton, Mifflin and Company, 1888.

Dang, Katherine. *Universal History, Volume I: Ancient History—Law Without Liberty.* Oakland: Katherine Dang, 2000.

Encyclopædia Britannica, The. Volume XI. Chicago: The Werner Company, 1893.

Famous Adventures and Prison Escapes of the Civil War. New York: The Century Co., 1913.

Fisher, Leonard Everett. *Tracks Across America.* New York: Holiday House, 1992.

Fiske, John. *The American Revolution,* Volumes I and II. Boston and New York: Houghton, Mifflin and Company, 1899.
The Dutch and Quaker Colonies in America, Volume I. Boston: Houghton, Mifflin and Company, 1899.

Ford, Henry. *My Life and Work.* New York: Doubleday, Page & Company, 1924.

Fritz, Jean. *The Great Little Madison.* New York: G. P. Putnam's Sons, 1989.

Frost, John. *Pictorial History of the World.* Hartford: O. D. Case & Co., 1855.

Gee, Henry and William John Hardy. *Documents Illustrative of English Church History.* London: Macmillan and Co., Limited, 1921.

Hall, Newton Marshall and Irving Francis Wood. *The Book of Life,* Volume 7. Chicago: John Rudin & Company, Inc., 1953.

Hall, Verna M. *The Christian History of the Constitution of the United States of America: Christian Self-Government.* San Francisco: Foundation for American Christian Education, 1966.
The Christian History of the American Revolution: Consider and Ponder. San Francisco: Foundation for American Christian Education, 1975.

Harte, Bret. *The Poetical Works of Bret Harte.* Boston and New York: Houghton, Mifflin and Company, 1904.

Henry, Matthew. *Exposition of the Old and New Testament.* London: James Nisbet & Co., Limited.

Hoare, H.W. *The Evolution of the English Bible.* New York: E.P. Dutton & Co., 1901.

Howard, John Tasker and George Kent Bellows. *A Short History of Music in America.* New York: Thomas Y. Crowell Company, 1957.

Irving, Washington. *Life of George Washington,* Volume 2. New York: G. P. Putnam & Co., 1855.
Knickerbocker's History of New York in *The Works of Washington Irving,* Volume I. New York: P.F. Collier.

Lincoln Library of Essential Information, Volumes I and II. New York: The Frontier Press Company, 1926.

Lossing, Benson J. *A Family History of the United States.* Providence: Murphy & McCarthy, 1881.
A History of the United States. New York: James Sheehy, Publisher, 1881.
The Pictorial Field-Book of the Revolution, Volumes I and II. New York: Harper & Brothers, Publishers, 1859.
Harpers' Popular Cyclopædia of United States History, Volume I. New York: Harper & Brothers, Publishers, 1892.
Harpers' Popular Cyclopædia of United

States History, Volume II. New York: Harper & Brothers, Publishers, 1893.

Mather, Cotton. *Lives of Bradford and Winthrop, Old South Leaflet,* No. 77. Boston: The Old South Association.

McMahon, John R. *The Wright Brothers: Fathers of Flight.* Boston: Little, Brown, and Company, 1930.

Montgomery, D.H. *The Leading Facts of American History.* Boston: Ginn and Company, 1910.
The Leading Facts of American History. New York: Ginn & Company, 1899.

Morison, Samuel Eliot. *The Oxford History of the American People.* New York: Oxford University Press, 1965.

Morrison, James E. *Janus.*

Neal, Daniel, M.A. *The History of the Puritans, Volume I.* New York: Harper & Brothers, 1843.

Paquette, Penelope. *The Battle of Saratoga.* Unpublished.

Penn, William. *A Letter from William Penn,* 1683.

Pittenger, Lieut. William. *Daring and Suffering: A History of The Great Railroad Adventure.* Philadelphia: J. W. Daughaday, Publisher, 1863.

Plumb, Albert H. *William Bradford of Plymouth.* Boston: The Gorham Press, 1920.

Prange, Gordon W. *Miracle at Midway.* New York: Penguin Books, 1982.

Raph, Theodore, *The Songs We Sang, A Treasury of American Popular Music,* New York: A. S. Barnes and Company, 1964.

Rose, James B. *A Guide to American Christian Education for the Home and School.* Camarillo: American Christian History Institute, 1987.
Spiritual Liberty is Causative to Religious and Civil Liberty. Granger: Pilgrim Institute and American Christian History Institute.

Schaff, Philip. *The Creeds of Christendom,* Volume I. New York: Harper & Brothers, 1877.

Slater, Rosalie J. *Teaching and Learning America's Christian History: The Principle Approach.* San Francisco: Foundation for American Christian Education, 1965.

Smith, Jeanette. *A Day at Hampton Court.* Unpublished work

Smith, John. *The Settlement of Jamestown. Old South Leaflets,* No. 167 (Boston: Old South Meeting House).

Swanson, Mary-Elaine. *The Education of James Madison: A Model for Today.* Montgomery: The Hoffman Education Center for the Family, 1992.

The Thompson Chain Reference Bible. Indianapolis, 1982.

Willard, Emma. *Universal History.* New York: A. S. Barnes & Co., 1848.

Webster, Daniel. *The Works of Daniel Webster,* Volume II, 1856.

Webster, Noah. *An American Dictionary of the English Language.* 1828. Facsimile, San Francisco: Foundation for American Christian Education, 1967.

Webster's New Collegiate Dictionary. Springfield: G & C Merriam Company, 1976.

Webster's Seventh New Collegiate Dictionary. Springfield: G & C Merriam Company, 1965.

Winsor, Justin. *Christopher Columbus.* Boston and New York: Houghton, Mifflin and Company, 1892.
Narrative and Critical History of America, Volume VII. Boston and New York: Houghton Mifflin and Company, 1888.

The World Book, Volumes 4 and 10. Chicago: W. F. Quarrie & Company, 1928.